Contesting Freedom

Warwick University Caribbean Studies

Contesting Freedom
Control and Resistance in the Post-Emancipation Caribbean

Edited by

Gad Heuman and David V. Trotman

MACMILLAN
CARIBBEAN

Macmillan Education
Between Towns Road, Oxford OX4 3PP
A division of Macmillan Publishers Limited
Companies and representatives throughout the world

www.macmillan-caribbean.com

ISBN 1-4050-6248-7

Text © Gad Heuman and David Trotman 2005
Design and illustration © Macmillan Publishers Limited 2005

First published 2005

All rights reserved; no part of this publication may be reproduced, stored in a retrieval system, transmitted in any form or by any means, electronic, mechanical, photocopying, recording or otherwise, without the prior written permission of the publishers.

Typeset by EXPO Holdings, Malaysia
Cover design by Gary Fielder AC Design
Cover photograph by Jerome Handler, reproduced from
http://hitchcock.itc.virginia.edu/Slavery

Printed and bound in Thailand

2009 2008 2007 2006 2005
10 9 8 7 6 5 4 3 2 1

Warwick University Caribbean Studies

Series Editors: Alistair Hennessy and Gad Heuman

Across Dark Waters
Ethnicity and Indian Identity in the Caribbean
Editors: David Dabydeen & Brinsley Samaroo   0–333–53508–1

Anatomy of Resistance
Anti-Colonialism in Guyana 1823–1966
Maurice St Pierre   0–333–73281–2

Caribbean Economic Policy and South-South Co-operation
Editor: Ramesh Ramsaran   0–333–58677–8

Caribbean Families in Britain and the Trans-Atlantic World
Editors: Harry Goulbourne & Mary Chamberlain   0–333–77679–8

Caribbean Transactions
West Indian Culture in Literature
Renu Juneja   0–333–62552–8

Charting Caribbean Development
Anthony Payne & Paul Sutton   0–333–73078–X

Contesting Freedom
Control and Resistance in the Post-Emancipation Caribbean
Editors: Gad Heuman & David V. Trotman   1–4050–6248–7

The Cultures of the Hispanic Caribbean
Editors: Conrad James & John Perivolaris   0–333–72604–9

The Debt Dilemma
IMF Negotiations in Jamaica, Grenada and Guyana
Horace A. Bartilow   0–333–67990–3

Democracy After Slavery
Black Publics and Peasant Radicalism in Haiti and Jamaica
Mimi Sheller   0–333–79263–7

Financing Development in the Commonwealth Caribbean
Editors: Delisle Worrell, Compton Bourne & Dinesh Dodhia   0–333–55204–0

The Fractured Blockade
West European-Cuban Relations During the Revolution
Editors: Alistair Hennessy & George Lambie   0–333–58365–5

French and West Indian:
Martinique, Guadeloupe and French Guiana today
Editors: Richard D.E. Burton & Fred Reno   0–333–56602–5

From Dessalines to Duvalier
Race, Colour and National Independence in Haiti
David Nicholls   0–333–65026–3

Islands, Forests and Gardens in the Caribbean:
Conservation and Conflict in Environmental History
Editors: Robert S. Anderson, Richard Grove & Karis Hiebert   1–4050–1271–4

'The Killing Time'
The Morant Bay Rebellion in Jamaica
Gad Heuman   0–333–49400–8

Marginal Migrations
The Circulation of Cultures within the Caribbean
Editor: Shalini Puri   0–333–96708–9

Narratives of Exile and Return
Mary Chamberlain   0–333–64826–9

Noises in the Blood
Orality, Gender and the 'Vulgar' Body of Jamaican Popular Culture
Carolyn Cooper   0–333–57824–4

No Island is an Island
Selected Speeches of Sir Shridath Ramphal
Editors: David Dabydeen & John Gilmore   0–333–79262–9

On Location
Cinema and Film in the Anglophone Caribbean
Keith Q. Warner   0–333–79211–4

Paradise Overseas
The Dutch Caribbean: Colonialism and its Transatlantic Legacies
Gert Oostindie   1–4050–5713–0

Prospero's Isles
The Presence of the Caribbean in the American Imaginary
Editors: Diane Accaria-Zavala & Rodolfo Popelnik   0–333–97455–7

Roots to Popular Culture
Barbadian Aesthetics: Kamau Brathwaite to Hardcore Styles
Curwen Best   0–333–79210–6

Sunset over the Islands
The Caribbean in an Age of Global and Regional Challenges
Andrés Serbin   0–333–72596 4

Trinidad Carnival
A Quest for National Identity
Peter van Koningsbruggen   0–333–65172–3

Trinidad Ethnicity
Editor: Kevin Yelvington   0–333–56601–7

The United States and the Caribbean
Anthony P. Maingot   0–333–57231–9

Writing West Indian Histories
B.W. Higman   0–333–73296–0

To Mildred Weinstock (GH)
and Mansa Trotman (DVT)

Contents

Acknowledgements ix
Contributors x
Introduction xiii
  Gad Heuman and David V. Trotman
Abbreviations xxix

SECTION 1 Aspects of justice and control

1 Popular and official justice in post-emancipation Jamaica   1
   Diana Paton

2 Race for power: people of colour and the politics of
   liberation in Barbados, 1816–c.1850   20
   Melanie Newton

3 'Working cutlass and shovel': labour and redemption
   at the Onderneeming School in British Guiana   39
   Juanita De Barros

4 Discipline, reform or punish? Attitudes towards juvenile
   crimes and misdemeanours in the post-emancipation
   Caribbean, 1838–88   65
   Sheena Boa

SECTION 2 Patterns of resistance

5 'You signed my name, but not my feet': paradoxes of
   peasant resistance and state control in post-revolutionary
   Haiti   87
   Mimi Sheller

6 'Is this what you call free?': riots and resistance in the
   Anglophone Caribbean   104
   Gad Heuman

7 Capping the volcano: riots and their suppression in
   post-emancipation Trinidad   118
   David V. Trotman

8   Different modes of resistance by British Indian and
    Javanese contract labourers in Suriname?   143
    Rosemarijn Hoefte

SECTION 3   Cultural conflicts

9   Afro-Cuban culture: within or outside of the nation?   157
    Christine Ayorinde

10 Reconsidering creolisation and creole societies   179
    O. Nigel Bolland

11 'Married but not parsoned': attitudes to conjugality in
    Jamaica, 1865–1920   197
    Brian L. Moore and Michele A. Johnson

12 The cloaking of a heritage: the Barbados Landship   215
    Marcia Burrowes

Index   235

Acknowledgements

The Workshop which preceded this volume was a joint project of the Centre for Caribbean Studies at the University of Warwick (CCS) and the Nigerian Hinterland Project at York University, Canada. The editors of this volume acknowledge the financial support of the CCS and the Canadian Social Science and Humanities Research Council through the York/UNESCO Nigerian Hinterland Project for the Workshop. The logistics for the Workshop were in the capable hands of Marjorie Davies who, together with the professionalism of the staff at the Conference Centre, made our stay at Warwick a memorable one.

The organisers of the Workshop also acknowledge the participation of Mary Turner, who acted as rapporteur and commentator for our presentations. Papers (which are not included in this volume) were also presented by Roseanne Adderley (Tulane University); Robert Hill (University of California, Los Angeles); Clem Seecharan (London Metropolitan University); and Verene Shepherd (University of the West Indies, Mona). Their contributions at the Workshop, as well as those of the participants who are represented in this volume, ensured that our discussions were stimulating and fruitful. It is our hope that this volume will reflect the dialogue initiated at Warwick.

Contributors

Christine Ayorinde was awarded her PhD by the University of Birmingham and lives in Oxford. Her publications include chapters in the forthcoming edited collections *The Yoruba in the Americas* (Indiana) and *Repercussions of the Atlantic Slave Trade: The Interior of the Bight of Benin and the African Diaspora* (Africa World Press). Her PhD thesis, 'Afro-Cuban Religiosity, Revolution and National Identity (*cubania/cubanidad*)', is under contract with the University of Florida Press.

Sheena Boa teaches history at the University of Warwick and the Open University. She is currently working on an examination of childhood experiences in the nineteenth-century Caribbean.

O. Nigel Bolland is the Charles A. Dana Professor of Sociology and Caribbean Studies at Colgate University. He is the author of several books on Belize. His book, *The Politics of Labour in the British Caribbean: The Social Origins of Authoritarianism and Democracy in the Labour Movement* (2001), won the Gordon K. Lewis Award of the Caribbean Studies Association and the Elsa Goveia Prize of the Association of Caribbean Historians. He is also the editor of *The Birth of Caribbean Civilisation: A Century of Ideas about Culture and Identity, Nation and Society* (2004).

Marcia Burrowes is Lecturer in History with Cultural Studies at the University of the West Indies, Cave Hill Campus, Barbados. Her areas of research are Caribbean Culture and African Diaspora Studies.

Juanita De Barros is Assistant Professor in the Department of History at McMaster University, Ontario. She is the author of *Order and Place in a Colonial City: Patterns of Struggle and Resistance in Georgetown, British Guiana, 1889–1924*. She has published articles on public health, popular cultural practices, and labour legislation in British Guiana. She is co-editor of a special issue of *Caribbean Quarterly* on the history of public health in the Caribbean and is currently working on the relationship between obeah, healing practices and the transition to freedom in British Guiana.

Gad Heuman is Professor in the Department of History and Director of the Centre for Caribbean Studies at the University of Warwick. His publications include *Between Black and White* and a study of the Morant Bay Rebellion in Jamaica, *The Killing Time*. He has edited books on slave resistance and on labour and is editor of the journal *Slavery and Abolition*.

Rosemarijn Hoefte is Head of the Department of Caribbean Studies of the Koninklijk Instituut voor Taal-, Land- en Volkenkunde/Royal Institute of Linguistics and Anthropology in Leiden, the Netherlands. She is also the managing editor of the *New West Indian Guide*. She has published extensively on the Dutch Caribbean. One of her most recent books is *Twentieth-Century Suriname: Continuities and Discontinuities in a New World Society* (2001), which she co-edited with Peter Meel.

Michele A. Johnson is Assistant Professor in the Department of History at York University (Toronto). Her publications include articles on domestic service in Jamaica, the West Indies Federation and, with Brian L. Moore, articles on Jamaican cultural history. She is currently working on publications, with Brian L. Moore, on Jamaican cultural history.

Brian L. Moore is Professor of Social and Cultural History at the University of the West Indies, Mona, Jamaica. His publications include *Race, Power and Social Segmentation in Colonial Society: Guyana After Slavery, 1838–1891* (1987) and *Cultural Power, Resistance and Pluralism: Colonial Guyana, 1838–1900* (1995). He is currently working with Michele A. Johnson on a cultural history of Jamaica in the late nineteenth and early twentieth centuries.

Melanie Newton is Assistant Professor of History at the University of Toronto. Her publications include '"New Ideas of Correctness": Gender, Amelioration and Emancipation in Barbados, 1810s-1850s' in *Slavery and Abolition* (December 2000) and 'Philanthropy, Gender and the Production of Public Life in Barbados, c1790–c1850' chapter in Pamela Scully and Diana Paton (eds.), *Gender and Emancipation in the Atlantic World* (Duke University Press, forthcoming, 2005).

Diana Paton is Lecturer in History at the University of Newcastle-upon-Tyne. Her edition of *A Narrative of Events Since the First of August, 1834, by James Williams, an Apprenticed Labourer in Jamaica* was published by Duke University Press in 2001. She is currently completing a book entitled *No Bond but the Law: Punishment, Race, and Gender in Jamaican State Formation, 1780–1870* (2004).

Mimi Sheller is Senior Lecturer in Sociology at Lancaster University. Her publications include *Democracy After Slavery: Black Publics and Peasant Radicalism in Haiti and Jamaica* (Macmillan, 2000), *Consuming the Caribbean* (Routledge, 2003) and a forthcoming co-edited volume *Uprootings/Regroundings: Questions of Home and Migration* (Berg). She is currently working on a book on the formation of gender, race and unequal freedoms in the Caribbean.

David V. Trotman teaches Caribbean History at York University in Canada and has published on crime, Yoruba religion and the Trinidad calypso. He is the former Director of Latin American and Caribbean studies and Master of Founders College at York University. He is currently the Associate Director of the York/UNESCO Nigerian Hinterland Project and the Harriet Tubman Centre for Research on the African Diaspora.

Introduction

Gad Heuman
David V. Trotman

Studies on the post-emancipation Caribbean are slowly replacing the understandable emphasis on the more dramatic studies of the period of slavery which tended to dominate the scholarship of previous years. Recent publications have been concerned with exploring some of the many issues faced by Caribbean societies as those societies grappled with the problems generated by the demise of slavery, the institution and social organisation which had been their defining characteristic since the region was first settled and colonised by the voluntary and involuntary migrants of Europe and Africa. The scholars concerned with post-slavery studies have struggled with the tendency to succumb to the seduction of seamless continuities and the equally perilous position of sharp definitive breaks with the past. Mindful of the increasing sophistication of those studies of the slave period, which have finally ungagged the slave from the silencing tendency of earlier studies of the institution of slavery, the scholars of the post-emancipation era have sought to ensure that the actions of the emancipated are similarly recognised and documented. Moreover, the historians of the post-slavery period have demonstrated that just as the slave period is not easily cast into a black and white drama, so too the post-emancipation period is replete with instances where varieties of black, white, shades of grey and a range of new colours have made the period intriguingly complex and requiring sophistication in theory, method and technique.[1]

The present volume seeks to contribute to the understanding of the post-emancipation period by taking as its jumping-off point the debate

---

[1] For bibliographic essays and assessments of the scholarship of the slave and post-slavery periods see Franklin W. Knight (ed.), *The Slave Societies of the Caribbean*, vol. 3, *General History of the Caribbean* (London and Basingstoke: UNESCO Publishing/Macmillan Education Ltd., 1997) and B.W. Higman (ed.), *Methodology and Historiography of the Caribbean*, vol. 6, *General History of the Caribbean* (London and Oxford: UNESCO/Macmillan Education Ltd., 1999). See also Bridget Brereton and Kevin A. Yelvington, *The Colonial Caribbean in Transition: Essays on Post-emancipation Social and Cultural History* (Barbados: Press University of the West Indies, 1999).

over continuity and change. It has as its central concerns the issues of conflict, control and resistance. All of the essays originated as shorter think-pieces presented at a workshop held at the University of Warwick in June 2000. The chapters on Cuba, Haiti and Suriname are attempts to provide points of comparison with Jamaica, Barbados, Trinidad and British Guiana (now called Guyana), the areas from the Anglophone Caribbean covered by the other chapters.

The experiences of the post-slavery period make the Caribbean a less homogeneous area of study than the slave period, where the commonalities are more obvious and compelling. The circumstances in which the slave systems were dismantled and the differences in the timing of the end of slavery combine with other factors (including environmental) to make the Caribbean an area of diverse post-emancipation experiences, despite some clearly obvious areas of real commonality.

There is now a general consensus that the dismantling of the slave systems of the Caribbean began with the heroic success of the enslaved and of the oppressed *affranchis* of St Domingue. This is not to deny validity to the anti-slavery struggles which contributed to undermining the viability and integrity of the system, but merely to emphasise the symbolic importance of the events of 1791–1804. Those actions not only put an end to the system of slavery but also created the first independent nation in the Caribbean. All of the major questions of the post-emancipation reconstruction of society and economy and, to be sure, the questions of post-colonial realities were first raised in Haiti. The revolutionary and violent circumstances of Haitian emancipation and its aftermath posed these questions in an acutely dramatic way perhaps peculiar to Haiti, but they nonetheless foreshadowed for the rest of the region the urgent and germane interrogations about the meaning of freedom. At the very least, the responses in Haiti, whether flawed or not, have to be judged against the constraining external realities (of being the sole free black republic in a region in which black slavery was still dominant) as well as the intransigence of the internal realities (infrastructural devastation coupled with the legacy of deep-seated race and colour divisions inherited from the slave period).[2]

The St Domingue Revolution and the creation of Haiti cast a long shadow on the region. The emancipation and reconstruction of the other Caribbean societies took place against a background of the unfolding drama taking place in Haiti. The pro-slavery advocates in the Caribbean used Haiti as a constant reference point for the post-slavery possibilities and the dangers of unfettered freedom when given to non-whites. The

---

[2] For an illuminating study see Mimi Sheller, *Democracy after Slavery: Black Publics and Peasant Radicalism in Haiti and Jamaica* (London: Macmillan, 2000).

revolution may have been silenced subsequently in the historical record, but the contemporaries of the nineteenth century were acutely aware of the importance of Haiti. The triumphant bondsmen of St Domingue did not hesitate to spread their revolutionary message of emancipation. In 1822 they liberated the enslaved of the neighbouring Spanish colony of Santo Domingo. This was an important step in the creation of the Dominican Republic. Although this emancipatory intervention on the part of the Haitians was never repeated elsewhere in the Caribbean, its significance was not lost on the slaveholders and the enslaved of the region.[3]

The second stage in the dismantling of Caribbean slave systems and the ushering in of the post-emancipation period involved the legislated abolitions of slavery in the British (1838), French (1848), Danish (1848) and Dutch (1863) colonies.[4] In all of these cases the local elites were forced to accept the imposition of freedom in their societies as an act of legislation by an external parliament. Without for a moment denying historical significance to the contributions of the enslaved to their freedom and including the dramatic intervention of the slaves of the Danish West Indies, we cannot ignore the fact that the thunder of self-emancipation was stolen by the legislative action of the metropole. The ideological possibilities for self-empowerment that should have come with emancipation were circumscribed, if not undermined, by metropolitan claims to overweening humanitarianism as the driving force of their actions. Even more importantly the act of emancipation, while it may have destroyed the property rights in humans characteristic of slavery, did not significantly change economic and political relations or, for that matter, and understandably so, social relations. The local elites, though damaged by the loss of their property rights (compensation for that loss notwithstanding), were nonetheless left with sufficient strength to recoup their political position, from which they continued to defend their economic, social and cultural interests.

The final episode in the story of *de jure* emancipation in the Caribbean is the case of the Hispanic Caribbean, though the focus is

---

[3] On Haiti and its impact see Michel-Rolph Trouillot, *Silencing the Past: Power and the Production of History* (Boston, Mass.: Beacon Press, 1995); David Barry Gaspar and David Patrick Geggus, *A Turbulent Time: The French Revolution and the Greater Caribbean* (Bloomington: Indiana University Press, 1997); David P. Geggus (ed.), *The Impact of the Haitian Revolution in the Atlantic World* (Columbia: University of South Carolina Press, 2001).

[4] For a general survey of the disintegration of the slave societies of the Caribbean see Franklin W. Knight, *The Caribbean: The Genesis of a Fragmented Nationalism*, 2nd ed. (New York: Oxford University Press, 1990) pp 159–92; also Eric Eustace Williams, *From Columbus to Castro: The History of the Caribbean, 1492–1969* (London: Deutsch, 1970) pp 280–327.

more on the situation in Cuba (1886) than on Santo Domingo (1822) or Puerto Rico (1873). Haitian intervention signalled the beginning of the demise of the system in the neighbouring colony of Santo Domingo. In Puerto Rico, a slave-based plantation system never got off the ground, so that it was not difficult for the island's representatives to the Spanish National Assembly to present a successful petition for the abolition of slavery. The Cuban system was the last of the Caribbean systems to come to maturity. But it virtually disintegrated under the impact of both uncontrollable internal forces and an increasingly unfavourable external climate. The enslaved of Cuba were more involved in both the struggle for their freedom and the birth of an independent nation than their counterparts in the other parts of the Caribbean, apart from Haiti. But whereas the enslaved of Haiti were the primary initiating agents of their emancipation, in Cuba the enslaved were used as pawns between the contending elites and their freedom used as bargaining chips both to win their allegiance and to up the ante in the colonial-metropolitan conflict. This is by no means to suggest that the enslaved were mute and malleable bystanders, for they soon used the situation to their own advantage and exploited the fissures in the structure of white control, showing initiative and agency both individually and collectively and in their own self-interest. As in Haiti, the emancipation of the slaves in Cuba was inextricably linked to the eventual rupture of the colonial relationship. But unlike Haiti, for Cuba the stifling embrace of a newly emerging imperial United States immediately compromised the moment of political autonomy. This neo-colonial relationship would influence in significant ways the options available for, and the responses of the recently emancipated to, the realities of freedom.[5]

Clearly, post-emancipation expectations and realities would differ between those who had been recently released from the thrall of servitude and those who had previously defined their freedom and their status on the basis of their ownership of property in humans. All of the

---

[5] On Cuba see Franklin W. Knight, *Slave Society in Cuba During the Nineteenth Century* (Madison: University of Wisconsin Press, 1970); Rebecca J. Scott, *Slave Emancipation in Cuba: The Transition to Free Labor, 1860–1899* (Princeton, N.J.: Princeton University Press, 1985); Louis A. Perez Jr, *Cuba between Empires, 1878–1902* (Pittsburgh: University of Pittsburgh Press, 1983); Louis A. Perez Jr, *Cuba under the Platt Amendment, 1902–1934* (Pittsburgh: University of Pittsburgh Press, 1986); Robert L. Paquette, *Sugar Is Made with Blood: The Conspiracy of La Escalera and the Conflict between Empires over Slavery in Cuba*, 1st ed. (Middletown, Conn.: Wesleyan University Press, 1988); Aline Helg, *Our Rightful Share: The Afro-Cuban Struggle for Equality, 1886–1912* (Chapel Hill: University of North Carolina Press, 1995); Ada Ferrer, *Insurgent Cuba: Race, Nation, and Revolution, 1868–1898* (Chapel Hill: University of North Carolina Press, 1999).

assumptions of the society – its economic organisation, its political structure and its social and cultural values and institutions – were in various ways open to contestation in a more dramatic way than the long-standing and endemic conflict around these issues which had characterised the societies during the period of legal slavery. At the very minimum, those who had been in various forms of subjection (slaves and the 'unappropriated') expected that life would be different from that which they had experienced during slavery in a number of immediate and significant ways. Certainly the overwhelming majority rejected all the worst aspects of a system that had depended on serious limitations on their actions as humans and that had aimed at putting control of their lives in the hands of others. The former slave owners expected cataclysmic changes but hoped for circumstances in which the spirit of the old order would remain, and they could successfully merge into the new without catastrophic disorder. It was expected that the end of slavery meant that things had to be different.[6] But the degree or magnitude of expectation of difference was dependent on or influenced by a variety of individual and often idiosyncratic factors.

Among the formerly enslaved there were those who expected that emancipation would allow them to fully exploit their skills and talents and to take advantage of the economic opportunities and options available and which may have been frustrated in the years of slavery. Slavery had demanded and used only those skills and talents that were of immediate value to the system of production and the reproduction of its way of life. The system had little use for the range and diversity of skills brought from Africa. On those occasions when those skills were utilised in the Caribbean, it was done despite the system rather than because of it and generally primarily in the area of cultural production. Yet there were Africans and Creoles who worked in areas other than as mere brute labour in the fields and who became indispensable skilled contributors to the successful production and reproduction of the economic system. In the post-emancipation period, they expected that these skills and talents, whether brought from Africa or developed in the Caribbean, would be the basis on which they could create themselves as autonomous economic actors. Some hoped that these skills would also be valuable bargaining chips in negotiations with the plantation order. Moreover, post-slavery life required skilled workers who could satisfy the material needs of the emancipated as the latter struggled to create an

---

[6] See for example Woodville Marshall, '"We Be Wise to Many More Things": Blacks' Hopes and Expectations of Freedom', in Hilary Beckles and Verene Shepherd (eds.), *Caribbean Freedom: Economy and Society from Emancipation to the Present* (Kingston, Jamaica: Ian Randle Publishers, 1993).

independent existence away from the controlling 'welfare-like' tentacles of the plantation and its 'wages and rent' entrapment. The establishment of villages and settlements with their accompanying physical structures – houses, churches, schools – was only one area in which these skills would be required outside of the plantation. But when the emancipated utilised their skills in non-plantation activity, it was viewed as a depletion of the skill pool available for plantation production purposes and therefore became a source of conflict.

The struggle over the restructuring of economic relations in the post-slavery era was a major area of contestation and the frequency and intensity of attempts at control and the consequent resistance to these attempts have encouraged historians to emphasise continuity rather than disjuncture with the slave period. The areas of contestation included wages, access to land and the ability to fully participate in all areas of the economy on terms negotiated rather than imposed. In short, the ability of the emancipated to test the real meaning of freedom depended on the way in which they could determine what portion of their economic activity was totally under their control, when and under what conditions they could sell their labour and to whom, and how they could maximise and benefit from their labour. This was the ultimate test of the end of slavery and the meaning of emancipation. For if slavery meant that the fruits of their economic activity were appropriated and its direction determined by others, then emancipation had to mean increased control over their labour and its products.

The struggle to control the economic life of the emancipated and the attempts to frustrate their search for autonomy form the background to the development of Caribbean peasantries.[7] Even those peasantries whose origins lay in the emergence of slave gardens in the pre-emancipation period found that their hold over land would be viewed as tenuous and problematic in the emancipation period. Land symbolised and actualised the kind of freedom which post-slavery elites did not have in mind for the emancipated. They therefore sought to prevent the

---

[7] The literature on Caribbean peasantries is quite large. See Woodville K Marshall, 'Notes on Peasant Development in the West Indies since 1838', *Social and Economic Studies* 17 (1968); Sidney Mintz, *Caribbean Transformations* (Chicago: Aldine Publishing Co., 1974); Trevor Marshall, *A Bibliography of the Commonwealth Caribbean Peasantry, 1838–1974* (Cave Hill: University of the West Indies, 1975); David Nicholls, 'Rural Protest and Peasant Revolt in Haiti (1804–1869)', in Malcolm Cross and Arnaud Marks (eds.), *Peasants, Plantations and Rural Communities in the Caribbean* (Leiden: Department of Caribbean Studies of the Royal Institute of Linguistics and Anthropology, Leiden, Netherlands, 1979); Dale Tomich, 'Houses, Provision Grounds and the Reconstitution of Labour in Post-Emancipation Martinique', in Mary Turner (ed.), *From Chattel Slaves to Wage Slaves* (Kingston, Jamaica: Ian Randle, 1995).

acquisition of land or circumscribe its use in such a way that the emancipated could not use land as the basis for a challenge to the economic, social and political dominance of the traditional elites. It is only against this background of conflict over land that one can appreciate Caribbean peasantries as both a mode of response and a mode of resistance. The slow, tortured and uneven emergence of the peasantry attests not only to the strength of the forces arrayed against them but also to their resilience. They struggled and earned the right to produce food for the internal market and to participate in the production of export crops and, in the process, carved for themselves some economic respect, social recognition and political representation.

The use of political power to restrict access to land, where this was possible, was only one strategy used by the elites to frustrate the ambitions of the emancipated to define the meaning of their freedom. In those situations where this was not feasible or completely effective, they resorted to the age-old solution of importing labour as a means of solving their problems with labour supply and control. With the support of their metropolitan allies, Caribbean planters took advantage of imperial connections to encourage the immigration of hundreds of thousands of indentured workers, primarily from the Asian sub-continent and with significant numbers from China. Their arrival, dispersal and use constitute another chapter in the long history of Caribbean labour, with its sub-themes of exploitation, control and resistance. The conditions of indentureship resembled those of its predecessor so much that it has encouraged some historians to see in it nothing more than 'a new system of slavery', in Hugh Tinker's phrase, and a seamless transition from the previous era. But there were important differences between the two systems of labour control. These led to critical divergences in the responses of the bonded and consequently, and importantly, in the aftermath of the experiences. But, nonetheless, the indentured and their descendants made important contributions in their own right to the history of struggle for the definition of the meaning of freedom in post-emancipation Caribbean societies.[8]

---

[8] The literature on indentureship is growing at a rate similar to that experienced in the 1960s and early 1970s by studies on slavery. See the relevant contributions in vol. 6 of the UNESCO General History of the Caribbean. In particular, see Hugh Tinker, *A New System of Slavery: The Export of Indian Labour Overseas, 1830–1920* (London: Oxford University Press for the Institute of Race Relations, 1974); K. O. Laurence, *A Question of Labour: Indentured Immigration into Trinidad and British Guiana, 1875–1917* (New York: St. Martin's Press, 1994); Walton Look Lai, *Indentured Labor, Caribbean Sugar: Chinese and Indian Migrants to the British West Indies, 1838–1918* (Baltimore: Johns Hopkins University Press, 1993); Rosemarijn Hoefte, *In Place of Slavery: A Social History of British Indian and Javanese Laborers in Suriname* (Gainesville: University Press of Florida, 1998).

The struggle of the emancipated and the newly-arrived indentured was also a struggle to be able to define themselves as much more than units of labour. The formerly enslaved were driven also by the need to express themselves culturally in ways which may have been restricted during slavery but which reflected their own cultural realities and which responded to their specific and subjective needs. In short, there was a struggle over their right to present themselves in everyday ways as a product of their particular histories, including their pre-slavery scripts, and as a self-creation and reflection of their contemporary realities. The vagaries of the slave trade and the constraints of slavery determined and configured the variety of ways in which cultural patterns and practices from African sources were transplanted and survived, just as surely as those two founding episodes profoundly contributed to the architecturing of the creole culture which inevitably emerged in Caribbean societies.[9]

The existence of large segments of the population born in Africa, for whom emancipation meant the possibility of reconstructing some aspects of their ancestral traditions in the Caribbean, constituted a major area of conflict. In the case of Haiti, large numbers of Africans from specific ethnic groups arrived up to the very morn of the outbreak of the revolution and the consequent emancipation. In the Anglophone Caribbean, although a full generation would separate the last of the African-born arrivals in 1807 from the general emancipation of 1838, the settlement of liberated Africans in some of the Anglo territories up to the late 1860s ensured the continuity of some traditions identified with specific ethnic groups. Similarly in Cuba, where Africans arrived as late as 1868 and slavery ended in 1886, it was possible to reproduce and maintain similar and other ethnic-specific cultural practices. Like their Creole counterparts, these African-born arrivals, given their age and the proximity of their arrival to emancipation, were the most likely to attempt to engage in the patterns of behaviour during the early years of freedom which for the elites constituted undesirable elements in the post-emancipation society. These practices evoked the fears of security

---

[9] The debate over the relative importance of Africanisation and creolisation in the creation of societies in the Caribbean has spawned a rich literature which includes Edward Brathwaite, *The Development of Creole Society in Jamaica 1770–1820* (Toronto: Oxford University Press, 1971); Sidney W. Mintz and Richard Price, *The Birth of African-American Culture: An Anthropological Perspective* (Boston: Beacon Press, 1992); John Kelly Thornton, *Africa and Africans in the Making of the Atlantic World, 1400–1680* (Cambridge; New York: Cambridge University Press, 1992); Richard Price, 'The Miracle of Creolization: A Retrospective', *New West Indian Guide* 75, nos. 1 and 2 (2001). See also the collection of articles in Verene A. Shepherd and Glen L. Richards (eds.), *Questioning Creole: Creolization Discourses in Caribbean Culture* (Kingston, Jamaica: Ian Randle Publishers, 2002).

and control which had plagued the ruling elites in the slave period and which continued to be active even after slavery. And their continued existence seemed to signal to the post-emancipation elites the possibility of a backsliding to barbarism. The attempts to eradicate these traces of the African elements in the post-emancipation period generated a pattern of conflict and resistance which tested the meaning of freedom.

But it was not only those clearly identified African practices that were under attack but also those creole practices which had developed during the slave period. Many of them had emerged as a result of intra-African and Afro-Euro cultural fusions as the enslaved responded culturally to the subjective reality of living in the new environments of the Caribbean. The enslaved were forced to come to terms with the reality of their condition in virtually every aspect of life. Over time they had created religious, ethical and aesthetic institutions and values which served the demands of their situation, including resistance. More often than not, the elite tolerated these created practices, except when they directly threatened the profits or the security of the slave system. In fact, tolerance of this Afro-creole culture was part of the mechanism of control, and its continued existence also often allowed slave holders to present justificatory testimony of the system of slavery.

In the post-emancipation period, although the concerns of profit and security remained prominent on the agenda of the elite, respectability and civilised living also emerged as their new and pressing concerns. The struggle to stamp out these practices in the post-emancipation period not only allowed the elite to distinguish themselves from the internal 'other' but also served to provide them with a claim to respectability and membership in the nineteenth-century club of the 'civilised' Christian bourgeois elite of Europe and Euro-America. Post-emancipation elites needed both internal distinction and external validation, both of which they sought in campaigns of moral reform and cultural cleansing. Still reeling from the charges of the anti-slavery movements that had characterised them as backward overseers of immoral regimes, post-emancipation elites ventured into areas that their predecessors had tolerated, ignored or encouraged for a variety of self-serving reasons. They sought to eradicate all traces of non-Christian religious practice and influences, and they sought to impose their versions of decency by trying to restructure family forms, mating patterns and sexual mores. Gender relations, roles and identities became charged areas of contestation in the post-emancipation period, as during slavery, and the formerly enslaved and the indentured newcomers struggled with the attempts at definition and re-definition of their gendered roles in the society. The post-slavery society was going to be recast in an image driven by the elites' concern for respectability and their understanding of civilised living.

Unlike their predecessors, the post-emancipation elites became more overtly interested in social engineering and cultural transformation. During slavery, slave owners turned a blind eye to, or even encouraged, 'objectionable' practices. These were excused as inevitable derivatives of their chosen social and economic system, dependent as it was on a peculiar pattern of labour recruitment and control, namely the Atlantic slave trade and the resultant racialised slavery. Many of the negative social and cultural practices were excused as the price one paid for the profits of the enterprise or as evidence of the congenital and therefore incorrigible backwardness of the African. Even in Europe this reasoning was fashionable and acceptable, and metropolitan elites colluded with their colonial counterparts in accepting the social and cultural status quo as natural and inevitable. But the ideological winds of change that had contributed to the removal of the slave trade and slavery, the props of the old society, had also facilitated the emergence of theories that supported attempts at social engineering and reconstruction. The elites of Europe themselves were engaged in campaigns of social reform as they tackled what they saw as the moral turpitude and degeneration of their working classes, who had to be disciplined into the social and cultural habits demanded by industrial capitalism. Ex-slaves also had to be disciplined and transformed into wage labour, and the cultural and social practices that seemed to subvert this aim had to be confronted and extirpated. Thus despite long-held ideas of African immutability and current ideas of scientific racism, the effort of reconstruction had to be made with their descendants in the Caribbean.

Post-emancipation elites welcomed missionaries to convert and minister to the emancipated with a zeal quite unknown to the slave period elites who, more often than not, considered the enslaved immune to salvation and missionaries subversive of the social order.[10] Even the

---

[10] The history of the churches, religions and missionary activities is yet to receive the sophisticated treatment which it deserves, especially for the post-emancipation period. See D. A. Bisnauth, *A History of Religions in the Caribbean* (Kingston: Kingston Publishers, 1989) but be extremely wary of its numerous errors and obvious biases. For the Anglo-Caribbean, see Mary Turner, *Slaves and Missionaries: The Disintegration of Jamaican Slave Society, 1787–1834* (Urbana: University of Illinois Press, 1982). See also Robert J. Stewart, *Religion and Society in Post-Emancipation Jamaica*, 1st ed. (Knoxville, Tenn.: University of Tennessee Press, 1992) and Robert Stewart, 'A Slandered People – Views on "Negro Character" in the Mainstream Christian Churches in Post-Emancipation Jamaica', in Darlene Clark Hine and Jacqueline McLeod (eds.), *Crossing Boundaries: Comparative History of Black People in Diaspora* (Bloomington and Indianapolis: Indiana University Press, 1999); Arthur C. Dayfoot, 'Themes from West Indian Church History in Colonial and Post-Colonial Times', in Patrick Taylor (ed.), *Nation Dance: Religion, Identity and Cultural Difference in the Caribbean* (Bloomington and Indianapolis: Indiana University Press, 2001); Juanita De Barros, 'Congregationalism and Afro-Guianese Autonomy', in Patrick Taylor (ed.), *Nation Dance: Religion, Identity and Cultural Difference in the Caribbean* (Bloomington and Indianapolis: Indiana University Press, 2001).

Roman Catholic Church, which, since Bartholomé de Las Casas, had been rather complicit by its silence during the period of slavery, belatedly found its voice and its energy in the post-emancipation period, especially in those societies where it competed with Protestant activists for the souls of the emancipated. Similarly its counterpart, the Anglican Church, dug deep to shake off its lethargy induced by a long-held preference for the support of the status quo and began to seriously compete with the Dissenters who were viewed as interlopers. But even these Dissenters – Baptists, Moravians, Wesleyans – whose role in the anti-slavery movement cannot be ignored or underestimated, often found themselves on the wrong side of the divide in the post-emancipation struggle for religious allegiance.[11]

For to the former enslaved, emancipation meant also the right to express themselves religiously in ways which sometimes did not meet the approval of their former allies against slavery. Their right to worship in their Africanised versions of Christianity as well as their reconstructed African religious rites became major areas of conflict. The religious activity of the emancipated was viewed as emblematic of cultural backwardness, and the struggle of the enslaved for autonomy in this sphere of life was construed as dangerous. In those countries where there were large populations of indentured workers from the Indian sub-continent, missionaries also saw in their presence an irresistible opportunity to convert another portion of the world's 'backward races'. The enticement to the emancipated and the indentured and their descendants was the control which religious bodies had over the major avenue to social mobility in the post-emancipation society, viz. education. For the missionaries, the road to Christian salvation passed through the schoolroom. But this was not an idea that was entirely and wholeheartedly shared by all of the elites: Christian salvation, yes, but education, no.

Post-emancipation elites did not depend only on religious ministrations to secure their continued control over the emancipated or to drive their project of social engineering. For one aspect of their ideological inheritance that they were slow to abandon was their understanding and belief in the persuasive power of coercion. They no longer had legal recourse to the whip and on-the-spot punishment, but they soon learned to appreciate the punitive and rehabilitative possibilities of the law and, in particular, the prison. Quite unlike their metropolitan counterparts, they were slow to appreciate the role of education in

---

[11] Missionary activity in post-emancipation Cuba is linked to the hegemonising efforts of the American occupation and therefore affects all Cubans in ways slightly different from what occurs in other parts of the Caribbean. On Cuba, see Louis A. Perez Jr, *Essays on Cuban History: Historiography and Research* (Gainesville: University Press of Florida, 1995) pp 53–72.

encouraging consent to and acceptance of the social order and therefore remained at worst hostile in their opposition to the provision of popular education and at best parsimonious in their disbursement of state support.[12] Rather than the civilising potential of the school, they preferred to place their bets on the coercive promise of the law, police and prisons. They used their continued control of the political apparatus in order in many instances to define the responses of the emancipated as criminal activity and therefore to use the brute force of the law to support their efforts to define the limits of emancipation and the meaning of freedom.

Politically the expectations of emancipation would have been varied. The emancipated ranged from those who would have preferred to be as far as possible from any interaction with state authority and control to those who appreciated that the protection of their freedom depended on the extent to which they were part of a decision-making process. We have to be extremely wary of implying a political consciousness, which may have been way beyond the ken or concerns of nineteenth-century contemporaries and reflects more our impositions on the past. At the risk of being overcautious, we can probably say that the emancipated may have expected and desired some semblance of universal citizenship, even if mitigated by the dominant current notions of class and gender deference. In the Caribbean as a whole, there was a difference in the political expectations (as well as what was expected of them) of those who lived in the new republics of Haiti and Cuba, where emancipation came with revolution and civil war, and those territories where emancipation was imposed by external legislative fiat. Moreover, there was a difference between those territories where the metropolitan influence had been removed or reduced and those where metropolitan colonial rule was deepened and intensified after emancipation.[13] In all cases, though, colour, race and racism would play determinative roles in defining the arenas of possibilities, expectations and realities.

In the new republics, the old elites of the slave period had been defeated or replaced by revolution and civil war and, in the other

---

[12] For the Anglo-Caribbean see Carl Campbell, 'Social and Economic Obstacles to the Development of Popular Education in Post-Emancipation Jamaica, 1834–65', *The Journal of Caribbean History* 1, November (1970); M.K. Bacchus, *Education as and for Legitimacy: Developments in West Indian Education between 1846 and 1895* (Waterloo: Wilfred Laurier University Press, 1994).

[13] On these 'expectations' see Thomas C. Holt, *The Problem of Freedom: Race, Labor, and Politics in Jamaica and Britain, 1832–1938* (Baltimore: Johns Hopkins University Press, 1992); Louis A. Perez Jr, *On Becoming Cuban: Identity, Nationality and Culture* (Chapel Hill and London: The University of North Carolina Press, 1999); Sheller, *Democracy after Slavery: Black Publics and Peasant Radicalism in Haiti and Jamaica*.

territories, the old elites seemed undamaged socially and politically. But in all areas of the Caribbean, there would be changes in the composition and definition of the elite in the post-emancipation period. Although racial origin still remained a formidable barrier to social advancement and recognition, occupational opportunities (especially in the military) and education provided a vehicle for social mobility for many non-whites. In the republics of Haiti and Cuba, the change was much more rapid and dramatic as the victors of revolution and civil war assumed leadership of the new states. New economic and social elites emerged to fill the power vacuum created by the wreckage of revolutionary and civil war. In the other territories, the exigencies of administering a colonial society, dependent less on coercion and increasingly more on consent, opened up spaces in the elite structure. The linear descendants of the free black and free coloured of the slave period made successful claims for inclusion in the post-emancipation elite. Their progress was not without considerable struggle and sacrifice. The ambiguity of their previous position of intermediacy in the social structure was exchanged for a more defined and secure position. In some instances the new additions, if only by their presence, challenged some of the assumptions of the old order. But in most cases, the new additions merely reinforced the old structures and gave a new lease on life to the ideas and habits of the old order. More fundamental changes had to await the democratic and socialist revolutions of the post-Second World War era and the nationalist struggles spearheaded in the main by organised labour seeking its own emancipation.

The contributors to this volume address all of these themes and others as well. They pay particular attention to the mechanisms of control used by former masters to ensure their continued dominance after emancipation. As Gad Heuman points out, these took a variety of forms. Across the Caribbean, legislators enacted laws designed to restrict the mobility of former slaves. In addition, planters sought to retain the services of freed people on the plantations by imposing a system linking rental of houses and lands to labour. In some cases, each member of a family was charged rent for their house. Planters also summarily ejected ex-slaves from their homes, often arbitrarily.

Faced with the prospect of free labour, planters resorted to importing rival labourers who were tied by strict contracts to the plantations. Rosemarijn Hoefte discusses the British Indians and the Javanese who were brought to Suriname. There, as indentured immigrants, they were subject to laws which not only controlled their movement off the estates but also regulated their labour. Writing about Trinidad, David Trotman supports this view and describes the system of indentureship as an important means of controlling freed people in the wake of emancipation.

In Trinidad as well as other Caribbean colonies, the authorities used other methods to maintain dominance. Faced with riots in the post-emancipation period, colonial officials turned to the military, the police, local militias and even imperial forces to subdue freed people. In the case of Cuba, Christine Ayorinde discusses the slaughter of several thousand blacks in 1912, less than 30 years after emancipation. The Cuban establishment saw blacks as a threat, especially since they organised a political party, the *Partido Independiente de Color*, which demanded social reform and full equality for Afro-Cubans. In this context, blacks were represented as a threat to civilisation; in addition, progress was equated with the undermining of black culture and the suppression of Afro-Cuban religious practices.

This negative view of Afro-Caribbean people was justification for a variety of repressive measures. In British Guiana, as Juanita De Barros shows, institutions were established to deal with recalcitrant juveniles. Reformatories, such as the Onderneeming School, were founded to control young children and, more specifically, to teach them industrial virtues. The aim was to transform them into agriculturalists, serving the interests of the planter class in British Guiana. Describing attitudes toward juvenile crimes in Jamaica, Sheena Boa reinforces the stereotypical view of freed people. Since the planters there believed that Caribbean labourers were a 'degraded people', it was necessary to reintroduce corporal punishments in the prison system. As Boa suggests, the way to discipline and reform the minds of the poor across the Caribbean was through punishing their bodies, largely through flogging. Yet control of the emancipated classes was not always maintained by a white planter class backed up by the colonial state. Mimi Sheller discusses the example of post-emancipation Haiti, in which new local non-white elites claimed to share the interests of the peasantry. The nineteenth-century Haitian elite consisted of *noirists* and *anciens libres*, blacks and browns who had profited most from the Haitian Revolution. In Barbados, some members of the new elite were also free people of colour. As Melanie Newton notes, many of these free coloureds had demonstrated considerable solidarity with the slave population and had supported the abolition of slavery. After emancipation, however, there were splits among the free coloured leadership. While the leader of the group, Samuel Jackman Prescod, was politically progressive, others distanced themselves from the ex-slave population. For Newton, then, some free coloureds were admitted into the elite but at the price of denying the broader democratic hopes of the emancipated classes. Co-optation of some leading free coloureds proved to be another form of control.

However, ex-slaves did not passively accept the attempts to limit their freedom after emancipation. In the process, freed people used a variety of tactics. In the aftermath of the Haitian Revolution, as Sheller points out, peasants used their feet to move beyond the reach of the state. In parts of the Anglophone Caribbean, former slaves moved off the plantations to establish freeholds of their own, and women left the estates in large numbers to work on their own account. This was often part of a family strategy to maximise the autonomy as well as the income of the family as a whole.

Throughout the post-emancipation period, freed people violently resisted the terms of emancipation. In the face of low wages and high rents, among other grievances, former slaves rioted across the region. In Dominica, six years after full emancipation, blacks protested because they believed they might be re-enslaved. In 1848, this time in Jamaica, ex-slaves again rioted, fearing a return to slavery; a year later in St Lucia they protested because of high taxes. Economic problems were partly to blame for island-wide riots in Trinidad in 1849, and the most significant outbreak of the post-emancipation period, the Morant Bay Rebellion in Jamaica, was caused by a combination of all these factors.

It was not just ex-slaves who protested; indentured labourers also struck work and rioted, largely because of poor conditions and low pay. In Suriname, Javanese indentured labourers preferred running away and turning to messianic cults rather than rioting, while Indian labourers were more likely to participate in collective defiance of the system. But as Hoefte concludes, the behaviour of both groups of indentured labourers was far less docile than the planters had hoped.

Blacks sought to manipulate the court system when they could, but in the face of a highly partial judicial system after emancipation, freed people sometimes developed their own alternative courts. As Diana Paton shows, these were independent, separate from the courts dominated by the planter class. They included the use of obeah to help resolve conflicts.

Obeah was an important part of Afro-Caribbean culture, and some societies, especially in the twentieth century, paid more attention to the culture of the former slaves. Christine Ayorinde notes the importance of the Afro-Cuban component of Cuban culture known as *Afrocubanismo*. Writing about Jamaica, Brian Moore and Michele Johnson describe a different aspect of popular culture: attitudes towards conjugality. For Moore and Johnson, the Jamaican people had their own ideas about marriage, which threatened to undermine the elite norms of the society. Many blacks believed that marriage followed the formation of a family rather than preceding it; moreover, this form of cohabitation often led to better relationships than the legal marriages of the middle and upper classes.

This type of cultural resistance was also important in Barbados and, more specifically, in the development of the Landship. Outwardly adopting British naval culture, the Landship, for Marcia Burrowes, reflected an African-Caribbean heritage. The followers of the Landship were therefore making use of masquerade and camouflage to practise their own traditions. The new culture which emerged in the Caribbean, as epitomised by the Landship, involved a process of creolisation. As Nigel Bolland suggests, the creation of this new culture arose from a process of negotiation, involving all the peoples of the Caribbean. As with contesting freedom, it is an ongoing process.

Abbreviations

AN	French National Archives
CO	Colonial Office Records, National Archives (formerly Public Record Office), London
GD	Governor's Despatches
IOJ	Institute of Jamaica
JA	Jamaica Archives
KVs	Koloniale Verslagen (Netherlands Colonial Reports)
MCC	Minutes of the Combined Court
MCP	Minutes of the Court of Policy
MMS	Methodist Missionary Society Records (London)
NAG	National Archives of Guyana
PP	British Parliamentary Papers

Section 1

Aspects of justice and control

1 | Popular and official justice in post-emancipation Jamaica

Diana Paton

A thief or any other criminal does not lose caste from having been in the penitentiary. On his discharge, he is as well received by his relatives, comrades and friends as if he had merely returned from a long journey. He does not feel the bitter disgrace that criminals in other countries do on being let out of prison.[1]

So commented H.B. Shaw, Jamaican General Inspector of Prisons, in a report arguing for the increased use of whipping as a punishment for crime. The stereotype embedded in his remarks was, from the mid-1850s, the common sense view of members of the Jamaican elite and British commentators on colonial affairs. Elite Jamaicans and British observers alike argued that the Jamaican masses rejected the decisions of the courts, perceived prison sentences as misfortune rather than disgrace, and welcomed convicted criminals back into their communities as 'martyrs' to an unjust and racist system. This powerful discourse was used to justify both the 1865 massacre at Morant Bay and the subsequent shift to an unrepresentative form of government.[2]

To what extent did this view accurately describe popular belief? Stripped of its racism, could it be accurate? Should we, following Ranajit Guha, treat Shaw's remark as an instance of the 'prose of counter-insurgency' and read his claims as inverted signs of popular adherence to an alternative 'moral economy'? Guha claimed that the 'words, phrases, and, indeed, whole chunks of prose' used in official documents 'have much to tell us not only about elite mentality but also about that to which it is opposed – namely, subaltern mentality'. He gives examples which seem highly pertinent to Jamaican history: official designations of 'fanatics' can be inverted to reveal 'rebels inspired by some kinds of

---

[1] H.B. Shaw, 'Report of the Inspector of Prisons', encl. in CO 137/388, Eyre to Cardwell, 30 March 1865, no. 69.
[2] On the Morant Bay rebellion and its aftermath see Gad Heuman, *'The Killing Time': The Morant Bay Rebellion in Jamaica* (London: Macmillan Caribbean, 1994); Thomas C. Holt, *The Problem of Freedom: Race, Labor, and Politics in Jamaica and Britain, 1832–1938* (Baltimore: Johns Hopkins University Press, 1992), pp. 263–309.

revivalist or puritanical doctrines', while 'lawlessness' indicates 'the defiance by the people of what they had come to regard as bad laws'.³

Guha's reading of the term 'lawlessness' could be transposed to the Jamaican context, where one might argue that claims like Shaw's reflected mass popular rejection of both the law and the courts. Before rushing to this conclusion, we should remember that Guha is writing here about moments of rebellion. Because it assumes both the unitary character of subaltern consciousness and that the terms encoded in elite discourse have easily discerned antonyms, Guha's technique is problematic in analysing moments of less intense conflict. In post-emancipation Jamaica, simply inverting the terms of such discourse to deduce popular consciousness invites us to turn a blind eye to the complexity and ambiguity of popular *mentalités*. Sherry Ortner has argued that too great a concern with 'resistance' in recent scholarship has led to 'ethnographic thinness': that is, to a tendency to overlook the relations of power that operate within subaltern communities, and a lack of precision about how oppositional mobilisations take place.[4] In some Jamaican post-emancipation historiography the focus on overt resistance has been at the expense of a broader analysis of the dynamics of daily life, so that we lack an understanding of how resistance takes place, as Douglas Haynes and Gyan Prakash put it, 'within the ordinary life of power'.[5] Instead, historians too often present a picture of heroic but uncomplicated people who 'endure when they had to' and 'resist however and whenever they could'.[6] Such historiography can lead to

---

[3] Ranajit Guha, *Elementary Aspects of Peasant Insurgency in Colonial India* (Delhi: Oxford University Press, 1983), pp. 14–17, quotes on pp. 16–17. Guha's attitude to this methodology of inversion is unstable, however: see also his 'The Prose of Counter-Insurgency', in Ranajit Guha (ed.), *Subaltern Studies II: Writings on South Asian History and Society* (Delhi: Oxford University Press, 1983), pp. 1–42, where he argues convincingly against a nationalist historiographic tradition that works by inverting colonialist paradigms.
[4] Sherry Ortner, 'Resistance and the Problem of Ethnographic Refusal', *Comparative Studies in Society and History* 37 (1995), pp. 173–93. For allied critiques in other contexts see Frederick Cooper, 'Conflict and Connection: Rethinking Colonial African History', *American Historical Review* 99, no. 5 (1994), pp. 1516–45; Lila Abu-Lughod, 'The Romance of Resistance: Tracing Transformations of Power Through Bedouin Women', *American Ethnologist* 17, no. 1 (1990), pp. 41–55.
[5] Douglas Haynes and Gyan Prakash, 'Introduction: The Entanglement of Power and Resistance', in Douglas Haynes and Gyan Prakash (eds.), *Contesting Power: Resistance and Everyday Social Relations in South Asia* (Delhi: Oxford University Press, 1991), p. 2.
[6] Michael Craton, 'Continuity Not Change: The Incidence of Unrest Among Ex-Slaves in the British West Indies, 1838–1876', in Hilary Beckles and Verene Shepherd (eds.), *Caribbean Freedom: Economy and Society From Emancipation to the Present* (Kingston: Ian Randle Publishers, 1993), p. 203.

false assumptions about both the ease with which opposition can be organised and the unproblematic nature of what might replace the status quo, and thus tends to produce a romantic and politically naive version of history. This chapter examines the ways in which non-elite Jamaicans understood their interactions with the courts in order to draw out the complexities that Ortner argues are essential to understanding resistance.

Everyday life, popular attitudes to 'crime', and the use of the courts

Court records demonstrate that in Jamaica, as in most societies, members of the elite made disproportionate use of the courts. For instance, in a collection of theft trial records from the parish of St Andrew, 62 of 141 prosecutors whose social standing could be identified were from the elite.[7] Nevertheless, there were also many prosecutions initiated by people who could not be considered part of the elite. Forty-nine of the theft prosecutors in these records are identifiable as small property-holders or skilled tradespeople, while 30 were described as or are otherwise identifiable as 'labourers'. They prosecuted for theft of crops, clothing, food, household items, livestock and cash. Armand Thomas, for instance, described in the trial record as 'labourer', brought a prosecution against two men for stealing 59 hills of yam from his ground.[8] James Clarke, a labourer who signed with a mark, prosecuted another labourer for stealing five quarts of flour, three towels and a small quantity of salt fish.[9] Despite their non-elite status, property rights were significant to these individuals, and they used the law to defend their relatively small amounts of property. In St Thomas in the East, between 31 and 43 per cent of petty sessions cases in the years 1863–65 – when popular disaffection was probably the highest it ever reached in the second half of the nineteenth century – were brought by people described as 'labourers'.[10] Although this is much lower than their proportion of the population, and is usually presented as evidence of the bias of the courts against them,

---

[7] Court's Office Records, Half Way Tree, St Andrew, 1A/2/2 Central Gov. Courts. Jamaica Archives, Spanish Town. This collection of 450 trial records, 325 of which involve theft, covers the period 1828–87; the bulk are from the 1850s and 1860s.
[8] Ibid., case 92, Quarter Sessions, April 1854.
[9] Ibid., case 182, Petty Sessions, 16 October 1857.
[10] Don Robotham, '*The Notorious Riot': The Socio-Economic and Political Base of Paul Bogle's Revolt* (Mona: Institute of Social and Economic Research, University of the West Indies, 1981), p. 61; PP 1866 (3683) XXXI Appendix: Part II A: 'Return of the number of cases, civil and criminal, heard in Petty Session at Bath, in the Parish of St. Thomas in the East, 1863–1865'.

these cases still reveal a significant degree of voluntary engagement with the official judicial system on the part of ordinary Jamaicans.

Willingness to engage with the state judicial system does not mean that those who used it believed it to be just in any abstract sense. As Douglas Hay remarks of English prosecutions, 'the notion that the poorer half of the population, because they sometimes were able to prosecute, believed that The Law was basically just seems most unlikely. Most people took a profoundly instrumental attitude to the law.'[11] In Jamaica, as well, popular attitudes to the law were instrumental, not supportive. As I will demonstrate, people used the courts to achieve a particular goal, rather than because they believed the state's claims to fairness or supported its desire to monopolise conflict resolution.

'Negro-house lawyers' and courtroom commentaries

Popular opinion about the state's legal system was not constructed only through direct experience of involvement as prosecutors or defendants. Throughout the early post-emancipation period elite observers noted – often with distaste – the many ordinary people who attended court sessions to observe and comment on the proceedings. Criminal trials were routinely attended by large numbers of people. Commenting on his decision to criticise a new statute privately rather than through a speech in court, Judge Henry Roberts wrote that he wanted to avoid his words having a negative effect on the 'large and shrewdly watchful audience' that would hear them.[12] A few years later a magistrate wrote of the need for sentencing policy to be aware of the effect on the 'audience' gathered in court that witnessed decisions.[13]

Courthouse 'audiences' were not the passive recipients of intended messages that these magistrates expected them to be. Especially in the major towns, elite commentators often described popular attendance at court as a nuisance. The *Morning Journal* wrote in 1842 of the problem of 'hale, hearty men and women wasting day after day, lounging about the [Kingston] Court-house, idling and making idle, when their time might be profitably employed, and themselves and their families benefited'.[14] Similarly, the *Falmouth Post* complained of the 'concourse of idlers' who

---

[11] Douglas Hay, 'Prosecution and Power: Malicious Prosecution in the English Courts, 1750–1850', in Douglas Hay and Francis Snyder (eds.), *Policing and Prosecution in Britain 1750–1850* (Oxford: Clarendon Press, 1989), p. 392.

[12] CO 137/306, Grey to Grey, 7 May 1850, no. 41, encl: Roberts to Grey, 20 April 1850.

[13] CO 137/336, Darling to Labouchere, 19 March 1858, no. 47, encl: T. Witter Jackson to Hugh W. Austin, 6 August 1857.

[14] *Morning Journal*, 13 May 1842.

attended the magistrates' court in Kingston.[15] The objection was to poor Jamaicans' habit of claiming the space of the courtroom for themselves, turning it into a place for their own sociability and enjoyment. If it was true, as the *Post* claimed, that 'the noise and confusion idlers occasion cause great interruption to the Court', then the popular presence effectively inverted the intended theatre of the law, forcing the officials to listen to the multiplicity of popular voices, rather than vice versa.[16]

Courtroom crowds frequently expressed loud opinions about the justice of decisions made. In 1855 Charles Wright, a Falmouth boatman, was charged with stealing coals. He had been employed to deliver coal from a brig to the wharf, and after delivering the contracted amount, had kept the remainder. In his defence he argued that this was accepted custom among boatmen, and was supported in this by the testimony of others. Despite being directed by the judge that such a 'monstrous doctrine' was not tenable as a defence, the jury acquitted Wright 'from conscientious motives'. The verdict was strongly welcomed by the courtroom crowd. According to the newspaper account it 'was received with a tremendous shout by the rabble, and it was some time before silence was restored.'[17] Similar cases involved prosecutions for the theft of a mare, the theft of bricks, a 'riot' on the part of Kingston Baptists involved in a dispute with their one-time minister, and the killing by a woman of her baby granddaughter.[18] In these cases, courthouse audiences 'shouted in approbation', gave 'triumphant shouts' at not-guilty verdicts, and created 'uproar' when defendants they supported were convicted.[19] Members of the crowd often accompanied the defendant they supported to his or her next location, whether prison or home. In so doing, they created an informal ceremony that used and transformed that of the state.

Individuals facing prosecution often turned to lay specialists from within their communities for advice and support. Some lay individuals, usually men, acquired experience with court procedures and gained reputations for their understanding of the law and ability to advise on it. These people were referred to by elites in a mixture of scorn and fear, as 'negro-house lawyers' or 'half-inch lawyers'.[20] The *Falmouth Post*

---

[15] *Falmouth Post*, 3 July 1855.
[16] Ibid.
[17] *Falmouth Post*, 15 May 1855.
[18] *Falmouth Post*, 12 May 1846, 18 August 1846, 1 August 1856, 18 November 1862; CO 137/326, Barkly to Russell, 26 April 1855, no. 45.
[19] *Falmouth Post*, 1 Aug. 1856; CO 137/326, Barkly to Russell, 26 April 1855, no. 45; *Falmouth Post*, 1 December 1857.
[20] The use of this term predates emancipation. See R.R. Madden, *A Twelvemonth's Residence in the West Indies, during the Transition from Slavery to Apprenticeship* (Philadelphia: Carey, Lea and Blanchard, 1835), pp. 103–7.

described one defendant as 'a sort of negro-house, second rate Lawyer',[21] while Peter Espeut, a coloured planter and assembly member, described the town of Morant Bay in 1862 as 'the nest of a set of characters whose principal occupation is that of "half-inch lawyers" and village politicians', singling out two men for particular designation as 'half-inch lawyers'.[22] Despite Espeut's descriptions of these men as poor and ignorant, they had both recently been involved in organising a public meeting to protest against the Governor's removal of the radical George William Gordon from his position as a magistrate. Their leading role in popular political organising indicates that, by the standards of their own communities, they were held in high regard. They were part of an emerging semi-urban artisan class that had connections to, but was not part of, the class of small settlers and squatters who made up the majority of the population. Such individuals could act as political brokers for the 'lower orders'.[23]

From emancipation on, then, Jamaicans actively approached the courts, participating as an audience, using them against one another, making clear their feelings about particular cases, and providing support to one another through amateur legal advice. There was dynamic popular engagement with the official judicial process, which did not defer to the judgement of the court but did understand it to be a significant space and source of power. Ordinary people perceived the significance of what went on in court and tried to exert control over the process. These patterns of interaction reveal that the events that precipitated the Morant Bay rebellion emerged out of long-standing patterns of behaviour. The rebellion began after a day in court, when a case of trespass was due to be heard. The defendant, Lewis Thomas, had consulted his cousin, Paul Bogle, who had advised him – in a way reminiscent of the complaints about 'half-inch lawyers' – to appeal against a previously imposed fine.[24] As well as advising his cousin, Bogle organised considerable numbers to attend the courthouse to support him. According to Gad Heuman, this mobilisation was deliberately designed by Bogle to develop into a confrontation with the authorities. Once they

---

[21] *Falmouth Post* 18 May 1842.
[22] CO 137/367, Eyre to Newcastle, 23 September 1862, no. 84, encl: P.A. Espeut, 'An analytical report of Mr. George W. Gordon's so-called public meeting holden at the Native Baptist Meeting House near Morant Bay, on the evening of Wednesday the 27th August 1862'.
[23] According to Mimi Sheller, one of the men, William Foster March, was also a reporter for some newspapers and worked as a clerk for George William Gordon. Mimi Sheller, *Democracy After Slavery: Black Publics and Peasant Radicalism in Haiti and Jamaica* (London: Macmillan, 2000), p. 220.
[24] Heuman, *Killing Time*, p. 5.

were in the courtroom, another case turned out to be more incendiary. The defendant's sister called out, 'Come out of the Court, let us go down in the market, and let us see if any d—d policemen come here if we don't *lick* them to hell.' As Mimi Sheller points out, this incident suggests 'the sense of female control over the market as a public space in which (unlike the courts) popular justice could prevail'.[25] While we should be wary of reducing all courthouse interventions to precursors to Morant Bay, we should also recognise the extent to which Bogle made use of long-standing strategies of engagement with the court system, transforming them from intermittent resistance into organised opposition. He could do this in part because of the existence of other forms of judicial practice that were intertwined with strategies involving the official system.

Alternative justice

There is evidence of the incipient development in the 1860s of a system of counter-official judicial practice, which some historians have labelled 'independent courts'. The small amount of evidence we have about these courts emerged during the course of the inquiry into the Morant Bay rebellion. William Miller, a magistrate and estate manager in St Thomas in the East, presented to the commission a 'summons' from such a court, which he claimed to have found on the person of one of his workers. The summons was addressed to James Miller, whom it charged with using 'abusive and calumnious language, tending to provoke a breach of the peace, in words following, to wit: "You are to give me your stick."' It commanded him to 'be and appear on Saturday the 4 day of March at the Court-house, Hundly Village, before such justices of the peacies [sic] as shall then be there to answer to the said charge, and to be further dealt with according to law'. According to a newspaper article published before the Morant Bay rebellion, 'sham courts' existed in St Thomas in the East, which tried real crimes and handed down real fines as sentences. The article stated that buildings 'arranged internally upon the same plan as parish court-houses' had been constructed.[26] After the rebellion, minutes of a meeting were found among the belongings of Paul Bogle. Echoing procedures regularly used in

---

[25] Mimi Sheller, 'Quasheba, Mother, Queen: Black Women's Public Leadership and Political Protest in Post-emancipation Jamaica, 1834–65', *Slavery and Abolition* 19, no. 3 (1998), p. 109.
[26] *Jamaica Tribune*, July 1865, in Evidence of His Excellency Edward John Eyre, Report of the Jamaica Royal Commission, 1866. Part II Minutes of Evidence and Appendix. PP 1866 (3683) XXXI, 1010.

political meetings at the time, the minutes recorded a process of decision-making in which proposals were made by one individual and seconded by another. The meeting appointed a 'State General' and two 'Justices of the Peace', including Bogle; it decided on the required 'Qualyfication of Baristers and Lawyers', fixed the dates of two 'Petty Sessions' courts and one 'Court of Arispagus', and established a procedure for summoning and ensuring the attendance of jurors. It further resolved 'that all Person or Persons who shall wilfully Missbehave themselves in the Vecinity of the Court the same shall be Commited for trial and if wont Submit be disbands as Unsivilise'.[27]

These documents are immensely suggestive, but difficult to interpret. Certainly a popular court system was developing in St Thomas in the East, modelling itself closely on the official system of justice. The rules regarding misbehaviour in the vicinity of the court reveal a concern to establish the authority of this new court system. William Miller claimed in 1866 that these courts had operated for the past three years, and that the punishments they imposed included fines and being required to work on the prosecutor's land. Despite his evidence, which may well be marked by a post-rebellion tendency to exaggerate the extent of popular organisation, we do not know how widespread these courts were, the degree to which they actually heard cases as opposed to making plans to hear them, or the extent of popular respect granted their decisions.

These courts have fascinated historians, many of whom downplay the difficulties involved in interpretation. Monica Schuler, for instance, refers in passing to 'a Creole system of justice which functioned independently of the colonial judicial system', while Don Robotham states matter-of-factly that these courts 'issued summonses, tried cases and imposed fines in the whole Serge Island-Plantain Garden River area, even as far as Manchioneal'.[28] Some have speculated that the courts acted like mutual aid societies; others that they gave people facing trials in the state's court system an opportunity to practise.[29] Others have

---

[27] PP 1866 (3683) XXXI, Appendix: Part VII: Miscellaneous Documents. B. 'Documents found among Paul Bogle's Papers produced by Governor Eyre as tending to show a disposition on the part of the Negroes to undertake the administration of justice by themselves.'
[28] Monica Schuler, *'Alas, Alas, Kongo': A Social History of Indentured African Immigration into Jamaica, 1841–1865* (Baltimore: John Hopkins University Press, 1980), p. 63; Robotham, *Notorious Riot*, p. 85. Schuler and Robotham base their claims on the evidence that I have presented here. See also Heuman, *Killing Time*, p. 73.
[29] Heuman, *Killing Time*, p. 73; Holt, *Problem of Freedom*, p. 289; Noelle Chutkan, 'The Administration of Justice in Jamaica as a Contributing Factor in the Morant Bay Rebellion of 1865', *Savacou* 11/12 (1975), pp. 78–85.

argued that the people turned to this alternative system of 'people's courts' because of their complete alienation from the official courts.[30] In the light of the evidence presented earlier, this is not a tenable interpretation; indeed, the involvement of Paul Bogle in both the alternative court system and in interaction with the official system shows that they operated together rather than separately.

As others have suggested, the courts in St Thomas in the East developed out of the traditions of community-directed conflict resolution established during slavery.[31] These traditions were organised around the leading role of headmen in deciding what should happen in cases of conflict among slaves. The St Thomas courts also drew on the judicial role of elders within religious communities. In some post-emancipation missionary churches, this role was formally established. The elders among the Hanover congregation of the Scottish missionary Warrand Carlile formed an autonomous court to resolve disputes among members, here described by the missionary's son, James Edward Carlyle [sic]:

> The people generally looked up to their pastor with great reverence. He and his venerable black session, composed then of four or five old negro elders, were a court of reference in all disputes as to property, &c. Few even of the most careless, and none of the church members, ever thought of going to a court of law. They brought their disputes before the minister and session, and though they stated their case with much vehemence, they always accepted the decision.[32]

---

[30] Robert J. Stewart, *Religion and Society in Post-Emancipation Jamaica* (Knoxville: University of Tennessee Press, 1992), pp. 131–2; Clinton Alexander Hutton, '"Colour for Colour; Skin for Skin": The Ideological Foundations of Post-Slavery Society, 1838–1865: The Jamaican Case' (PhD dissertation, University of the West Indies, 1992), pp. 189–92.

[31] On these systems of conflict resolution see Diana Paton, 'No Bond But the Law: Punishment and Justice in Jamaica's Age of Emancipation, 1780–1870' (PhD dissertation, Yale University, 1999), pp. 90–9; Orlando Patterson, *The Sociology of Slavery: An Analysis of the Origins, Development and Structure of Negro Slave Society in Jamaica* (London: Macgibbon and Kee, 1967), pp. 230–1; Robert Dirks, *The Black Saturnalia: Conflict and its Ritual Expression on British West Indian Slave Plantations* (Gainesville: University of Florida Press, 1987), p. 141. For the claim that post-emancipation courts developed out of slavery-era informal judicial practice see Chutkan, 'Administration of Justice'; Heuman, *Killing Time*, p. 74.

[32] James Edward Carlyle, *Thirty-Eight Years' Mission Life in Jamaica: A Brief Sketch of the Rev. Warrand Carlile, Missionary at Brownsville, by One of His Sons* (London: James Nisbet & Co., 1884), pp. 52–3. The two spellings of Carlyle/Carlile are in the original: presumably the son changed the spelling of his name from the more unusual version used by the father.

While Carlyle stresses respect for the white missionary, it seems likely that the moral authority of the black (and almost certainly male) elders gave this institution its real power.[33]

The court in which Paul Bogle served as a JP represented, it seems likely, an attempt to formalise and institutionalise the system of justice associated with the dissenting churches and the plantation community. Like the procedures described by Carlyle, it arose out of a desire on the part of many Jamaicans for an additional space, beyond the official system, wherein their conflicts could be adjudicated.

Most interpretations of the informal courts have examined them primarily for what they tell us about the relationship between the Jamaican people on one hand and the state or the elite on the other, focusing in particular on their function as resistance. But the independent courts also provide suggestive evidence about the power dynamics operating within Jamaican communities. Scholars who have examined similar institutions in other colonial societies have tended to see popular justice in a less straightforwardly celebratory light than have historians of Jamaica, and their work is helpful for a re-examination of the Jamaican independent courts. As Clifton Crais notes in relation to a similar 'people's court' in the Transkei in the 1950s, it is more useful to ask questions about the political imaginaries of participants in informal judicial practices than to take a straightforwardly evaluative approach.[34] That is, we should not be satisfied with asking whether such practices constituted resistance to the colonial state, but should also seek to understand what other issues, problems and power relations they articulated.

In the Jamaican case, although Bogle's court did not have access to state force to enforce its decisions, it expressed and perpetuated relations of power and authority within the peasant community. For instance, it allocated the right to judge to men alone. All the officers named in the minutes of the meeting found in Bogle's house were men. Moreover, it confined this power primarily to smallholding farmers who formed the 'respectable' peasantry. Such smallholders – rather than landless workers – also formed the backbone of support for the Morant Bay rebellion.[35] The elders in Carlile's congregation, like Paul Bogle

---

[33] For an account of a similar practice see Claude McKay, *My Green Hills of Jamaica* (Kingston: Heinemann Educational Books (Caribbean), 1979), pp. 60–1.
[34] Clifton Crais, 'Of Men, Magic, and the Law: Popular Justice and the Political Imagination in South Africa', *Journal of Social History* 32, no. 1 (1998), pp. 49–72. See also Richard L. Abel (ed.), *The Politics of Informal Justice* (New York: Academic Press, 1992).
[35] Holt, *Problem of Freedom*, pp. 299–300.

and his fellow JPs, were part of this group. People who had authority to mediate disputes were also those who played respected roles in the churches. The threat, quoted above, by Paul Bogle's meeting to declare those who misbehaved 'Unsivilise' suggests a belief among this group that there was an important, if fluid, distinction between the civilised and the uncivilised within the Afro-Jamaican population. The content of this concept of civilisation remains to be explored, but civilisation was certainly a complex attribute, probably requiring the conjunction of status based on class, gender, age and religion.[36]

Obeah and myalism

The alternative court system described above has attracted much attention from historians, but was probably not the most widespread unofficial judicial practice engaged in by ordinary Jamaicans. The beliefs and practices labelled obeah and myalism provided another means of pursuing conflict and responding to harm and wrongdoing. They have been much studied for what they tell us about African cultures in Jamaica, but rather less so for their use as a method of obtaining justice. Unlike both the official court system and the systems of justice associated with the black dissenting churches, obeah held out the possibility of gaining redress even in conflicts with people of superior status, including planters. Obeah was also available to women as much as to men: many obeah practitioners were women.

Precise definitions of obeah and myalism have proved elusive. In part, this is because the evidence about them comes almost entirely from outside, from efforts to define them for purposes of legislating against them. Obeah was the name Europeans gave to all aspects of Caribbean popular belief that they found alien and threatening. In addition, obeah and myalism comprised a very broad system of beliefs and practices that does not correspond to any of the realms into which scholars are accustomed to dividing social life. These beliefs and practices cannot be categorised as medicine, law, religion, magic or judicial practice; they encompassed all of these but were not confined to any one of them, or even to all of them collectively. Mindie Lazarus-Black puts it well in arguing that obeah 'defies neat categorization'; it is, she argues, 'an empowering phenomenon, a discourse and practice concerning rights, crime and punishment, and varying forms of domination and

---

[36] For a preliminary analysis of Jamaican 'respectability', see Patrick Bryan, *The Jamaican People 1880–1902: Race, Class and Social Control* (London: Macmillan Caribbean, 1991).

resistance'.[37] It is, additionally, characteristic of a worldview in which discourses about health, the spiritual world and responsibilities of people to one another remain tightly connected.

Ordinary Jamaicans could use the power of obeah to counter that of the state. Individuals charged with crime sometimes made direct use of obeah in the hope that this would prevent their conviction. For instance, two men accused of horse theft consulted an obeahman in order to ensure that they were not convicted; this was revealed because they failed to pay the obeahman and he testified against them.[38] In another case, two women charged with assault were reported to have sacrificed a cock on the courthouse steps prior to their trial to protect themselves from conviction; they were found guilty.[39] Despite the failure of these specific instances, obeah's power seemed to work often enough for people to remain convinced of its usefulness.

Obeah did not, however, primarily involve direct interaction with state judicial practice. As Mindie Lazarus-Black recognises, obeah 'may be directed against an exploiting class, but the justice it expresses also permeates relationships between neighbours, lovers, and kin'.[40] Obeah practitioners – those with specialist knowledge of how to mobilise supernatural power for concrete ends – were consulted for the purpose of pursuing goals and conflicts beyond the realm of formal law. Evidence about these purposes comes from descriptive accounts of white observers, and also from court cases involving accusations of obeah. Such cases included the use of obeah to heal sickness which was believed to have been caused by obeah. Joseph Hudson, for instance, allegedly 'pretended to suck pieces of glass and other like rubbish', from the body of Catherine Manford, an old woman who died a few days later. He was convicted of obeah.[41] Obeah could also allow its user to gain sexual power over an actual or hoped-for partner. Such practice was revealed in a case in which Lewis Thomas, on trial for obeah, was said to have provided 'charms' to a man who used them to entice the wife of another man to live with him.[42] Obeah could be used to harm enemies, especially those who occupied a higher social position than the person who made use of obeah's power. A former headman who had been dismissed was prosecuted for engaging an obeahman to attack the

---

[37] Mindie Lazarus-Black, *Legitimate Acts and Illegal Encounters: Law and Society in Antigua and Barbuda* (Washington: Smithsonian Institution Press, 1994), pp. 40, 54.
[38] PP 1854 (1848) XLIII Barkly to Newcastle no. 1 report of Bell.
[39] *Falmouth Post*, 20 May 1859.
[40] Lazarus-Black, *Legitimate Acts and Illegal Encounters*, p. 259.
[41] *Falmouth Post*, 20 November 1857.
[42] *Falmouth Post*, 20 March 1857.

attorney who he believed had cheated him, while in another case a witness testified that the defendant had asked him for a draught to render an estate's overseer unconscious.[43] Others consulted obeah practitioners to discover who had committed a crime, and to find out why someone had become sick. Obeah mobilised power in ways that partially overlapped with the formal state system of justice. It disciplined people involved in practices recognised by the state as criminal, such as theft, but also those who transgressed community norms in ways that were not defined by the state as criminal, such as by firing somebody from their employment.

It is difficult to read popular values from obeah cases, because its use often reveals an area of conflict rather than consensus. Like lower-class use of the courts, obeah was primarily used as a way of taking forward conflicts within communities, rather than as a weapon against the state or the elite. It structured sexual relationships between men and women, revealing the conflict involved in many of them. It could also organise gendered hierarchies among men, as in the case cited above in which one man uses obeah in order to win another man's partner, thus increasing his own status and prestige. The use of obeah had complex consequences: it organised conflict within Afro-Jamaican communities and simultaneously provided an alternative way of understanding wrongdoing and responsibility that countered the hegemonic goals of the elite.

The conflict inherent in the practice of obeah was revealed most profoundly in collective popular attempts to banish obeah practitioners. These disciplinary actions were known in Jamaica as myalism. Many historians have described rituals undertaken in order to rid a community of the evil power that was causing misfortune, rituals that often included violent attacks on individuals accused of practising obeah. In 1841–42 many such events took place in St James and Trelawny. According to Monica Schuler, the movement began on Spring estate, St James, where there had recently been several deaths. Myal leaders came to the estate and performed a ceremony designed to cleanse the area of hostile obeah forces; this ceremony involved the use of violence against men who were identified as obeah practitioners.[44] This was an Afro-Creole religious-judicial process in which individuals accused of

---

[43] *Falmouth Post*, 1 July 1845 and 7 August 1849.
[44] Schuler, '*Alas, Alas, Kongo*'; Richard D.E. Burton, *Afro-Creole: Power, Opposition, and Play in the Caribbean* (Ithaca: Cornell University Press, 1997); Diane J. Austin-Broos, *Jamaica Genesis: Religion and the Politics of Moral Order* (Chicago: University of Chicago Press, 1997), pp. 51–3. Similar ceremonies on other estates are recorded in contemporary newspapers: see, for instance, *Falmouth Post*, 19 October 1842.

the crime of obeah were punished and purified. The process did not take the same form as that of the formal courts, because it relied on a different interpretation of evidence and proof of guilt. It also understood the significance of punishment quite differently from the state system. Adam Black, whom myalists accused of obeah, reported that he had been tied up, brought to Gale's Valley estate, the centre of the movement in Trelawny, and beaten. He testified that a group of myalists:

> tied his arms behind him with a rope – called him a wicked man, and forced him to Gale's Valley Estate, some shoving him, and a man on a mule pulling him along with a rope. Arrived at Gale's Valley, he was placed in confinement, his thumbs and fingers were tightly bound with a cord; he was also tied round his head, with so much force as to cut him. He asked for water, but it was refused, unless he would tell them about Obeah. When they danced, men and women thumped him on his sides, and on the third night of his endurance, the prisoner Mary Shand, assisted to hold his feet, while the parties, male and females inflicted several blows on his ____. [sic][45]

We do not know what Black was alleged to have used obeah for, or with what results. In the cases at Spring estate, however, the accused obeahmen were said to have caused the deaths of local young men, and the accusations in Trelawny probably involved similar charges.[46] Such anti-obeah activities combined religious and judicial processes.

Myalists and others who attacked obeah practitioners understood misfortune to result from the use of hostile supernatural power. The law likewise assumed that obeah practitioners could cause harm, but interpreted their ability to do so as resulting from the use of poison or the power of 'suggestion'. The crime of obeah was defined as '*pretend[ing]* to the possession of supernatural power'.[47] The law also refused to recognise the distinction between obeah and myalism. Thus, there was a profound break between popular and official assessments of judicial processes. Adam Black's assailants did not believe that a satisfactory result could be obtained through legal channels. Having Black convicted of obeah would not break his powers of sorcery, nor release the shadows he had caught. Even if they had wanted to prosecute, it is unlikely

---

[45] *Falmouth Post*, 26 October 1842.
[46] Schuler, '*Alas, Alas, Kongo*', pp. 40–1.
[47] My emphasis. This phrase was used in the first anti-obeah law, in 1760, 'An Act to remedy the evils arising from irregular assemblies of slaves', 1 Geo. III c. 22, and maintained in subsequent anti-obeah legislation.

that Black's attackers would have obtained a conviction. Despite obeah's illegality, the evidence that convinced his assailants that Black was an obeahman was unlikely to convince a court. The assumptions and standards of proof of the formal system of criminal justice operated very differently to those of most Jamaicans, for whom obeah was a real and ever-present threat. In this case, people had to go beyond the law in order to achieve what they considered to be justice. The two systems of justice relied on profoundly different assumptions about all stages of the judicial process.

Obeah was first made illegal in 1760 in response to its use in a major slave rebellion.[48] There is plenty of other evidence that elites feared it because of its power to mobilise Afro-Jamaicans to political ends. Nevertheless, neither obeah nor myalism was an inherently oppositional practice: in many cases they were used against the same poor and marginal individuals who were also likely targets of court procedures. However, the persistence of the belief that harm was caused by obeah, with its corollary belief that the remedy for such harm was a spiritual-judicial practice designed to counter obeah, created a profound cultural block against popular acceptance of the monopolisation of penal power by state institutions. Because obeah represented an alternative system of law and justice, a different way of understanding and responding to harm, the colonial legal system found it at once very threatening and very difficult to respond to. Laws against obeah had to perform the contradictory task of denying the reality of the practice while providing a mechanism by which those who 'pretended' to its power could be punished.

What do all these events, practices and case studies reveal about Jamaican conceptions of justice and of popular interactions with the official court system? We can confirm the claim that the judicial system was widely perceived to be unfair. However, belief that the system was unjust and racially oppressive did not usually lead to total rejection of that system. Most Jamaicans also tried to make use of the legal and penal system when it suited them, and tried to manipulate court proceedings to their advantage. Many expressed deep interest in individual cases, commenting on the justice of particular decisions in ways that imply neither the absolute rejection of the system described by many members of the Jamaican elite, nor the passive acceptance of the law as the only mechanism for mediating conflict that elites would have liked to see. As in any society, Jamaican popular attitudes to the law and to justice were complex and contextual. Elite claims about popular

---

[48] Adolph Edwards, 'The Development of Criminal Law in Jamaica up to 1900' (PhD dissertation, University of London, 1968), p. 263.

alienation from the law, such as H.B. Shaw's remarks quoted at the beginning of this chapter, built on real feelings of injustice, but those feelings existed within a much more complex matrix of instrumental and other uses for and oppositions to the law than this discourse allowed.

My purpose is not to replace a complacent portrait of unceasing resistance and clear-sighted popular understanding of oppression with a facile one in which 'the people' accept the rule of law and find it basically legitimate. Neither picture is appropriate, most fundamentally because the wide range of ways in which ordinary Jamaicans interacted with the state's system of justice demonstrates that there was not one unitary 'popular belief' with regard to the law. A common analytic move in such circumstances is to invoke the Gramscian concept of 'hegemony', arguing not that the people believe that the status quo is just but that there are certain limits beyond which change is unthinkable, and that struggle takes place within such limits. Framed in this way – as 'the language of contention' in which conflict is conducted, as William Roseberry puts it – hegemony does provide a useful way of thinking about non-elite Jamaicans' interactions with the state's system of justice after emancipation.[49] Nevertheless, 'hegemony' is such a broad concept that it can be used to describe almost any situation short of revolution, and yet it is clear that if most societies are dominated by some kind of coerced consent, some hegemonic situations are more fragile than others. We need to be able to distinguish between hegemonic situations: when, for instance, are the boundaries within which contention takes place likely to shift? In a situation like that in Jamaica, in which circumstances and popular attitudes shifted widely over time, it is necessary to explain how and in what circumstances one type of understanding of the role of the courts, the law and the state – such as that which operated in Morant Bay in 1865 – came to predominate.

The hegemony of the courts and the state was always unstable in Jamaica because state institutions faced deep and ongoing competition for dominance as the mechanism of conflict resolution. As well as using the official courts, non-elite Jamaicans resorted to a series of other methods for resolving or mediating conflicts, building on institutions and practices developed within the slave community. Although historians have paid most attention to the fragments of evidence that reveal the existence of a network of popular or independent courts, this chapter

---

[49] William Roseberry, 'Hegemony and the Language of Contention', in Gilbert M. Joseph and Daniel Nugent (eds.), *Everyday Forms of State Formation: Revolution and the Negotiation of Rule in Modern Mexico* (Durham: Duke University Press, 1994), pp. 355–66.

has argued that the juridical role of obeah, and in particular its countervailing explanation of harm and redress, was the most powerful source of this competition.

In looking at popular interactions with the official courts and efforts to implement justice, we find on the one hand an ongoing and intense engagement with the state legal system, in which many people made great efforts both to use the system in their favour and to prevent it being used against them, and on the other the vibrant counter-hegemonic juridical practices contained within the traditions of obeah, myalism and Native Baptism. Both traditions could be transformed at significant moments of crisis into weapons that challenged the power and authority of the island's rulers. Equally important, both were significant ways in which ordinary Jamaicans expressed their understandings of the proper social and spiritual order, and organised and challenged hierarchies within their communities.

Note

This is a shortened and revised version of a chapter that will appear in my book, *No Bond but the Law: Punishment, Race, and Gender in Jamaican State Formation, 1780-1870* (Durham: Duke University Press, 2004). I would like to thank the organisers and participants of the conference on 'Control and Resistance in the Post-Emancipation Caribbean' for comments on an earlier version, and Yale University for financial support of the research for this article.

2 Race for power: people of colour and the politics of liberation in Barbados, 1816–c.1850

Melanie Newton

Introduction

During the closing decades of slavery and the first years of emancipation, class and ideological conflict shaped free black and coloured politics in Barbados. Although historiographical emphasis has been placed on the struggle by the non-white elite for improvements in civil rights, this chapter places these essentially conservative efforts within the wider context of free black and coloured and slave politics during the final decades of slavery. In this period a counterculture of radical and abolitionist politics emerged which challenged the political authority of both the plantocracy and the black and coloured elite. Through this radical opposition free people of colour, mainly but not exclusively of lower-class background, expressed their sense of political solidarity with slaves.[1]

The emergence of progressive voices from within the overwhelmingly conservative black and coloured elite after emancipation was part of the legacy of this pre-1834 current of non-white radicalism.[2] Upper-class demands for the desegregation of the island's political institutions temporarily converged with the desires of lower-class free people of colour and former slaves for political representation.

---

[1] In the article I have chosen to use the terms 'free people of colour', 'free black and coloured' or 'free non-white' interchangeably when referring to the group of people of African and mixed European-African descent who were legally free in Barbados during slavery. To describe this same group after emancipation and distinguish them from those freed between 1834 and 1838, I have added the qualifiers 'pre-emancipation' or 'pre-1834'. Despite the cumbersome or problematic nature of these terms, I have chosen them in preference to the more commonly used phrases 'free coloureds' and 'freedmen', which are ambiguous and frequently inaccurate.

[2] For discussion of the concept of 'currents of radicalism' see Eugene Biagini and Alastair Reid (eds.), *Currents of Radicalism: Popular Radicalism, Organised Labour and Party Politics in Britain, 1850–1914* (Cambridge: Cambridge University Press, 1991), Introduction.

This racial solidarity, however, was constrained by the same conflicts of ideology and interest which had defined free black and coloured politics during slavery. The democratic hopes of the disenfranchised majority were ultimately dashed by the combined efforts of white and non-white elites.

There are few studies of the political role of pre-emancipation free non-whites in post-slavery politics and society. Historians such as Michael Craton and O. Nigel Bolland have emphasised the continuity in patterns of control and resistance before and after slavery. However, the existing literature on free people of colour in Barbados during this period by implication suggests a contradictory discontinuity. Given that pre-emancipation non-white politics are represented as largely pro-slavery in their views, historians have a difficult time accounting for the sudden rise to prominence of a radical coloured figure, Samuel Jackman Prescod, who became the leading political advocate of disenfranchised non-whites during and after apprenticeship. Hilary Beckles attempts to bridge the divide between the free elite of colour and slaves by stating rather vaguely that, sometime around emancipation, Prescod 'became associated with anti-slavery opinions emanating from the slave yards', emerging out of the ether to lead the emancipated.[3]

The struggle between the plantocracy and the ex-slave estate labour force has been the traditional fault-line between control and resistance in the post-emancipation Caribbean. This study locates this boundary within an intracommunal context, among a group of people usually ignored, as a group, in the study of post-emancipation Barbados. It suggests that conflicts of class and political ideology reflected the political permeability of apparently rigid boundaries of race and legal status. Wealthy whites and wealthy free people of colour often united against the more radical reformist demands of the majority of Afro-Barbadians. At the same time the chapter analyses the existence of political networks among elite people of colour, using the recurrence of the names of certain individuals to reveal the shifts and continuities in black and coloured politics over the time period.

---

[3] Hilary Beckles, *A History of Barbados: From Amerindian Settlement to Nation-State* (Cambridge: Cambridge University Press, 1990), p. 116; O. Nigel Bolland, 'Systems of Domination After Slavery: The Control of Land and Labour in the British West Indies After 1838' and Michael Craton, 'Continuity Not Change: The Incidence of Unrest among Ex-Slaves in the British West Indies, 1838–1876', in Beckles and Verene Shepherd (eds.), *Caribbean Freedom: Economy and Society From Emancipation to the Present* (Kingston: Ian Randle, 1993), pp. 107–23 and 192–206 respectively.

'Enlightened, respectable and wealthy': the conservative tradition in non-white politics, 1799–1831

By the time of emancipation in August 1834 two distinct and frequently conflicting currents of political activity had emerged among Barbados' free people of colour in their struggle for greater civil rights. The earliest and most organised strand of civil rights activity took the form of petitions sent to the House of Assembly by quite select groups of men of colour, predominantly drawn from the island's non-white elite of Bridgetown merchants.[4]

The black and coloured elite's cautious pursuit of civil rights stood in stark contrast to the more radical activities of many of their counterparts elsewhere in the Lesser Antilles during the era of the French and Haitian revolutions.[5] From their first petition in 1799 these elite men addressed the Barbados House of Assembly in the most pro-planter terms, stressing their support for slavery. They requested a crucial, but limited, increase in civil rights, namely the right to give testimony in court. The petitioners sought to draw a clear distinction between themselves and 'their' slaves, emphasising their free status, their financial wealth and their legal entitlements as British imperial subjects. A petition of 1829 was the first to request the right to vote for the small number of free men of colour who could satisfy the island's property-based franchise.[6]

These petitions were part of a process during the late eighteenth and early nineteenth centuries by which this newly emergent elite sought to distinguish itself from lower-class people of colour, slave as well as free. During the 1780s and 1790s an urban merchant class emerged whose material circumstances and educational background were significantly superior to those of the majority of free people of colour. Very few free people of colour were part of this wealthy stratum.

---

[4] Petitions were sent in 1799, 1803, 1811, 1812, 1817, 1823, 1829, 1830 and 1833.
[5] Hilary Beckles, 'On the Backs of Blacks: The Barbados Free-Coloureds' Pursuit of Civil Rights and the 1816 Slave Rebellion', *Immigrants and Minorities,* vol. 3:2 (July 1984), pp. 167–88; David Geggus, 'The Slaves and Free Coloreds of Martinique during the Age of the French and Haitian Revolutions', in Robert L. Paquette and Stanley L. Engerman (eds.), *The Lesser Antilles in the Age of European Expansion* (Gainesville: University Press of Florida, 1996), pp. 280–301.
[6] See Lucas Mss, Minutes of the Barbados Council, 15 October 1799, 'The Humble Memorial and Remonstrance of the Free Coloured People...', 14 October 1799, and 'The Humble Petition of the Free Coloured People, Inhabitants of the Island', in Lucas Mss, Minutes of the Barbados Council, 1 November 1803, cited in Jerome Handler, *The Unappropriated People: Freedmen in the Slave Society of Barbados* (Baltimore: Johns Hopkins University Press, 1974), pp. 76, 147; CO 31/51, 14 July 1829.

Most free black and coloured people were quite poor and shared their working and recreational lives with non-agricultural slaves.[7]

The Barbadian legislature rewarded this elite for its fidelity on two occasions. The first was in 1817, after the suppression of the 1816 slave revolt. Several free militiamen of colour displayed their loyalty to the slave-owning cause by helping to suppress the rebellion and the legislature responded with a bill allowing certain free men of colour to testify in court. The member of the assembly who proposed the bill specified that it applied only 'to the most enlightened class of the free people of colour' and not 'to the vulgar class, many of whom have no idea of the nature or Solemnity of an Oath'. In 1831 the legislature passed an act allowing free people of colour to vote, but its application was even more class-specific than the legislation of 1817. It set a franchise qualification of £30 for free men of colour, £20 higher than the qualification for white men.[8]

These concessions to the elite of colour may have served to ensure the loyalty of the wealthy few who benefited but they also alienated the non-white elite politically from the majority of free people of colour, who were excluded from the privileges granted. Additionally the petitions expressed views, particularly on the issue of slavery, with which, as will be shown, many free blacks and coloureds were not in agreement. Thus, these petitions and the favourable response they received from the legislature helped to consolidate ideological and class conflicts among free people of colour and provided focal points of political dissent from other free non-whites and slaves.

Black and coloured popular radicalism, 1816–34

Only rarely did radical and dissenting sentiments break through the carefully crafted script of political consensus which the conservative white and non-white elites composed during the early nineteenth century. Nevertheless these moments were frequent enough to suggest a

---

[7] Handler, *Unappropriated People*, pp. 122–133; Barry Higman, *Slave Populations of the British Caribbean, 1807–1834* (Barbados: The Press, University of the West Indies, 1995), pp. 226–59; Handler and Charlotte Frisbie, 'Aspects of Slave Life in Barbados: Music and its Cultural Context', *New West Indian Guide/Nieuwe West-Indische Gids*, 71 (1997), pp. 183–225; Melanie Newton, 'Philanthropy, Gender and the Production of Public life in Barbados, c1790–c1850', in Diana Paton and Pamela Scully (eds.), *Gender and Emancipation in the Atlantic World* (Duke University Press, forthcoming 2005).
[8] About 75 people of colour could meet this franchise qualification (CO 31/47, Minutes of the House of Assembly, 8 October 1816; CO 30/21, no. 538, 'An Act to remove certain restraints and disabilities imposed by Law on His Majesty's Free Coloured and Free Black Subjects…', 9 May 1831; Handler, *Unappropriated People*, p. 103.

pattern of anti-racist, anti-elitist and frequently abolitionist political activity which crossed the lines of legal status, with non-white radicals – including some elites but mostly lower-class free blacks and coloureds and slaves – coming together to challenge the authority of the upper classes.

The first evidence of the existence of this current of free black and coloured radicalism comes from the 1816 rebellion. Four free non-white men were executed on trumped-up charges for allegedly leading the revolt. While it is of course possible that these individuals participated in the uprising, it seems more likely that the rebellion provided the plantocracy with a convenient opportunity to dispose of individuals who held dangerous political opinions. Such a supposition seems especially fitting in the case of one of the men, Joseph Franklin, singled out by the Assembly as the rebellion's principal leader. Twenty years later, during the final months of apprenticeship, the editors of the island's first abolitionist newspaper, two free men of colour, asserted that Franklin had been executed because he was 'a man of bold, independent spirit' who, like themselves, was '*too troublesome* to the Great'. They claimed him as well as 'dozens of others whom we can *now* point to with pleasure and pride as co-operators in a good cause' as abolitionist heroes.[9]

Lower-class free coloured and black resistance to state authority and the conservative elite erupted onto the public stage in the 1820s, at the height of the struggle between abolitionists, the imperial government and West Indian planters over slavery. In October 1823, following a historic debate on slavery in the British parliament in May and the Demerara slave revolt in August, racial tensions were high in Barbados; a 'white mob' destroyed the Methodist church in Bridgetown, whose congregation was composed almost entirely of free people of colour. In response 'Mobs' of people of colour began 'assembling about the Town' and organising political meetings. Frightened by this display of extra-parliamentary political opinion, a group of self-described 'enlightened, respectable and wealthy' men of colour, who had received the right to testify in 1817, sent an address to the House of Assembly, professing to speak for the 'free coloured community at large'. They condemned abolitionism and lauded planters for 'efforts ... [to teach the slaves] to be contented and happy in their present highly improved condition'. They

---

[9] Barbados House of Assembly, *Report... into the origin, causes, and progress, of the late Insurrection* (Barbados and London: T. Cadell and W. Davies, 1818, afterwards the '1818 Report'); Handler, *Unappropriated People*, pp. 86, 114; *Liberal*, 7 March 1838 (emphasis in the original); H.A. Vaughan, 'Joseph Pitt Washington Francklyn, 1782–1816', *The Democrat* (January 1971), cited in Beckles, *Black Rebellion*, p. 95.

also stressed that they would not take advantage of the 'disturbed' political situation to press the legislature for civil rights.[10]

The address provoked a mass meeting of other free people of colour who had not been consulted on its contents and 373 men signed a counter-address in which they distanced themselves from the pro-slavery comments and obsequiousness of the original address. Some of the men were wealthy and had signed earlier petitions, but the names of the overwhelming majority do not appear in any other public document, not even taxation records, indicating that they were men of low socio-economic status. A shocked and infuriated House of Assembly held an inquiry into the petition, which revealed deep resentment among poorer and younger men of colour towards the old elite, outrage at the claim regarding the slaves' 'improved condition' and a view that Barbadian people of colour should 'fight' for the right to vote for, and be elected to, the island's legislative assembly.[11]

There is no evidence that the extra-parliamentary and anti-elite opposition which was expressed in the 1823 counter-address was politically organised, but the pro-planter *Barbadian* newspaper referred in 1825 to the existence of a political group of free people of colour called the 'Radicals' and accused some instigators of the counter-address of being involved with it.[12] Black and coloured opposition to the collaboration between the non-white elite and the legislature surfaced repeatedly during the final decade of slavery. In contrast to elite men of colour, who stated their collective requests through the accepted political channel of petitions to the House of Assembly, the stage of the 'radicals' and lower classes was the streets and other public spaces of Bridgetown.

The targets of this non-violent but vocal political dissent were elite men of colour perceived to be on the side of the assembly and institutions which epitomised the principle of racial inequality. In 1824, just months after the counter-address controversy, the leader of the elite petitioners, Jacob Belgrave Jr, and several of his friends 'of the most respectable class' were verbally assaulted by a 'number of free black and coloured persons' and slaves at the Bridgetown wharf. The protest occurred as Belgrave was leaving the island for England, where he intended to present himself to the Secretary of State for the Colonies to

---

[10] CO 31/49 Minutes of the Barbados House of Assembly 21 October 1823, containing "The Humble Address of the free coloured Inhabitants..." dated 20 October 1823; CO 28/93, Governor Henry Warde to Secretary of State for the Colonies Lord Bathurst, 4 February 1824.
[11] The *Globe*, 22 January 1824, cited in Handler, *Unappropriated People*, pp. 94–7; CO 28/93, Warde to Bathurst, 4 February 1824; CO 31/49, 4 February 1824.
[12] *Barbadian*, 29 July 1825.

answer any questions regarding the island's free people of colour. The crowd of slaves and free people of colour had assembled at the wharf for the specific purpose of protesting against Belgrave and his friends.[13]

Although the *Barbadian* dismissed the slaves at the protest as 'mobs' who would always 'join in any disturbances', their presence suggests that the demonstration was a collective expression of political solidarity between slaves and free people of colour against men seen to be traitors to their own colour. As one of the island's few planters of colour, Belgrave had long been a target for expressions of opposition by slaves and lower-class free people of colour. On two occasions just days before the outbreak of the 1816 rebellion, slaves had accosted him on public roads, accusing him of being responsible for withholding their freedom. No white planters experienced such personal vilification and Belgrave's estates sustained the third highest damage in the revolt, suggesting that he was personally targeted by the rebels.[14]

In 1825, 1831 and 1833, groups of free people of colour staged demonstrations against racial segregation by occupying the sections of churches reserved for whites, twice in St Michael's Cathedral in Bridgetown and once in Christ Church parish church. The first such occupation occurred in 1825 during a service at the Cathedral for a whites-only school, whose establishment was widely viewed by free non-whites as an insult.[15]

Elites of both colours found it especially disturbing when lower-class non-whites and slaves intervened on the stage of formal politics. This happened on the eve of emancipation in 1834, when a liberal white lawyer, Attorney-General Henry Sharpe, ran for a seat in the House of Assembly. Planters were vehemently opposed to Sharpe – he was a trusted ally of Governor Lionel Smith, who had been sent to the island in 1833 to force the recalcitrant assembly to pass an emancipation bill. Sharpe's support for merchant-friendly policies and franchise reform endeared him to elite Bridgetown merchants of colour, who threw themselves wholeheartedly behind his campaign.[16]

---

[13] Ibid., 8 October 1824.
[14] Ibid. and 29 July 1825; '1818 Report', pp. 38–9 and 59–63; Karl Watson, *The Civilised Island Barbados: A Social History, 1750–1816* (Ann Arbor: University of Florida, 1977), p. 256.
[15] *Barbadian*, 1 March 1825 and 8 March 1825; St Michael vestry minutes, 7, 13 and 19 December 1831, 2 January 1832; *Barbadian*, 17 December 1831; Christ Church vestry minutes, 31 December 1833 and 8 December 1834.
[16] CO 28/111, Governor Lionel Smith to Secretary of State for the Colonies Lord Stanley, 12 October 1833; *Barbadian*, 31 May 1834; CO 28/116, Smith to Glenelg, 8 August 1835, no. 31.

On the day of the elections both 'the respectable individuals of the coloured class' and whites were horrified when the hustings in St Michael's Cathedral were thronged by masses of 'vulgar' lower-class 'negroes and coloured persons – of the lowest degree ... who filled up the pews, and made the walls of that sacred place re-echo with their profane "hurras", several times'. Hundreds of slaves and free people of colour, both men and women, were 'swaggering up and down the aisles of the cathedral, with the bows of blue ribbon on their arms, the distinguishing badge of those, respectable as well as vulgar, who professed to be the supporters of Sharpe'.[17]

Thus, people of colour, both slave and free, began emancipation deeply divided over what resistance to racial discrimination should aim to achieve. For many elite men of colour, lower-class free non-whites had no particular right to participate directly in the political process. Most saw slaves as people from whom they needed political protection, not as members of their own community. Lower-class free people of colour and slaves, however, tended to see slave emancipation as a democratic opportunity for the non-white poor and politically disenfranchised, regardless of legal status.

Anti-segregation and radicalism, 1833–38

Until the very end of slavery, black and coloured urban merchants refused to embrace abolition, even phrasing their demands for greater political representation in terms of a need to protect themselves and their property from the chaos of emancipation. However, during apprenticeship, a sea change occurred in the attitudes of elite men of colour towards majority demands for greater political representation. Even the most conservative men of colour began to assert their demands for political appointments and franchise reform on the grounds that the racial desegregation of politics would provide for better representation of all people of colour, including ex-slaves.[18]

While emancipation was certainly the catalyst for this shift, it was firmly rooted in pre-1834 developments in free black and coloured politics. Although class exerted a strong influence on ideological divisions among free people of colour, some elite merchants had supported radical positions at least since the 1820s, when several of them participated

---

[17] *Barbadian*, 4 June 1834.
[18] See for example CO 31/51, 24 March 1834, 'Petition from inhabitants of St. Michael's Parish, praying for an augmentation of their representation'; J.A. Thome and J.H. Kimball, *Emancipation in the West Indies: A Six Months' Tour of Antigua, Barbados and Jamaica in the Year 1837* (New York: American Anti-Slavery Society, 1838), pp. 72–5.

in the agitation which produced the 1824 counter-address. Nevertheless, elite individuals who sympathised with emancipation and a democratic concept of desegregation remained marginal within the most influential circle of free coloured and black politics. This changed during apprenticeship, largely in response to the plantocracy's steadfast resistance to the desegregation of the island's military and civil institutions, symbolised by the 1831 Franchise Reform Act, which once again upheld the principle of racial inequality and only benefited a tiny minority even among the merchant elite. This intransigence lent new legitimacy to progressive and more confrontational voices among free people of colour.

At the same time, several individuals who had studied in Europe during the 1820s and either participated in or been influenced by the European abolitionist and political reform movements returned to the island and became politically active. Between 1833 and the end of apprenticeship such individuals, particularly Samuel Jackman Prescod, Thomas Harris Jr and Nathaniel Roach, emerged as the leading voices of the popular current of non-white political radicalism. The most outspoken of these three individuals, Prescod rose to prominence in 1833 when he called a public meeting in support of a leading merchant of colour, Thomas Cummins, after the legislature refused the Governor's request to appoint Cummins to an officership in the island's militia. The meeting represented the first time that the anti-elitist confrontationalism of the non-white majority successfully overruled the more conciliatory approach of the elite. Hundreds attended and voted for a strongly worded address of protest to the legislature, condemning its decision as racist and unjust, over the objections of conservative men of colour who were used to having a free hand in preparing such petitions.[19]

The status of Prescod, Harris and Roach as popular leaders was confirmed after they became the editors of the *Liberal* and *New Times* newspapers during apprenticeship and used their newspapers as a forum for disenfranchised people to voice their opinions on formal politics. The *Liberal* was especially popular, advocating bourgeois franchise reform to include some lower-class free people of colour and former slaves, in order for 'a number of the poor and middle classes of every complexion [to] be admitted to a share in legislation'. In the first years after apprenticeship the editors organised annual anti-slavery dinners, attended by pre-1834 free people of colour and ex-slaves, to celebrate emancipation and demand a broad extension of the franchise.[20]

---

[19] *Barbadian*, 15 May 1833; Handler, *Unappropriated People*, p. 106.
[20] *Liberal*, 10 March and 1 December 1838; 8 May 1839.

The *Liberal* and the *New Times* went beyond demanding franchise reform and became active opponents of the apprenticeship system and early post-emancipation labour policies. The *Liberal* saw it as the role of the 'middle classes' to mediate in the struggle between planters and labourers, and warned planters that 'the respectable coloured community' would not 'quietly ... suffer the laborer to be imposed upon for the want of that knowledge, and talent, and influence which they possess'. Harris sometimes went to court to speak on behalf of estate labourers unfairly prosecuted by employers, and labourers would frequently come to the *Liberal*'s office in Bridgetown for advice and assistance.[21]

Most upper-class men of colour saw Prescod as a rabble-rouser but, perhaps inspired by the recent success of the British parliamentary reform movement, temporarily rested their political hopes on the possibility that his immense and unprecedented popularity would influence the Barbadian legislature. Thus, at an August 1839 dinner commemorating the first anniversary of the end of apprenticeship, Joseph Kennedy, a prominent merchant, admitted that he had once opposed Prescod because he thought his methods 'ill-timed, but that was years ago now'. Kennedy proclaimed that 'so long as the colored classes were united and firm, nothing could prevent them from moving forward'. That year, 18 non-white businessmen, including politically cautious men like Kennedy and Joseph Thorne, closed their businesses in commemoration of emancipation day, and sold tickets for the dinner at their stores.[22]

Divide and rule: the state co-opts the non-white elite

The desires of upper-class free people of colour for public office found supporters in the Colonial Office before and during apprenticeship. Imperial policymakers saw pre-1834 free people of colour as the 'natural' representatives of ex-slaves' interests because of their colour, as well as potentially effective instruments of social and labour control over former slaves after emancipation. The imperial government's interest in appointing men of colour to political posts applied only if they were of the right socio-economic status.

---

[21] *Liberal*, 10 March, 26 May, 18 September and 10 October 1838; 23 and 26 January, 18 September 1839.
[22] See minutes of free coloured and black mass meeting, *Barbadian*, 15 May 1833; *Liberal*, 20, 27 July and 4 August 1838, 4 August 1839.

The Governor at the time of emancipation, Sir Lionel Smith, was determined to appoint men of colour to civil and military posts.[23] He appointed the Grenadian Joseph Garraway and the Antiguan Henry Loving, both men of colour, to the special magistracy during apprenticeship. Loving, an abolitionist, had been a popular figure among progressive free people of colour in pre-emancipation Barbados. In 1837 and 1838, Smith's successor Sir Evan MacGregor appointed Garraway and seven local planters and merchants of colour, including Cummins, to commissions of the peace, which toured the island explaining to apprentices their rights and duties under apprenticeship – with emphasis placed, unsurprisingly, on their duties. [24] MacGregor also appointed Nathaniel Roach, the editor of the radical *New Times*, as police magistrate of St Lucy, a surprise decision which outraged some whites.[25] In 1839, after several other government appointments and years of being re-elected to the St Michael vestry, Thomas Cummins was appointed to the island's legislative council, and became police magistrate for St George parish. Between 1840 and 1842, he presided over the Court of Grand Sessions, the highest judicial appointment for a local magistrate. In 1841, he began his first of several terms as churchwarden of the St Michael vestry.[26]

With the exception of Roach, none of the men appointed or elected to political office was associated with radical non-white politics. Like the legislative concessions of 1817 and 1831, these post-

---

[23] CO 28/111, Governor Sir Lionel Smith to Stanley, 23 May 1833. Smith's successor as Governor of Barbados, Sir Evan MacGregor, had a similar policy while he was Governor of Antigua (see Susan Lowes, '"They Couldn't Mash Ants": The Decline of the White and Non-White Elites in Antigua, 1834–1900', in Karen Fog Olwig (ed.), *Small Islands, Large Questions: Society, Culture and Resistance in the Post-emancipation Caribbean* (London: Frank Cass, 1995), pp. 31–52, p. 38.

[24] In 1832 a group of free men of colour threw a party in Loving's honour when he stopped in Barbados on his way back to the West Indies from England, where he had testified in favour of abolition before the 1831–32 commission on slave emancipation (*Barbadian* 6 and 10 October 1832); PP 1831–32, vol. 20, *Report of the Select Committee [on] Slavery*, pp. 156–67. On Garraway's appointment see the *Barbadian*, 2 November 1836; On Loving's see CO 28/119, Governor Evan MacGregor to Secretary of State Lord Glenelg, 19 May 1837, no. 112, and CO 28/120, MacGregor to Glenelg, 30 October 1837, no. 248.

[25] CO 28/119, MacGregor to Glenelg, 2 January 1837, no. 1; CO 28/123, MacGregor to Glenelg, 11 August 1838, no. 214, encl: no. 11; *Barbadian*, 5 December 1838; CO 28/127, MacGregor to Glenelg, February 7 1839, no. 14; *Liberal* and *Barbadian*, 13 March 1839.

[26] *Barbadian*, 9 December 1835 and 19 January 1842; CO 28/127, MacGregor to Glenelg 7 February 1839, no. 14; *Liberal*, 28 July 1842; Minutes of the St Michael vestry 25 March 1844, 2 March 1845 and 2 March 1846.

emancipation political appointments provoked discord among political activists of colour, silenced opposition and reinforced elite non-white support for the plantocracy. The appointments gave political influence to men like Cummins and Thorne who proved to be deeply committed to maintaining post-emancipation social order, even if this meant curtailing the freedom of ex-slaves. In the case of Roach, elevating him to office proved to be an effective way of dividing the radical opposition of colour. Upon taking office as a magistrate, Roach immediately gave up his post as editor of the *New Times* and reversed his earlier opposition to planters' labour policies. Roach's shift in allegiance outraged Prescod, who publicly accused Roach of having been 'bought' by the Governor and the legislature with his appointment. In January 1839, when Prescod called a meeting to establish a Franchise Reform Committee, Roach was not even invited. The meeting rapidly degenerated into political factionalism, with Roach's supporters showing up to disrupt the meeting's procedures and interrupt speeches by Prescod's contingent.[27]

Similarly, after Thomas Cummins was elected to the St Michael vestry during apprenticeship, he came under fire for supporting vestry policies which other people of colour considered discriminatory. At the franchise meeting in January 1839 Cummins admitted that his vestry votes were influenced by careerist rather than populist considerations, stating that he was 'aware that my tenure is by permission of the Vestry, and that were I to incur their displeasure by opposing any of their views they might prevent my re-election.' He added that he supported franchise extension as his best hope of keeping his seat 'in opposition to the caprice of the old members'.[28]

Thus, after 1838, although non-white activists all now spoke the language of racial equality, emancipation divided them much as slavery had done. Many conservative elite individuals continued to pursue their own political interests largely at the expense of the black and coloured majority. Once apprenticeship ended, these long-standing divisions of class and ideology found a new expression in the debate over ex-slaves' rights to control their labour.

Free people of colour and the indentured emigration debate

Apprenticeship came to an end across the British Caribbean amidst strikes, evictions and violent confrontations between labourers on one

---

[27] *Liberal*, 29 August 1838; CO 28/123, Private, MacGregor to Glenelg, 8 September 1838; *Barbadian*, 8 May 1839; *Liberal*, 23 and 26 January, 7 and 21 August 1839; *Barbadian*, 9 October 1841.
[28] *Liberal*, 31 October 1838 and 23 January 1839.

side, and estate authorities, estate constables, the police force and magistrates on the other. Barbadian ex-slaves voted with their feet against repressive terms of estate labour, and went to neighbouring territories such as Trinidad and British Guiana to work for higher wages.[29] In response to this new threat to planters' interests the Barbadian legislature passed repressive labour laws and anti-emigration acts during the apprenticeship period and the first years of full freedom. Under the 1840 'Act to regulate the Hiring of Servants', or contract act, labourers who refused to sign one-month contracts with the estates on which they lived faced immediate eviction. Furthermore, anyone found guilty of 'enticing' a labourer away from an employer could be fined £10.[30]

The *Liberal*'s advocacy of the right of rural labourers to resist labour coercion increased its popular support among both the rural and lower-class non-white poor. As committed liberals, Prescod and Thomas Harris opposed any attempt to regulate the labour market, whether in the form of labourers who organised 'combinations' or planters who tried to limit labourers' freedom. They promoted emigration as the only way to stop planters' interference with the free movement of labour. Before Roach's defection to the planter camp the *Liberal* and *The New Times* offered advice to potential emigrants in their offices, and their newspapers became the platform for the pro-emigration lobby. Many other elite men of colour were uncomfortable with the *Liberal*'s radical positions on labour issues, and they worried that Prescod's methods, his popularity among the urban and rural poor, especially former slaves, and his corresponding unpopularity with the government would damage the credibility of the franchise reform struggle. At the January 1839 franchise meeting, one of his supporters felt compelled to publicly dismiss claims that Prescod 'had not the support of the respectable colored community' and that 'it was only the lower orders, the rabble, who viewed his conduct with approbation'.[31]

---

[29] Gad Heuman, 'Riots and Resistance in the Caribbean at the Moment of Full Freedom in the Anglophone Caribbean', *Slavery and Abolition*, vol. 21, no. 2, (August 2000), pp. 135–49; Trevor Marshall, 'Post-emancipation Adjustments in Barbados, 1838–1876', in Alvin O. Thompson (ed.), *Emancipation I: A Series of Lectures to Commemorate the 150th Anniversary of Emancipation* (Barbados: National Cultural Foundation and the History Department, UWI Cave Hill, 1984), pp. 88–107.
[30] William A. Green, *British Slave Emancipation: The Sugar Colonies and the Great Experiment, 1830–1865* (Oxford: Clarendon Press, 1976), p. 193; Beckles, *A History of Barbados*, p. 109.
[31] See articles and editorials on labour relations in the *Liberal*, 26 May and 22 September 1838, 6 March 1839 and 15 July 1840; see minutes of franchise reform meeting, *Liberal*, 23 January 1839.

The stage was set for a political crisis among people of colour. It began in September 1839, when a new agent for British Guiana, Thomas Day, arrived in Barbados. According to the Governor, Day had a 'higher motive' for being an agent, namely, 'to raise the wages of Labor in Barbados which he considered ... too low ...' Whether or not Day's political claims were genuine, his mission endeared him to the editors of the *Liberal*. In articles, editorials and advertisements, Day and the *Liberal* ran a pro-emigration campaign, supported by letters from the public.[32]

In order to counteract the threat from Day and the *Liberal*, Governor MacGregor nominated Joseph Thorne to the newly-created position of Assistant Harbour Master of the Bridgetown port. Thorne represented a perfect example of how conservative men of colour reconciled their stated commitments to emancipation and racial liberation with the coercion of rural workers. His task was to convince agricultural labourers who came to the harbour with emigration certificates to remain. In October 1839 the *Liberal* accused Thorne of misleading and coercing potential emigrants in order to prevent them from emigrating to British Guiana as indentured agricultural labourers. An indignant Thorne responded that he felt 'perfectly justified as a man of colour' in advising them not to go because he had heard that the work to be performed in British Guiana was too arduous. He invoked the anti-slavery cause to support his opinion, stating that his actions were 'borne out by one of the best friends that the negro race ever had, namely [British abolitionist John] Scoble'.[33]

In 1840, Day was prosecuted under a new act which the *Liberal* immediately dubbed the 'Gagging Act', since the law made it illegal even to voice a positive opinion about emigration. The act provoked a political crisis among non-white political leaders. On 23 March 1840, the Barbados Auxiliary Anti-Slavery Society met to draw up a

---

[32] Governor's correspondence with magistrates, 2 September 1839 (Bridgetown Public Library); CO 28/128, MacGregor to Normanby, 19 September 1839, no. 95, and MacGregor to Normanby, 9 October 1839, no. 102, encl: no. 7, Memorial of Thomas Day, 19 September 1839; *Liberal*, 19 February and 18 April 1840; *Barbadian*, 2 May 1840.

[33] CO 28/128, MacGregor to Normanby, 19 September 1839, no. 95, encl: no. 17, Thorne to Garraway (24 September 1839); *Liberal*, 12 and 16 October 1839; CO 28/129, MacGregor to Secretary of State Lord Russell, 20 December 1839, no. 131, encl: no. 1, Meeting of the Court of Error (3 December 1839); CO 28/133, MacGregor to Russell, 21 March 1840, no. 26 encl: 'An Act to empower the Governor... to appoint an Assistant Harbour Master...' and encl: D, Joseph Thorne to Joseph Garraway (21 March 1840); CO 28/139, MacGregor to Russell, 8 February 1841, no. 17, encl: 'The memorial of Thomas Day, of British Guiana...', and MacGregor to Russell, 17 March 1841, no. 25.

resolution regarding the act. The Society's committee consisted of 12 men of colour, as well as Solicitor-General Robert Bowcher-Clarke, and some white clergymen and planters. At the meeting Clarke, the House of Assembly's leading advocate of planter interests, introduced motions to condemn indentured emigration. The majority voted in favour of the motions, but seven dissenters, among them Prescod and Harris, issued a counter-statement publicly opposing the 'Gagging Act'. After the meeting the *Liberal*'s staff distributed handbills condemning the act on behalf of the society.[34]

The disagreement was a victory for elites of colour. Joseph Thorne was among those who, opposed to Prescod and labour emigration, took the opportunity to characterise him publicly as a hypocrite. Thorne cemented his political ties to the planter interest in 1840 by campaigning for Solicitor-General Clarke, who was the leading voice of planters' interests in the assembly, in the latter's bid to be returned as the representative for the parish of St Michael. Thorne's involvement in Clarke's campaign probably helped him in his later campaign for election to the St Michael vestry, of which he was churchwarden for several years during the 1840s.[35]

The containment of popular radicalism, 1840–44

Within a decade of emancipation the radical and lower-class struggle which had sought to shape the politics of racial liberation in a more democratic fashion was systematically undermined by the combined efforts of the local aristocracy and members of the black and coloured elite. In 1840, several men of colour and the plantocracy colluded in an unsuccessful state-orchestrated attempt to shut the *Liberal* down. After Prescod wrote a scathing article accusing him of being a tool of the planters, Thomas Cummins' successor as police magistrate for St George, a white planter named Frederick Watts, assembled a delegation of 54 St George estate 'headmen' in his office. The men signed their Xs to an address contradicting Prescod's claims, and delivered it to the Governor's residence 'on behalf' of all the labourers from St George,

---

[34] *Barbadian*, 28 March 1840; PP 1842, vol. 29, 'Quarterly Reply…' 1 January-31 March 1840, no. 3, St George; CO 28/134, MacGregor to Russell, 9 April 1840, no. 35, encl: B, police magistrate of St Philip to Garraway (3 April 1840); *Liberal*, 18 April 1840; CO 28/134, MacGregor to Russell, 9 April 1840, no. 35.

[35] *Barbadian*, 3 June 1840; *Liberal* 3 June 1840; CO 28/134, MacGregor to Russell, 9 April 1840, no. 35; PP 1842, vol. 29, 'General Reports for 1840', Thorne to Felix Bedingfeld, Governor's Private Secretary, 11 December 1841, pp. 131–2; St Michael vestry, March 1844–March 1846.

none of whom was consulted regarding its contents. Watts then sued Prescod for libel.[36]

The trial was a victory for the supporters of elitist racial integration. Thomas Cummins was the Chief Justice of the 1840–41 Court of Grand Sessions – the first time a man of colour had filled that post – and presided over the case. Three 'respectable coloured and black gentlemen', merchants Joseph Kennedy, Henry Brathwaite and Henry Wilkins, sat on the jury which sentenced Prescod to five months in prison and fined him £200.[37]

Prescod was pardoned and, in 1843, became the first man of colour to be elected to the House of Assembly as the representative for Bridgetown under a new electoral law of 1842. Prescod's essentially bourgeois views on franchise reform and his economic liberalism gained him the respect of some white merchants, who supported his 1843 campaign as a candidate for his own newly-formed Liberal Party. Even so, in 1844, a white merchants' newspaper described Prescod's supporters as 'paupers, the majority of them', 'without a doubloon that they could honestly call their own' and his opponents as 'gentlemen, the *Elite* of the wealth and respectability of the city ... two of whom probably contribute to the Treasury of this Island fully as large a sum as the grand total of the Radical faction all put together ...' Prescod harnessed lower-class street protest as part of the theatre of his campaign. His supporters would gather in the streets and at the hustings to express their hostility towards the wealthy. During the 1843 elections various reports mentioned that the planters' candidates – one of whom was, ironically, Attorney-General Henry Sharpe – were hissed at in the streets by Prescod's lower-class supporters, who heckled the conservatives' supporters at the polls, attempted to steal their ribbons and greeted them with derisive cheers of 'Prescod forever!'[38]

Prescod's 1843 election victory was a victory for progressive forces in Barbados over the plantocracy.[39] However, it also summed up the political tragedy of emancipation that the election of this popular

---

[36] *Liberal*, 16 and 20 November 1839; *Barbadian*, 20 November 1839; CO 28/133, MacGregor to Russell, 24 January 1840, encl: C no. 1, 'Address from the Laborers of the Parish of St. George'; CO 28/134, MacGregor to Russell, 26 December 1840, no. 118, encl: the *West Indian*, 21 December 1840, report on the proceedings of the court of grand sessions; *British Anti-Slavery Reporter*, 12 February 1840. Headmen were male estate employees who supervised labourers in the field and in the boiling house.
[37] CO 28/134, MacGregor to Russell, 26 December 1840, no. 119, encl: MacGregor to the Provost Marshal General, 24 December 1840.
[38] CO 28/156, Grey to Stanley, 17 June 1843, no. 47; *Liberal*, 17 and 21 June 1843 and 27 July 1844, letter entitled 'The Globe's say'.
[39] Beckles, *History of Barbados*, p. 118.

hero came at the expense of the democratic and anti-racist tradition which had brought him to prominence. The same law which redrew the electoral boundaries in favour of Prescod's urban supporters also equalised the franchise requirement at £20, which made no difference to either the size or composition of the electorate. Less than one per cent of the population could vote in 1843, a figure which would not change substantially until the twentieth century. Although Prescod's election gave 'great pleasure to the numerous class of colored Inhabitants', few if any of the disenfranchised masses of people of colour who had supported him ever won the right to vote.[40] The lower-class people of colour who took to the streets supporting his campaign were reduced to a supporting and, ultimately, non-threatening role in the theatre of politics.

As with previous politicians of colour, imperial and colonial authorities gained by Prescod's elevation into the circle of elite formal politics. In elected office Prescod compromised somewhat with his political adversaries and, in the process, was divested of the most dangerous aspect of his radicalism as a voice of the disenfranchised labouring majority. Prescod stopped publicly advocating emigration, probably out of political prudence and possibly because it was a hopeless cause. By the mid-1840s the authorities were no longer worried that emigration or labour unrest would lead to a decrease in the size of the labour force. As in many other post-slavery societies, harsh labour legislation and the absence of any fundamental redistribution of wealth, land or political power forced most ex-slaves to accept the repressive terms of Barbadian estate labour. He also stopped calling for franchise reform. Prescod's voting record in the House of Assembly indicates that he remained consistent in his liberal views, advocating lower taxes for working people and urban businesses and reduced state spending as an answer to the island's financial woes and increasingly desperate poverty.[41]

Thus, whether they opposed or supported the plantocracy, emancipation brought political benefits for some elite men of colour without enfranchising the majority. The anti-establishment popular politics which had been born among free people of colour and slaves in the 1820s became a manipulated part of the spectacle of hustings in the 1840s. Politicians now made crowd participation in the name of one candidate or another a 'legitimate' part of electoral politics. The

---

[40] CO 28/139, MacGregor to Russell, 2 April 1841, no. 29; CO 28/140, Lieutenant-Governor Henry Darling to Stanley, 28 October 1841, no. 27, encl: Prescod to Russell, 13 July 1840; CO 28/156, Governor Charles Grey to Stanley, 17 June 1843, no. 47.

[41] See, for example, CO 31/53, 3 October 1843, 13 May 1845 and 9 May 1848.

political establishment thereby absorbed the energy and vitality of lower-class black and coloured public demonstrations while stripping them of their force as expressions of non-white and lower-class political autonomy.

Conclusion

At an anti-slavery dinner in September 1840, a few months before his libel trial, Prescod expressed the bitter irony of legal freedom without either political enfranchisement or social reform for the majority of people of colour when he asked the audience: 'Why should it be called liberality, and so much credit assumed for the act, when a black or coloured man [is] appointed to fill a public situation[?]'[42] Prescod's question remains as challenging for the post-slavery and, officially at least, desegregated and post-imperial societies of the twenty-first century Atlantic world as it was 160 years ago.

Reintegrating the history of popular politics and non-white radicalism before and after 1834 into the historiographical debate on slave emancipation is crucial for our understanding of how race, class and imperialism shaped and continue to shape public life in the Atlantic world. For the disenfranchised non-white majority in the British Caribbean, both free and slave, slave emancipation seemed to herald a new era of political change after years of popular agitation. However, the political careers of prominent men of colour, including liberals such as Prescod, flourished under oligarchic rule. Ultimately, they participated in the institutionalisation and containment of demands for radical political change which had predated emancipation. Thus, emancipation ushered in an era of deradicalisation and reaffirmed the exclusion of the majority from political influence.

On one level, this trend of deradicalisation was not unique to the Caribbean. It was equally a feature of politics in Britain where, less than two decades after mass mobilisation for emancipation and the reform of parliament, Chartism was in decline and a rather more conservative 'working class Liberalism' was emerging. Far from being 'the fruit of the ideological success of "bourgeois ideology"', this represented 'the institutionalisation of older and genuinely plebeian traditions'.[43] Yet, on another level, the political dynamic between elite conservatism and popular radicalism in nineteenth-century Barbados must be understood as more than just an imperial political trend – it is intrinsic to understanding the legacy of racial slavery for Caribbean politics and society.

---

[42] *Liberal*, 19 September 1840.
[43] Biagini and Reid, *Currents of Radicalism*, p. 10.

Racial discrimination was integral to the structures which excluded people of colour from politics. During slavery the struggle against racial discrimination became the most powerful factor mobilising and uniting people of colour across boundaries of class and legal status. Demanding that men of colour be accepted into politics was central to popular hopes for change, but it was also symbolic of the more radical, democratic desires of lower-class non-whites and slaves. By accepting a few elite men of colour into the political fold without also being forced to make fundamental socio-political changes, the imperial and colonial regimes were able to absorb and deflect mass discontent while reaffirming the exclusion of the majority from public life. The presence of men of their own colour in government positions, which had served as such a forceful rallying cry for lower-class free people of colour in the final years of slavery, brought no real benefits. Instead, the broader, democratic hopes of these people and former slaves remained unfulfilled in their lifetimes.

3 'Working cutlass and shovel': labour and redemption at the Onderneeming School in British Guiana[1]

Juanita De Barros

In the early 1880s, the superintendent of the boys' reformatory in British Guiana, the Onderneeming School, visited the Red Hill Industrial School in Great Britain. F.A. Gall noted differences in architecture – the school in Surrey had five houses, each with two dormitories, whereas the one in British Guiana was but a single building with one dormitory – but concluded that both institutions were conducted in much the same fashion, 'having due regard to the class of boys and climate'.[2] Gall's assessment was in part accurate: founded some 30 years before Onderneeming, Red Hill, like the school in British Guiana, was established to house 'destitute and criminal juveniles'.[3] The similarity doubtless owed much to Onderneeming's provenance: British legislation and policies influenced the form of nineteenth-century juvenile institutions in British Guiana. Yet the mitigating factors cited by Gall – the 'class of boys and [the] climate' – ensured that Onderneeming evolved differently from British reformatories.

Established in 1879 to reform criminal and vagrant boys, Onderneeming reflected the ideological and economic exigencies of colonial life. Training was geared towards recovering the largely Afro-Guianese inmates for the colonial economy – in the long term, by creating a pool of unskilled agricultural labourers, and more immediately, by helping maintain the reformatory and other colonial institutions and contributing to efforts to diversify British Guiana's sugar-dependent

---

[1] I would like to thank Sheena Boa, Douglas Hay and David Trotman for reading and commenting on the paper. I also appreciate the comments of the participants in the workshop on 'Control and Resistance in the Post-emancipation Caribbean and Africa' held at the Centre for Caribbean Studies, University of Warwick, July 2000, where I presented an earlier version of this paper. Any errors remain my responsibility.

[2] *Report of the Superintendent of the Government School at Onderneeming for the Year 1881*, p. 139.

[3] Alexander Scholes, *Education for Empire Settlement: A Study of Juvenile Migration* (London: Longmans, Green and Co., 1932), p. 16.

economy. It also served the implicitly racialist project of encouraging young Afro-Guianese males to return to the agricultural sector.

In terms of their inception and nature, reform schools in the nineteenth century were similar regardless of their location. Their British and American founders aimed to remove young offenders from 'contaminating' contact with adult criminals, to save them from joining the 'criminal classes', and to inculcate industriousness. A highly regimented schedule consisting of minimal academic instruction and long hours of industrial and agricultural training and labour was believed to be the route to reformation.[4] This model was also used in Britain's colonies, but the form it eventually took was influenced by the colonial environment. In Britain, before the mid-nineteenth century, children convicted of crimes were punished in the same manner as adults. Their subsequent detention in specialised penal institutions was part of larger changes in nineteenth-century methods of dealing with all offenders.[5] According to Margaret May, prison reforms due to concerns about crowded prisons (themselves resulting from an increasing reliance on incarceration) and the introduction of a system to classify inmates by the nature of the offence illuminated the 'special problem' of convicted juveniles, and raised doubts about whether children belonged in jail. These developments coincided with an apparent rise in the rate of juvenile crime as new methods of acquiring data were introduced.[6]

In Great Britain, private efforts to address the 'problem' of juvenile delinquency and remove young criminals from adult prisons received legislative sanction in the 1850s, when a system of privately run charitable reformatories which mixed education and detention was established, regulated and partially funded by the British government.[7] The nineteenth-century reformer and founder of 'ragged schools', Mary Carpenter, influenced the form these institutions eventually took. She maintained that children could be divided into a 'dangerous class' and a

---

[4] See, for example, Steven Schlossman, 'Delinquent Children: The Juvenile Reform School', in Norval Morris and David Rothman (eds.), *The Oxford History of the Prison: The Practice of Punishment in Western Society* (New York: Oxford University Press, 1995), pp. 363–89. See also David Rothman, *The Discovery of the Asylum: Social Order and Disorder in the New Republic* (Boston: Little, Brown, and Co., 1971).

[5] Margaret May, 'Innocence and Experience: The Evolution of the Concept of Juvenile Delinquency in the Mid-Nineteenth Century', *Victorian Studies* 28: 1 (September 1973), pp. 7, 9; see also John Stack, 'The Juvenile Delinquent and England's "Revolution in Government"', 1825–1875', *The Historian* XLII: 1 (November 1979), p. 44.

[6] May, 'Innocence and Experience', pp. 9–11, 14–16, 21.

[7] W.J. Forsythe, *Penal Discipline, Reformatory Projects and the English Prison Commission 1895–1939* (Exeter: University of Exeter Press, 1991), p. 45; David Garland, *Punishment and Welfare: A History of Penal Strategies* (London: Gower Publishing Company Limited, 1985), p. 8.

'perishing class'. Legislation passed in 1854 established reformatories for children who made up the former category, those who had been convicted of crimes. Under this act, convicted juvenile offenders under 16 years of age could be sent to a reformatory for between two and five years.[8] It was followed three years later by a law that instituted industrial schools for destitute children and 'incipient criminal[s]'.[9] It was amended in 1866 to include young children considered to require 'care and protection', that is, children under 14 years of age who associated with thieves or who had been found begging, or who lacked proper homes. In addition, the amended legislation stipulated that convicted offenders under 12 years of age be sent to industrial schools rather than to the reformatories to which their offences would have destined them had they been older.[10]

This distinction between these institutions, though, was never absolute, both in terms of their clientele and their function. Contemporary and more modern scholars have argued that the two kinds of reform schools dealt with the same kind or 'class' of children. Mary Barnett, in a 1913 account, argued that the 'boys and girls in Reformatory and Industrial Schools belong[ed] to the same social class'.[11] According to Ivy Pinchbeck and Margaret Hewitt, a key difference lay in anticipated as opposed to actual criminality. Reformatories housed convicted offenders, whereas industrial schools dealt with those children who, 'from their ignorance, destitution, and the circumstances in which they [were] growing up', were believed likely to become criminals 'if a helping hand [were] not extended to them'. The recognition in 1896 by the Departmental Committee on the Education and Maintenance of Pauper Children in the Metropolis that reformatories and industrial schools functioned in a similar fashion led it to conclude that they should be 'treated as one',[12] a recommendation that found expression in the Children Act of 1908. As Pinchbeck and Hewitt have argued, the difference between reformatories and industrial schools

---

[8] May, 'Innocence and Experience', p. 26.
[9] May, 'Innocence and Experience', pp. 22, 25; see also Ivy Pinchbeck and Margaret Hewitt, *Children in English Society Volume II. From the Eighteenth Century to the Children Act of 1948* (London: Routledge & Kegan Paul, 1973), p. 472.
[10] May, 'Innocence and Experience', p. 27; see also Jane Martin, '"Hard-headed and large-hearted": Women and the Industrial Schools, 1870–1885', *History of Education* 20:3 (1991), pp. 187–201.
[11] Mary Barnett, *Young Delinquents: A Study of Reformatory and Industrial Schools* (London: Methuen & Co., Ltd, 1913), p. 44.
[12] Pinchbeck and Hewitt, *Children in English Society*, p. 489.

eventually became 'largely artificial',[13] and finally ended under the Children and Young Persons Act of 1933.[14]

When legislation establishing specialised juvenile institutions was transferred to parts of Britain's empire, this distinction between destitute and criminal juveniles accompanied it. Yet, as historians of Britain's empire have argued in other contexts, the transfer of metropolitan institutions to the colonies was neither smooth nor complete,[15] an observation borne out by studies of reformatories. Linda Chisholm, for example, has demonstrated that the Porter Reformatory in the Cape Colony was 'based on the British model'. Its goal of removing young criminals from 'degrading surroundings' and bringing them 'within the ranks of wage earners' echoed the reasons provided for the establishment of reformatories in Great Britain. Yet the particular social and economic environment of the Cape Colony altered the nature of the Porter Reformatory: a racialist ideology and a concern to educate boys as agricultural labourers influenced daily operations.[16]

Likewise, in Britain's Caribbean colonies, reform schools based on British forms were established to rescue young offenders and incipient criminals and to reclaim them as industrious workers. Patrick Bryan has argued that in nineteenth-century Jamaica, ideological 'contamination' played an important role in the introduction of these institutions, citing the influence of 'the movement for reform of juveniles' in Great Britain and North America.[17] The dearth of scholarly research in this field makes it difficult to draw firm conclusions, but an intriguing coincidence in the timing of the introduction of reformatories suggests that something more than 'contagion' may have been at work: the Stony Hill Reformatory in Jamaica was founded by at least 1878, the Porter Reformatory in the Cape Colony in 1879, and the Onderneeming School in British Guiana in the same year.[18]

However, as Chisholm has shown in the case of the Cape Colony's Porter Reformatory, provenance aside, the colonial environment

---

[13] Pinchbeck and Hewitt, *Children in English Society*, pp. 489, 494–5; see also Barnett, *Young Delinquents*, p. 44.
[14] Schlossman, 'Delinquent Children', p. 383.
[15] See, for example, David Arnold, 'The Colonial Prison: Power, Knowledge and Penology in Nineteenth-Century India', in David Arnold and David Hardiman (eds.), *Subaltern Studies VIII*, (Delhi: Oxford University Press, 1994), pp. 148–87.
[16] Linda Chisholm, 'The Pedagogy of Porter: The Origins of the Reformatory in the Cape Colony, 1882–1910', *Journal of African History* 27 (1986), pp. 482–3, 485–6.
[17] Patrick Bryan, *The Jamaican People 1880–1902* (London: Macmillan Caribbean Ltd., 1991), p. 124.
[18] Chisholm, 'The Pedagogy of Porter', p. 486; Bryan, *The Jamaican People*, pp. 124, 126.

determined the form these institutions would take. British West Indian industrial schools and reformatories developed in a context that was significantly different from that of Great Britain (and indeed, from that of the Cape Colony): they were established during the 40-odd years of social, legal, and economic adjustments that followed the end of slavery. With formal emancipation in 1838, colonial governments throughout the region responded to a range of new challenges with the old mindset developed during slavery. Colonial governments became responsible for services and institutions that previously had fallen under the purview of slave owners. Thus the court system was expanded, jails were built, police forces were established and, in colonies such as British Guiana, a local judiciary was instituted.[19]

This new or expanded penal/judicial complex attempted to deal with what colonial elites considered to be an unfortunate consequence of emancipation: increased freedom of movement. Despite the introduction of vagrancy legislation and other restrictions on mobility imposed by colonial governments, former slaves used their new freedom to leave the plantations for villages and urban centres, thereby threatening planter control over estate labour. Local political and economic elites represented the young men (and women) congregating in the streets as idle and criminal and thus as threats to public order. Such anxieties and a determination to maintain plantation agriculture dominated official discourse, both in the colonies and the Colonial Office.

These individuals (along with other free people who left the estates) were also seen as posing a threat to the viability of the plantations. Caribbean sugar production had long depended on cheap, dependent labour, but the industry's decline after the 1840s – due to British trade policies and the competition of cane sugar from Latin America and beet sugar from Europe – made such a workforce even more necessary. The 'unreliable' and increasingly expensive Afro-Creole labourers seemed to threaten the viability of plantation agriculture. But as David Trotman has argued, 'the production of sugar by a large labour force tied to large plantations and ... run by either resident European owners or the representatives of absentees' was much more than an economic arrangement: in the eyes of the plantocracy, it represented 'civilisation'. Thus, '[d]espite all the moral clamorings, this concept inherited from the days of slavery was still dominant in the nineteenth century'.[20]

---

[19] See, for example, William Green, 'The Apprenticeship in British Guiana, 1834–1838', *Caribbean Studies*, 9:2 (July 1969), pp. 47–8.
[20] David Trotman, *Crime in Trinidad: Conflict and Control in a Plantation Society 1838–1900* (Knoxville: The University of Tennessee Press, 1986), p. 41.

These colonial concerns were expressed within an imperial ideological matrix. After the 1840s, views of Afro-Creoles as idle and savage, existing in an Eden-like setting that made work unnecessary, dominated colonial and imperial discourse. They were also expressed in more popular works. Thomas Carlyle's 1849 'Discourses on the Nigger Question', though one of the more infamous examples, was hardly unique. Carlyle described idle 'Quashee' eating pumpkin 'while the sugar-crops rot[ted] ... uncut, because labour [could not] be hired or so cheap [were] the pumpkins'.[21] The attitudes expressed in this discourse were manifested in colonial policies. Political leaders throughout the region attempted to compel the freed population to continue to labour on the sugar plantations by exploiting tenancy arrangements, introducing discriminatory taxes, and establishing prohibitively high prices for Crown land; in British Guiana, the colonial government, as well as instituting similar policies, neglected the small farms and villages established after 1838, and discouraged exploitation of gold and timber industry by the small-scale largely Afro-Guianese miners.[22]

Afro-Creole adults, though, were not the only labourers in the British Caribbean. Before 1834, enslaved African and Afro-Creole children worked on the sugar estates. The very young children gathered grass, whereas those in their early to late teens weeded and 'trashed' the cane fields.[23] Emancipation, however, led to the partial decline of involuntary child labour on the estates, thereby validating planters' fears.[24] In 1840, for example, a Guianese magistrate observed that 'the number of women and children occupied in agricultural employment [had] ... considerably, [even] ... alarmingly, diminished'.[25] As Thomas Holt has argued, these negative views of the Afro-Creole population as a whole

---

[21] Thomas Carlyle, 'The Nigger Question,' John Stuart Mill, 'The Negro Question,' ed. Eugene R. August (New York: Crofts Classics, 1971); quoted in Thomas Holt, *The Problem of Freedom: Race, Labor, and Politics in Jamaica and Britain, 1832–1938* (Baltimore: The Johns Hopkins University Press, 1992), p. 280.
[22] Alan Lancaster, 'Proposals for Hinterland Settlement and Development of British Guiana, 1884–1890', *History Gazette* 59 (August 1993), p. 17; see also Walter Rodney, *A History of the Guyanese Working People, 1881–1905* (Baltimore: The Johns Hopkins Press, 1981; 1982).
[23] Barry Higman, *Slave Populations of the British Caribbean 1807–1834* (Mona: The Press University of the West Indies, 1995; 1984), pp. 166–7, 189.
[24] Green, 'The Apprenticeship in British Guiana, 1834–1838', p. 58.
[25] Bridget Brereton, 'Family Strategies, Gender and the Shift to Wage Labour in the British Caribbean', in Bridget Brereton and Kevin Yelvington (eds.), *The Colonial Caribbean in Transition: Essays on Postemancipation Social and Cultural History* (Kingston: The Press University of the West Indies, 1999), p. 87; see also Holt, *The Problem of Freedom*, p. 151.

had implications for the juvenile reform system: '[O]nce one accepted that black Jamaican adults were demoralized wretches, it was easier to justify removing children from their authority to that of the planters.'[26] And planters, local politicians and members of the Colonial Office increasingly accepted this view of the free Afro-Creole masses, not only in Jamaica but throughout the Anglophone Caribbean. Colonial governments rationalised the establishment of reformatories by citing the supposedly 'poor' training and models provided by Afro-Creole parents. Thus, when Onderneeming was founded, British Guiana's Governor Young expressed the hope that it would remedy the poor training provided by Guianese parents. He hoped it would inculcate in the boys the discipline and self-control they had not been taught by their parents[27] and would, more generally, 'create a powerful influence for good on the rising generation'.[28]

Reform schools emerged from a similar context in British Guiana. As elsewhere in the region, local political and economic leaders claimed that crime and idleness were rampant among the Afro-Creole population, particularly among the young people. H.V.P. Bronkhurst, a Methodist missionary who ministered to Indians in British Guiana between 1860 and 1889, spoke for many when he argued that crime was pervasive. He and others attributed much of this crime to the Afro-Guianese who, he argued, spent 'much of their time in idleness, ... debauchery' and thieving.[29] Former Demerara Magistrate Henry Kirke, who had been in the colony from 1872 to 1897, believed that 'the children of the poor' were particularly prone to such behaviour: '[t]he boys [were] idle and dissolute, the girls dirty, foul-mouthed and dishonest', and both were liable to drift into thieving and prostitution.[30] Similar accounts continued to fill newspapers and other contemporary sources well into the early twentieth century as groups of unemployed and marginally-employed boys and men, known locally as 'centipede gangs', were blamed for urban crime and unrest.[31]

Of even greater concern was the apparent idleness of the Afro-Guianese population. Though this representation dominated post-

---

[26] Holt, *The Problem of Freedom*, p. 287.
[27] CO 111/415, Lt-Governor William Young to Hicks Beach, 4 November 1879; no. 241, encl: W. Hayne Smith, Attorney General to Young, 1 November 1879.
[28] CO 111/415, Lt-Governor William Young to Hicks Beach, 4 November 1879, no. 241.
[29] H.V.P. Bronkhurst, *Among the Hindus and Creoles of British Guyana* (London, 1888), pp. 41, 49; Rodney, *A History of the Guyanese Working People*, p. 177.
[30] Henry Kirke, *Twenty-five Years in British Guiana* (Westport: Negro Universities Press, 1970 [1898]), pp. 46–7.
[31] Rob Sindall, *Street Violence in the Nineteenth Century: Media Panic or Real Danger* (Leicester: Leicester University Press, 1990), pp. 29–30, 164.

slavery colonial discourse throughout the British West Indies, it was articulated with particular force in British Guiana, where the relatively late development of plantation slavery had resulted in a comparatively smaller labouring population. Since the end of slavery, planters and politicians in British Guiana had complained about a scarcity of plantation workers, castigating freed Afro-Guianese for refusing to work on the estates for the low wages on offer. Choosing from peripatetic livelihood strategies which could range from the docks in Georgetown to the gold diggings in the interior to small plots of land along the rivers – all of which could be combined with temporary labour as cutters on the estates – they frustrated planters and estate attorneys who wanted to control the terms under which workers laboured.[32] Walter Rodney, like many Guianese historians, has argued that this labour 'shortage' was more apparent than real and that it was solved with the importation of indentured labourers after the late 1830s from Portugal, China and India.[33] Despite the arrival of hundreds of thousands of contract workers, mostly from India, complaints about the lack of plantation labour continued into the twentieth century, when the 'new' public health with its eugenicist undercurrents provided additional urgency to the calls for more workers; high mortality rates, particularly among infants, seemed to aggravate the labour problem.[34]

Within this ideological and economic context, the colonial government began to establish institutions designed to control and educate juveniles. As well as the Onderneeming School, it founded an orphan asylum, industrial schools and public schools. As Hazel Woolford has argued, the same economic and social concerns underlay the introduction of compulsory education in British Guiana in 1876.[35] Indeed, according to Attorney-General William Hayne Smith, compulsory education in British Guiana and the consequent 'remodelling' of the educational system was incomplete without the 'proper provision ... for training the waifs and strays of the community'.[36]

---

[32] See, for example, GO 3272, *Report of Labour Commissioner, Together with Minutes of Sittings, and Evidence of Witnesses* (Georgetown: C.K. Jardine, 1890).
[33] Walter Rodney, 'Barbadian Immigration into British Guiana 1863–1924', paper presented at the Ninth Annual Conference of Caribbean Historians (ACH), Cave Hill, 1977, p. 16.
[34] See *Report on the Census Results, 1911*, v; *Report of the Register General for the Year 1892*, p. 390; *Report of the Register General for the Year 1891–1892*, p. 383; see also The Baby Saving League of British Guiana, *The Fifth Annual Report, 1918*, p. 7.
[35] Hazel Woolford, 'Social Issues Behind the Introduction of the Compulsory Denominational Education Bill of 1876', *History Gazette* 26 (November 1990), pp. 2–4, 8, 12–13.
[36] CO 111/415, Lt-Governor William Young to Hicks Beach, 4 November 1879; no. 241, encl: W. Hayne Smith, Attorney General to Young, 1 November 1879.

The first such institution was the orphan asylum. It opened in 1852 and provided the basis for later institutions dealing with destitute and delinquent juveniles. In the early 1850s, the colonial government expressed a concern for the increasing number of orphaned and destitute children, 'waifs and strays'. It blamed neglectful parents as well as the high mortality rates consequent upon the arrival of indentured immigrants from the late 1830s onwards. According to the Attorney-General, William Arrindell, many of the colony's 40 000 children were 'destitute orphans … whose condition, in too many instances [was] servile, degraded, and miserable'.[37] Governor Barkly argued that British Guiana's lack of a large resident upper or middling class made it 'essential that the state should assist' in this area.[38] Thus, in 1852, legislation establishing an orphan asylum was passed to 'reserve some of these children from want and misery and … render them useful members of society'.[39]

The orphan asylum was later transformed to deal with additional 'classes' of children, a transformation that was due in part to official pressure but was also in response to contemporary concerns about apparently idle and criminal youth.[40] As had Great Britain before the 1850s, British Guiana lacked institutions for convicted juveniles, who were thus compelled to serve out their sentences in adult prisons.[41]

---

[37] CO 111/289, Barkly to Grey, 24 March 1852, no. 45, encl: Arrindell to Barkly, 24 March 1852.

[38] CO 111/289, Barkly to Grey, 24 March 1852, no. 45; An Ordinance to establish an Orphan Asylum and School of Industry in the Colony of British Guiana, in CO 111/289, Barkly to Grey, 24 March 1852, no. 45.

[39] CO 111/289, Barkly to Grey, 24 March 1852, no. 45; encl: Arrindell to Barkly, 24 March 1852; CO 111/368, Hincks to Duke of Buckingham, 8 July 1868, no. 100; encl: Attorney General to Hincks, 5 July 1868.

[40] The institutional arrangements for delinquent girls are uncertain. Although orphaned and indigent girls were sent to the Orphan Asylum in Georgetown, it is unknown whether, following the changes instituted by the 1868 legislation, delinquent girls were sent there as well. Indeed, colonial officials were divided on the need for such an institution. In 1879, when Onderneeming was founded, Attorney General W. Hayne Smith argued that there was no 'want for any such institution for girls', implying that the reconfigured orphan asylum, recast in 1868 as an Industrial School for boys and girls, served such a purpose. Less than a decade later, however, the colonial government established a girls' reformatory, but it was short-lived and did not survive the 1890s. So far, I have been unable to discover anything further about the Girls' Reformatory, including the reason why it closed. CO 111/415, Lt-Governor William Young to Hicks Beach, 4 November 1879, no. 241, encl: W. Hayne Smith to Young, 1 November 1879; CO 111/410, Londen to Earl of Carravon, 1 February 1877, no. 22; CO 111/452, Gormanston to Knutsford, 23 May 1890, no. 177; encl: Report on the Girls' Reformatory, 1888.

[41] *British Guiana Directory and Almanac for 1891* (Georgetown: C.K. Jardine, 1891), p. 178; See, for example, *The Creole*, 10 April 1865.

Some ten years after the orphan asylum's establishment, the directors of the board proposed that it could include a 'reformatory for juvenile offenders'. The plan was abandoned in the face of opposition from the incoming chair, but in 1867 the directors again put it forward. Governor Hincks agreed, and introduced an act to divide the orphan asylum into an industrial school and a reformatory. Based largely on the British Reformatory and Industrial Schools Acts of 1866 (Stat. 29 and 30 Vict. cap. 117 and 118), the 1868 Guianese ordinance ordered that '[d]estitute Orphans' would be sent to the industrial school and 'youthful offenders ... to the Reformatory'.[42] According to Attorney-General Hayne Smith, this act followed the 'English system of dividing youthful "wastrels" into two classes requiring one class to be sent to an Industrial School and the other to a Reformatory'.[43] The two categories of children were to be kept 'apart from each other', housed in separate buildings in the orphan asylum.[44]

Colonial officials, however, soon concluded that this separation could not be maintained on practical grounds. Hayne Smith contended that the institution's 'structure' did not lend itself to 'classification of the inmates' and that its small scale prevented compliance with the 1868 legislative stipulation that 'the children in the Industrial and Reformatory schools ... be kept apart from each other'. He believed that this proviso was crucial: it reflected the popular view that the orphans should not be 'exposed to the evil influences of children already conversant with bad habits'.[45] The revamped orphan asylum was also too small to hold all those juvenile offenders who should have been sent there; prison records detail the relatively high numbers of juveniles serving time in the colonial prisons as late as the mid-1870s, implying that the capacity of the orphan asylum was inadequate. In 1873, for example, British Guiana's six prisons contained almost 300 'juveniles' who had been sentenced to periods ranging from three months to five years.[46]

Despite these concerns about the 'contaminating' influence of juvenile offenders, the colonial government established an institution

---

[42] CO 111/368, Hincks to Duke of Buckingham, 8 July 1868, no. 100, encl: Attorney General to Hincks, 5 July 1868.
[43] CO 111/415, Lt-Governor William Young to Hicks Beach, 4 November 1879, no. 241, encl: Attorney General W. Hayne Smith to Young, 1 November 1879.
[44] CO 111/368, Hincks to Duke of Buckingham, 8 July 1868, no. 100, encl: Attorney General to Hincks, 5 July 1868.
[45] CO 111/415, Lt-Governor William Young to Hicks Beach, 4 November 1879, no. 241, encl: W. Hayne Smith, Attorney General to Young, 1 November 1879.
[46] See the *British Guiana Blue Book, Gaols and Prisoners* for 1873, 1874 and 1875, pp. 5–6.

that continued to contain both groups previously incarcerated at the expanded orphan asylum. In 1879 it purchased Plantation Onderneeming in Essequibo for this purpose.[47] It was to house both groups of boys who were the targets of the 1868 legislation, that is, all boys under the age of 16 who, under the British legislation, could have been sent 'either to an Industrial or to a Reformatory school'. Thus, boys under 16 years of age whose parents had left them destitute (either through death or imprisonment), or who had been found begging or consorting with thieves, or who lacked a 'settled place of abode' were sent to Onderneeming. It also admitted boys under the age of 16 who had been charged with an offence 'punishable by a summary conviction'.[48] Though this new institution did not appear to solve the perceived problems of the old orphan asylum, that is, the proximity of the two 'classes' of boys, the Attorney-General at least supported this approach, arguing British Guiana's '[w]astrels under the age named [were] not vicious; they [were] simply ... "sans discernement"'.[49] Officials in the colonial government and at Onderneeming debated the accuracy of this assessment. Some were adamant that the boys were 'more or less from the criminal classes',[50] whereas others claimed that most had committed crimes of a 'trivial character' and were guilty of little more than 'loitering'.[51] Although the source material is patchy, examining records over a period of five years suggests that most were admitted for a variety of petty crimes, including theft, vagrancy and begging (see Table 1). As the sources do not provide details of these crimes, it is impossible to conclude whether the boys were convicted for relatively minor thefts or more serious offences.[52] However, an 1891 report shows that 22 of 36 boys were convicted of theft (61 per cent), many of them having stolen

---

[47] CO 111/415, Lt-Governor William Young to Hicks Beach, 4 November 1879, no. 241, encl: W. Hayne Smith, Attorney General to Young, 1 November 1879.
[48] CO 113/6, An Ordinance to Make Provision for the Establishment and Regulation of a School for the Proper Instruction and Training of Vagrant Boys and Youthful Male Offenders (5 of 1879), ss. 12, 13, M&S Project.
[49] CO 111/415, Lt-Governor William Young to Hicks Beach, 4 November 1879, no. 241, encl: W. Hayne Smith, Attorney General to Young, 1 November 1879.
[50] *Report on the Onderneeming School for the Year 1904–1905*; encl: Minutes of the Governor with Regard to Future Conduct of Onderneeming Reformatory School, 24 March 1905, p. 494; *Report on the Onderneeming School for the Year 1906–1907*, p. 469.
[51] *Report on the Onderneeming School for the Year 1897–1898*, p. 269; CO 111/545, Hodgson to Lyttelton, 9 May 1905, no. 18744, no. 132.
[52] *Report on the Orphan Asylum for the Year 1855*, pp. 213–4; *Report on the Chairman, Poor Law Commissioners, for the year 1907–1908*, p. 354; *Report of the Chairman, Poor Law Commissioners, for the Year 1908–1909*, p. 401; *Report of the Chairman of the Poor Law Commissioners on the Orphan Asylum for the Year 1916*, pp. 337, 339; *Report of the Chairman, Poor Law Commissioners, for the 9 Months April-December, 1915*, p. 332.

Table 1: Convictions of boys committed to Onderneeming[54] (percentage)

Year	Theft	Vagrancy/ begging	Assault	Cruelty to animal	False pretence	Undesirable inmate at orphan asylum	Refractory conduct	Breach of peace	Not attending/ misbehaving at industrial day school
1915	67 %	19 %	7 %	4 %	4 %	n/a	n/a	n/a	n/a
1916	63 %	33 %	4 %	n/a	n/a	n/a	n/a	n/a	n/a
1918	76 %	2 %	13 %	n/a	n/a	n/a	7 %	2 %	n/a
1920	84 %	5 %	5 %	n/a	n/a	n/a	5 %	n/a	n/a
1926	n/a	24 %	n/a	n/a	n/a	n/a	13 %	n/a	63 %

trifling items: tobacco, sugar cakes and nuts, coconuts, fowl and, in one case, money; seven boys were convicted for lodging under verandas, in unoccupied buildings or under bridges (19 per cent); one was sentenced for receiving stolen property, another for being found on private property 'for some unlawful purpose', another for having escaped, and four more were convicted for an unspecified crime.[53]

Officials, though, believed that Onderneeming contained sufficient numbers of serious offenders to pose a threat of 'contamination' to those guilty of more trivial crimes and tried repeatedly to re-establish the principle of segregation. W.J. West, the official visitor, was concerned that 'criminals' were mixed with 'those who [were] not',[55] which one-time superintendent Bayley was worried would ensure that a 'small minority of criminal lads' held a 'corrupt influence ... over others'.[56] For West '[i]t [was] only human to degenerate in the presence of those worse than' oneself.[57] He proposed a classification system which would divide the boys by seriousness of offence, ensuring that the boys admitted for 'loitering' be kept apart from those charged with 'stealing and other crimes'.[58] The sources do not indicate whether such a system was implemented. Some years later, however, officials attempted to distinguish the boys by their behaviour within Onderneeming, rather than by the nature of their offences before committal. These were temporary measures, designed to reform and punish those boys found guilty of repeatedly breaking the institution's rules. A 'penal class' was set up but after little more than a year it proved unsuccessful; inadequate staff and space made Bayley conclude in despair that it was impossible to 'completely isolate the boys whose propensities [were] known to be entirely degraded'.[59]

Having concluded that physical separation was impossible, officials experimented with a form of social segregation. The Governor's proposal of an 'incorrigible class' was accepted as one means to achieve this end. Its members were to wear a 'distinctive uniform'; they were 'not permitted to join the other boys at play, at meals or in School [and] [w]hile at work, they [were] directly under the eye of an officer and [were] given the least congenial kind of labour'.[60] By

---

[53] *Report on the Onderneeming School for the Year 1891–1892*, p. 240.
[54] *Report on the Onderneeming School, 1915, 1916, 1918, 1920, 1926.*
[55] *Report on the Onderneeming School for the Year 1898–1899*, p. 301.
[56] *Report on the Onderneeming School for the Year 1907–1908*, p. 482.
[57] *Report on the Onderneeming School for the Year 1897–1898*, p. 269.
[58] Ibid.
[59] *Report on the Onderneeming School for the Year 1906–07*, p. 469; *Report on the Onderneeming School for 1907–1908*, p. 482.
[60] *Report on the Onderneeming School for the Year 1907–1908*, p. 482.

1909, Bayley was certain that this punishment was effective: being 'placed in the Blue-sleeve class … [was] felt to be a disgrace and degradation apart from its punitory provisions'.[61] It was a 'drastic punishment' which was attended with 'ostracism, degradation and forfeiture of recreation for a period of one month, during which time the offender [had to] keep a clean record to entitle him to re-instatement'.[62]

Yet regardless of the reasons why boys were sent to reformatories or their classification once there, work was to be their salvation. Whether this labour was agricultural or industrial, it was designed to redeem young delinquents for the labour market by teaching them workplace discipline and by inculcating industriousness. Steven Schlossman has argued that nineteenth-century reformatories in the United States emphasised this kind of instruction in values rather than teaching children particular workplace skills.[63] Likewise, Guianese officials and political leaders agreed that the delinquent and vagrant boys housed at Onderneeming should be taught these industrial virtues. Yet the aims expressed by these officials were more specific than this: the Onderneeming boys were to become agriculturalists, a goal that served colonial ideological and economic ends.

Onderneeming's enabling legislation stated that its inmates were, 'as far as practicable', to be 'employed in agricultural pursuits'.[64] As Governor Kortwright observed a decade later, producing artisans at Onderneeming meant that the boys' 'services as … agricultural labourers … [were] lost to the colony'.[65] Although provisions were made to train some boys as artisans by the early 1890s, these were exceptional cases, boys considered ill-suited to agricultural work or with previous artisanal training.[66] Achieving such an aim contributed to fulfilling wider ideological goals, that is encouraging the population to work in agriculture. Indeed, Onderneeming's establishment was part of a larger educative project that encouraged/compelled young Guianese males to engage in agricultural labour. The 1876 compulsory education ordinance established 'day industrial schools', frequently located on

---

[61] *Report on the Onderneeming School for the Year 1908–1909*, p. 517.
[62] *Report on the Onderneeming School for the Year 1909–1910*, p. 423.
[63] Schlossman, 'Delinquent Children', p. 369.
[64] CO 113/6, An Ordinance to Make Provision for the Establishment and Regulation of a School for the Proper Instruction and Training of Vagrant Boys and Youthful Male Offenders (5 of 1879), ss. 12, 13. s. 3.
[65] CO 111/416, Governor Kortright to Sir M.E. Hicks-Beach, 23 March 1880, no. 44.
[66] *Report on the Onderneeming School for the Year 1892–93*, pp. 234, 236, 239.

plantations, to provide children 'with industrial training [and] elementary instruction'[67] and to employ them in 'agricultural pursuits'.[68]

Onderneeming served this same aim, whether tacitly or not. Indeed, its ability to compel juvenile offenders and destitute boys to labour in agriculture and its expressed ultimate goal of reclaiming them for the agricultural sector ensured that the school served the racialised end of returning Afro-Guianese to the fields. The annual reports indicate that most boys were Afro-Guianese (see Table 2) and that their numbers were disproportionate to their size in the overall population.[69] According to the colonial census reports, in the wider population Afro-Guianese males under 20 years of age were outnumbered by Indian and Indo-Guianese males in the same age group by 1911. (Afro-Guianese comprised 38 per cent and Indians and Indo-Guianese 42 per cent, numbers that remained almost unchanged by the time of the 1921 census, when they were 43 per cent and 37 per cent respectively.)

The reasons for the large number of Afro-Guianese in Onderneeming are unclear. Some scholars have argued that in Trinidad, young East Indian and Indo-Trinidadian offenders were sent to the orphan asylum rather than to the reformatory; whether or not this was the case for British Guiana is uncertain.[70] The explanation may lie in the origins of the boys or the sites of their crimes. Georgetown's Indian and Indo-Guianese population was substantially smaller than that of the Afro-Guianese: in 1891, Indo-Guianese under 20 years of age comprised just five per cent of the total male population of the city and its environs, whereas Afro-Guianese made up 47 per cent. (In 1911, the figures were ten per cent and 47 per cent, and in 1921, 11 per cent and

---

[67] CO 111/410, Londen to Earl of Carravon, 1 February 1877, no. 22.
[68] CO 111/410, Londen to Earl of Carravon, 1 February 1877, no. 22, encl: The Attorney General's Report on Ordinance no. 14 of 1876, to Governor James Londen, 31 January 1877.
[69] Changes in racial categorisation make it difficult to draw conclusions about the racial composition of Onderneeming. Before 1904, its records included 'creole', which likely meant blacks because Afro-Guianese were not listed anywhere else. From 1904 to 1915, the category 'creoles of the colony' was included. As no other racial groups were identified as being inmates at Onderneeming in these years, it is possible that 'creoles of the colony' included every inmate, regardless of race. Or perhaps only Afro-Guianese were admitted in these years. In 1915, the classification system changed again. Inmates were listed as 'black creoles', 'East Indian creoles', and 'Portuguese' or 'Portuguese creoles'. *Report on the Onderneeming School* for 1881, 1882, 1883, 1885, 1886, 1891–2, 1892–3, 1894–5, 1898–9, 1903–4, 1904–5, 1905–6, 1906–7, 1907–8, 1908–9, 1909–10, 1915, 1916, 1918, 1920, 1926.
[70] Conversation with David Trotman, July 2000.

Table 2: Racial breakdown of inmates at Onderneeming

Year	Black	Portuguese	East Indian	Mixed Race	Sierra Leonian	Chinese	Aboriginal	BWI	Surinamese	Dutch	Total
1881	79 %	3 %	7 %	n/a	n/a	n/a	n/a	5 %	n/a	n/a	112
1882	87 %	2 %	6 %	n/a	n/a	n/a	n/a	5 %	n/a	n/a	121
1883	87 %	3 %	3 %	n/a	n/a	n/a	n/a	9 %	n/a	n/a	117
1885	84 %	2 %	9 %	n/a	n/a	1 %	n/a	2 %	n/a	n/a	137
1886	88 %	0.7 %	7 %	n/a	n/a	1.4 %	n/a	3 %	n/a	n/a	142
1891–2	90 %	2 %	5 %	n/a	n/a	n/a	n/a	3 %	n/a	n/a	195
1892–3	90 %	3 %	5 %	n/a	n/a	n/a	n/a	2 %	n/a	n/a	187
1894–5	91 %	1 %	2 %	n/a	n/a	1 %	n/a	4 %	n/a	1 %	157
1895–6	87 %	1 %	4 %	n/a	n/a	n/a	n/a	7 %	n/a	1 %	143
1897–8	91 %	n/a	n/a	n/a	1 %	n/a	n/a	8 %	n/a	n/a	143
1898–9	91 %	n/a	1 %	n/a	1 %	n/a	n/a	6 %	n/a	n/a	139
1903–4	96 %	n/a	1 %	n/a	n/a	n/a	n/a	1 %	n/a	n/a	107
1904–5	99 %	n/a	n/a	n/a	n/a	n/a	n/a	1 %	n/a	n/a	117
1905–7	99 %	n/a	n/a	n/a	n/a	n/a	n/a	1 %	n/a	n/a	91
1906	100 %	n/a	n/a	n/a	n/a	n/a	n/a	n/a	n/a	n/a	93
1907	100 %	n/a	n/a	n/a	n/a	n/a	n/a	n/a	n/a	n/a	100
1908–9	100 %	n/a	n/a	n/a	n/a	n/a	1 %	n/a	n/a	n/a	101
1909–10	100 %	n/a	n/a	n/a	n/a	n/a	n/a	n/a	n/a	n/a	98
1915	75 %	3 %	12 %	9 %	n/a	n/a	n/a	n/a	n/a	n/a	127
1916	81 %	3 %	10 %	7 %	n/a	n/a	n/a	n/a	n/a	n/a	136
1918	82 %	2 %	10 %	5 %	n/a	n/a	n/a	n/a	n/a	n/a	164
1920	85 %	n/a	7 %	7 %	n/a	n/a	n/a	n/a	n/a	n/a	163
1926	79 %	n/a	8 %	n/a	n/a	n/a	n/a	n/a	n/a	n/a	154

46 per cent respectively.)[71] In that year, over half the boys (21, or 58 per cent) sent to Onderneeming had been sentenced by P.H.R. Hill, the police magistrate for Georgetown, implying that most were either from the Georgetown area or had committed their crimes there.[72] However, as the records generally do not indicate the origins of the boys, the site of their crimes, or the jurisdiction under which they were tried, it is unclear whether or not the large number of Georgetown cases for 1891 was an aberration. Though the causes of Onderneeming's racial composition are unclear, its consequences are not: young males of African descent were compelled to perform unskilled agricultural labour.

As was the case in North American and British reformatories, the officials at British Guiana's Onderneeming School attempted to transform juvenile delinquents into diligent, industrious workers through a combination of academic and workplace instruction. Industrial discipline was inculcated through carefully regimented days, the structure of which did not seem to vary overly much across national and colonial boundaries.[73] As Chisholm has pointed out, the daily regime of the Porter Reformatory was copied from Redhill and Parkhurst in Britain.[74] At Onderneeming, as elsewhere, the careful regimentation of the boys' days was designed to teach them to follow a workday schedule: they rose early (at 5:00 or 5:15) and, at set intervals, worked, prayed, ate, studied and played.

Labour, though, was the principal means by which the boys were to acquire this discipline. Academic instruction was consequently underemphasised, consisting of little more than an hour or two a day. The dismal conclusion of the inspector of schools, W. Blair, that Onderneeming was a 'total failure' as an educational institution[75] did not perturb one official, who pointed out that '"a high standard of Education" [had] ... never [been] contemplated'; instead, the boys were to receive 'a good sound, practical and moral education, with as little interference with the present routine of work as practicable'. The limited attention directed towards teaching the boys to read, write and cipher made sense to Onderneeming's first superintendent, F.A. Gall. Like

---

[71] See *Report on the Census Results, 1891* (Georgetown: 1891); *Report on the Results of the Census of the Population, 1911* (Georgetown: 'The Argosy' Company, Limited, 1912); *Report on the Results of the Census of the Population, 1921* (Georgetown: Argosy Co., 1921).

[72] *Report on the Onderneeming School for the Year 1891–1892*, p. 240.

[73] See, for example, Anthony Platt, *The Child Savers: The Invention of Delinquency* (Chicago: The University of Chicago Press, 1969; 1977); see also Rothman, *The Discovery of the Asylum*.

[74] Chisholm, 'The Pedagogy of Porter', p. 485.

[75] *Report on the Onderneeming School for the Year 1891–2*, pp. 16–17.

many of his contemporaries, he considered an academic education largely irrelevant to a population destined for agricultural work. He argued that 'the class of boys ... sent to this School [would] not derive much benefit from a high standard of education' which would 'make them despise trade and agricultural pursuits' even more than at the present.[76] Though the number of hours devoted to the 'three Rs' increased after the turn of the century, Onderneeming remained 'primarily an agricultural school'.[77]

Thus work dominated the boys' days. In the 1880s and 1890s, they worked seven hours a day; in the early 1900s, this was reduced to six hours.[78] Those who completed their tasks quickly were rewarded, but laggards were compelled to finish these during 'free time'. Members of the Onderneeming Committee believed in the efficacy of this system, noting that 'the best boys [took] pleasure in completing their tasks and keeping clean sheets'.[79] The boys acquired this discipline gradually. The labour performed by the youngest lads kept them under 'more direct control' and '[broke] them to harness'.[80] In preparation for the 'outside' world, the older boys worked increasingly longer days, from six hours at first to eight hours – Onderneeming officials had learned that children accustomed to working in the fields six hours a day found it 'difficult to work steadily for eight or nine hours when suddenly required to do so after discharge'.[81]

The nature of the Guianese economy determined that this redemptive labour would be largely agricultural.[82] The number of boys performing unskilled agricultural work significantly exceeded the number of those labouring as artisans.[83] In 1905–06, for example, the ratio was close to three to one, but this remained more or less constant throughout the 1910s.[84] Most boys (an average of 38 per year over nine years)

---

[76] *Report on the Onderneeming School for the year 1892–3*, pp. 234, 239.

[77] *Report on the Onderneeming School for the Year 1907–08*, pp. 480, 483.

[78] *Report of the Superintendent of the Government School at Onderneeming* for 1881, 1885, 1891–2, 1895–6, 1903–4, 1904–5, 1905–6.

[79] *Report on the Onderneeming School for the Year 1905–06, 480; Report of the Onderneeming School for the Year 1909–1910*, p. 422.

[80] *Report on the Onderneeming School for the Year 1905–06*, p. 480.

[81] *Report on the Onderneeming School for the Year 1907–1908*, pp. 479–81.

[82] This can be compared with the work the inmates of the girls' reformatory were compelled to perform: they had to look after the 'whole of the household duties of the Institution, such as cooking, cleaning, clothes washing, weeding paths, &c'. CO 111/452, Gormanston to Knutsford, 23 May 1890, no. 177, encl: Report on the Girls' Reformatory, 1888.

[83] Alleyne Leechman, *The British Guiana Handbook 1913* (London: Dulau & Co.), p. 118.

[84] *Report on the Onderneeming School for the Year 1905–1906*, p. 479.

did the same kind of work they would have performed as slaves. They laboured as 'weeders, shovelmen, forkers, and woodcutters'. The tasks varied according to age: at 12 years of age, boys cut grass and acted as orderlies, but by 16 they began performing heavier work 'with shovel, fork, cutlass and axe'. Those who were convalescent swept the yard and kept the grounds tidy. There were some exceptions. Boys working in coffee and cocoa cultivation (about 23 a year) seem to have been taught a wider range of skills, 'practically everything ... from the setting of the beans to the time the product [went] from the curing house to the store'. The few boys who worked as bakers, cooks, tailors or washers (an average of six each year over nine years) and as carpenters (an average of three for the same period) likewise seem to have to been taught skilled work.[85] However, the rigor of this artisanal training is uncertain. In the mid-1920s, Governor Rodwell claimed that the 'industrial training ... appear[ed] to be a farce', the 'tools ... scanty and worn out'.[86] It is likely that such had been the case for some time.

Boys were also trained through a system of licences. This functioned as a kind of parole, designed to ready a boy for life on the 'outside'. During a boy's last year or year-and-a-half at the school, he could live with 'any trustworthy or respectable person', usually his parents and guardians, while working for an employer chosen for him.[87] If he failed, he would be returned to Onderneeming, where he would 'be deprived of certain of the privileges given to the other boys and be treated as "under punishment"' until he was willing to 'take up another employment and remain in it as required'. The institution's yearly reports indicate that from at least 1883, several boys were licensed in this fashion each year.[88] Many of these attempts ended in failure as the boys either ran away or were so troublesome that their employer returned them to the school.[89] However, Superintendent William Craigen noted several instances of relatively successful work terms. In 1903, the boys who worked at the Botanic Gardens seemed to have done well, as had the five boys 'allotted' to Thomas Wardle of Berbice's Washington Farm.[90]

---

[85] See *Report on the Onderneeming School* for 1905–1906, 1906–1907, 1907–1908, 1908–1909, 1909–1910, 1915, 1916, 1918, 1920.

[86] GD, CSO 6060/25, Confidential, Governor C. H. Rodwell to Secretary of State Amery, 23 February 1926, NAG, encl: Copy of Memorandum by His Excellency the Governor, 18 January 1926.

[87] No. 5 of 1879, ss. 24, 25.

[88] See *Report on the Onderneeming School* for 1883; 1885; 1886; 1891–2; 1892–3; 1894–5; 1895–6; 1897–8; 1898–9; 1905–6; 1907–8; 1908–9; 1916.

[89] *Report on the Onderneeming Industrial School for the Year 1918*, p. 422.

[90] *Report on the Onderneeming Industrial School for the Year 1903–1904*, p. 451.

This labour served Onderneeming's immediate needs. The young artisans, like their fellow agriculturalists, contributed to the maintenance of the institution, the profits accrued defraying the costs of operation and their work supplying its daily needs and keeping the buildings and grounds in order. Linda Chisholm has noted the same for the Cape Colony's Porter Reformatory. She has argued that the 'industrial training' it provided did not teach the boys skills by which they could earn a livelihood but rather contributed to the reformatory's maintenance: boys made uniforms and repaired buildings and equipment.[91] Likewise, in Jamaica, the production of cash crops and items such as furniture at the Stony Hill reformatory earned money for the school.[92] The same can be seen in British Guiana. From Onderneeming's inception, the Governor believed that '[t]here seem[ed] ... a prospect that the institution [could] be made to pay a fair proportion of its expenses'.[93] Indeed, soon after it opened, the inmates had cultivated 12 acres of land.[94] In 1891, though the average cost of keeping each child was over £15 a year, the money earned 'reduced the cost per boy'.[95]

Most of the inmates worked on Onderneeming's 'farm' – some 70 acres where coffee, cacao, rubber, lime, nutmeg and fruit trees were cultivated and livestock raised.[96] The farm was successful: in 1885, for example, it produced over 200 000 pounds of grass, over 30 000 pounds of cassava, 150 pounds of yams, 72 pounds of cocoa and 403 pounds of rice, as well as pumpkins, charcoal, arrowroot, potatoes, coconuts, coffee and limes, all earning over $1600. These amounts steadily increased. In 1894, five pigs arrived at the farm, joining the donkeys and cattle already resident. By the following year, there were horned cattle, and the piggery contained 54 pigs; in 1898, five buffaloes were sent from India and they, too, multiplied yearly.[97] As well as producing the goods that earned specie for Onderneeming, the boys contributed to the institution's daily upkeep. Young agriculturalists kept the grounds and pasture tidy, and carpentry trainees built such needed items as latrines and were responsible for minor repairs.[98] The young bakers provided bread

---

[91] Chisholm, 'The Pedagogy of Porter', pp. 488–9.
[92] Bryan, *The Jamaican People*, p. 126. For the United States, see also Schlossman, 'Delinquent Children'.
[93] CO 111/415, Lt-Governor William Young to Hicks Beach, 4 November 1879, no. 241, encl: W. Hayne Smith, Attorney General to Young, 1 November 1879.
[94] CO 111/416, Governor Kortright to Sir M.E. Hicks-Beach, 23 March 1880, no. 44.
[95] PP, *Annual Report for 1891* (1891: 1893–94 LIX.423), p. 447.
[96] PP, *Report for 1909–1910* (1911 Cd. 5467–7 li.359), p. 380.
[97] *Report on the Onderneeming School* for 1886, 1894–95, 1895–96, 1898–99.
[98] *Report on the Onderneeming School for the Year 1905–1906*, pp. 478–9; *Report on the Onderneeming School for the year 1906–1907*, p. 468; *Report of the Onderneeming School for the Year 1895–6*, p. 260.

for the school itself, and the tailors clothing for the boys and the staff as well as such items as pillowcases and cot covers.[99] Their labour also benefited other colonial institutions. Onderneeming frequently sent cattle to the Penal Settlement and milk to the Suddie Public Hospital.[100]

The boys contributed to the colonial economy in another way: they participated in the effort to diversify British Guiana's agricultural sector, to develop crops other than sugar. As a government institution, the reformatory was central in this endeavour. Its farm was part of the Board of Agriculture and under the Director of Science and Agriculture, Professor Harrison, who would periodically arrange experiments with such 'economic plants' as cacao, coffee, limes and rubber, making sure that he received the 'careful' records that were kept. As Superintendent Bayley noted, Onderneeming, '[w]hile ... affording a means of profitably employing the labour of the boys and training them in agriculture', also clearly 'possess[ed] a further value to the Colony'.[101] Thus, the lads worked in the experimental cotton field and helped with the cultivation of coffee and cocoa, looking after plants sent by Harrison.[102] Lime production was particularly encouraged. Bayley believed that as the county where Onderneeming was located (Essequibo County) was 'so eminently suitable for the cultivation of limes', the reformatory had a 'special responsibility ... to encourage [this] ... industry'. He hoped to inspire the small farmers on the Essequibo coast and invited them to inspect the school's plants. The limes flourished. Plantains and cassava had been planted among the lime trees, and Bayley believed this should show the local small farmers the ease with which they could 'establish what may be regarded as a "permanent cultivation" without interfering to any extent with [their] ordinary provision crops'. So determined was Bayley to use Onderneeming as an agricultural model that he planned to have limes and plantains planted on the school's grounds adjoining the public road to ensure 'that every one who passe[d] along the road [would] be able to observe the methods adopted'. In this fashion, he hoped 'to stimulate interest, and encourage owners of even small plots of land to follow the example'.[103]

---

[99] *Report on the Onderneeming School for the Year 1920*, p. 451; *Report on the Onderneeming School for the Year 1926*, p. 381.
[100] *Report on the Onderneeming School for the Year 1905–6*, p. 485.
[101] *Report on the Onderneeming School for the Nine Months April-December 1915*, pp. 501–2.
[102] PP, *Report for 1919* (1921 Cmd. 1103–11 xxiv.187), p. 15.
[103] *Report on the Onderneeming School for the Year 1907–08*, p. 486; *Report on the Onderneeming School for the Year 1908–09*, pp. 520–1; *Report on the Onderneeming School for the Year 1909–10*, pp. 428–9.

In 1905, a riot paralysed Georgetown, British Guiana's capital city. It was blamed in part on 'centipedes', the urban youth gangs held responsible for much of the petty crime that was believed to plague Georgetown. A year later, a correspondent with the *Daily Chronicle* newspaper argued that Onderneeming should be closed, as it had not served its purpose.[104] Although F.W. Sandy of Golden Grove village did not mention the riot, the timing of his missive and its criticism of Onderneeming suggested his belief that the school had failed to prevent the kind of unrest that so concerned respectable Guianese. Onderneeming's officials shared Sandy's ambivalence about the institution's achievements, their assessment turning on the ability of those discharged to avoid prison and find employment, preferably in the agricultural sector. Yet ultimately, it was the inmates and their parents who determined the extent of Onderneeming's success.

Onderneeming's first superintendent, F.A. Gall, worried about discharged boys 'gravitat[ing] to their old haunts'.[105] Without 'parent or friend to receive him, [the discharged boy] ... [was] liable to join bad companions and loiter about the nearest village without any fixed purpose'.[106] Gall suspected that one boy, working on a steamer and living at his mother's house, would join his old friends, 'the street city Arabs', and 'naturally lapse into habits of vice'.[107] Indeed, some went even farther and asserted that once discharged, the boys 'became new recruits to the criminal classes'.[108] Though information about their whereabouts once they left Onderneeming is elusive (officials found it difficult to trace the boys once they left),[109] attempts to track them revealed that for some years, many remained outside the penal system. The discovery that none of the boys released in 1903 had ended up in prison was heartening to the members of the Onderneeming committee, seeming to demonstrate that the period of incarceration had exerted a positive influence on them.[110] In 1907, J.B. Harrison, the Acting Official Visitor, noted that only six of the 69 boys discharged from the Reformatory in the past years had 'lapsed into disorderly modes of life'. He, too, saw this as indicating the 'good results of Onderneeming School

---

[104] *D.C.*, 2 December 1906, p. 8.
[105] *Report on the Onderneeming School for the Year 1886*, p. 210.
[106] *Report on the Onderneeming School for the Year 1881*, pp. 138–9.
[107] *Report on the Onderneeming School for the Year 1882*, p. 125.
[108] MCC, 188/1904, *Report of the Onderneeming School Committee, for the Year 1903*, p. 5, NAG.
[109] *Report on the Onderneeming School for the Year 1909–1910*, p. 425.
[110] MCC, 188/1904, *Report of the Onderneeming School Committee, for the Year 1903*, p. 5, NAG.

training'.[111] From about 1905 to 1910, fewer than 12 per cent of the boys discharged ran foul of the law, 'leaving 88 per cent of the boys who [had] passed through the School as having been reclaimed'.[112] Onderneeming's officials attempted to facilitate the boys' reintegration into society. Upon being discharged, each boy was given a ticket to Georgetown and a letter to the Secretary of the Onderneeming Committee. Once in the city, he would receive any money he might have earned while at the reformatory and be placed in a job, perhaps chosen for him by the Committee.[113]

Onderneeming's primary goal, though, was to produce industrious workers for the agricultural sector. The admittedly sparse records imply that this mission was not successful. One superintendent suspected that the boys' training would lead them to choose other occupations once they left the school.[114] A 1905 source, for example, observed that 21 boys found work in a range of skilled and unskilled occupations – as tailors, bakers, agricultural workers and gold diggers.[115] Many, though, ended up 'idling about the stellings and wharves'.[116] According to Superintendent Bayley, many boys who found jobs did not keep them; he suspected that 'after having been subjected to strict discipline for years and having been cared for, [they did] not value the situations provided for them immediately on discharge and either work[ed] so carelessly as to cause their dismissal or themselves [threw] ... up their places'.[117]

Bayley's observations must be considered within the context of British Guiana's economy and fluctuations in employment levels. 1905, for example, the year that Bayley made these points, saw particularly high rates of unemployment. But these comments may suggest a determination on the part of Onderneeming boys to order their own working lives in opposition to the demands of the institution's administrators. One such example is provided by a boy who, trained as a carpenter and placed in the Georgetown Public Works Department, quit after less than a year. Onderneeming officials claimed that the boy had been 'taken under the wing of a relative who [was] a "carpenter of sorts", and together they work[ed] at the trade as odd jobs turn[ed] up'.

---

[111] *Report on the Onderneeming School for the Year 1907–1908*, p. 479.
[112] *Report on the Onderneeming School for the Year 1909–1910*, p. 426.
[113] *Report on the Onderneeming School for the Year 1905–06*, p. 482; see also *Report on the Onderneeming School for the Year 1907–1908*, pp. 480–1.
[114] *The Report on the Onderneeming Schools for the Year 1891–1892*, p. 239.
[115] *Report on the Onderneeming School for the Year 1905–1906*, p. 482.
[116] *Report on the Onderneeming School for the Year 1909–1910*, p. 425.
[117] *Report on the Onderneeming School for the Year 1905–06*, p. 483.

Onderneeming officials did not surrender the boy 'without a struggle'; they reminded him that serving the rest of his apprenticeship would see him 'qualify for a certificate and thereafter command a higher wage than was possible if he threw away his opportunity'. The institution's superintendent concluded that the boy was clearly 'overwhelmed by the temptation ... to enjoy the easy life which no doubt he saw his relative enjoying, working from time to time instead of steadily from Monday morning to Saturday evening'.[118]

Although these observations were biased, they reflect what many Caribbean historians have observed: former slaves in the British Caribbean attempted to control their own working lives. After having laboured according to the whims of others for so long, they determined to dictate the terms of their labour. Thus the decision of the young carpenter to work 'at odd jobs' with his relative was not unusual or surprising. The sources imply, though, that Afro-Creole parents also rejected the attempts of colonial officials to control when and how work would be performed. In particular, they refused to allow their sons to engage in agricultural labour at industrial schools.[119] One example is Berbice's Rose Hall Industrial School, which failed in the early 1890s. The 40-odd boys enrolled spent most of their days performing agricultural labour to the disapproval of their parents, some of whom declared that they 'would not let their children "work cutlass and shovel"'.[120] Subsequent attempts to encourage parents to apprentice their children in agriculture likewise met with little success. A government scheme established in 1907 to induce parents to enrol their sons as 'Agricultural Apprentices' netted only 25 boys despite an advertising campaign that saw much of the colony seemingly papered in advertisements. The Inspector of Schools concluded that parents who were farmers either preferred to train their sons themselves or were generally 'not particularly desirous that their sons should be instructed in Agriculture on the practical and scientific lines pursued by the Government'.[121]

Such sentiments were of long standing and were not unique to British Guiana. During the apprenticeship system that followed slavery's end in 1834, parents contested planters' attempts to apprentice their young children to the estates. Intended as a four-year transition between slavery and freedom, the apprenticeship system demanded that all former slaves provide some 40 hours a week of free labour; children

---

[118] *Report on the Onderneeming School for the Year 1907–1908*, pp. 480–1; *Report on the Onderneeming School for the Year 1908–1909*, p. 516.
[119] *Report of the Inspector of Schools for the Year 1894–1895*, p. 229.
[120] *Report of the Inspector of Schools for the Year 1892–1893*, p. 197.
[121] *Report of the Inspector of Schools for the Year 1910–1911*, p. 378.

under six years of age were excepted and became legally free on 1 August 1834. Yet former masters throughout the British West Indies, including British Guiana, attempted to compel the labour of these free children, demanding that they be apprenticed to work the estates in exchange for 'allowances', that is, the free food, clothes and health care slaves had traditionally received.[122] For the most part, Afro-Creole parents refused to cooperate, often sending their children to stay with relatives and friends.[123] These attitudes continued to be expressed after 1838. According to Bridget Brereton, field labour was permitted only as a last resort, if the family was in dire circumstances. Instead, parents preferred their children to work on the family land, labour that became particularly important as small-scale farming developed throughout the region after 1838.[124]

Part school, part gaol, Onderneeming was established to 'save' criminal and vagrant boys. Although this aim was not unique, Onderneeming's final form was. Indebted to British legislation and influenced by British practices, it evolved within the economic and ideological climate of colonial British Guiana. By placing the Onderneeming School within the context of a 'colonial carceral project',[125] this paper has traced the metamorphosis of a metropolitan institution within the colonial context. Though the source material on Onderneeming is not as comprehensive as that available for British historians examining nineteenth- and early twentieth-century reformatories and industrial schools, government reports and official correspondence allow historians to detail the emergence of such institutions and thus begin to recover some aspects of subaltern experience.[126] Despite several notable exceptions, historians of the Anglophone Caribbean have been slow to use this material to explore the penal institutions that emerged in the nineteenth century. Yet their importance is clear: they represented part of the ongoing effort of colonial elites to exercise control over former slaves and to ensure that their labour continued to serve the colonial economy. Such studies can also illuminate the relationship between colonial and metropolitan institutions, not only showing the impact of metropole upon colony, but revealing as well the

---

[122] Monica Schuler, 'Plantation Labourers, The London Missionary Society and Emancipation in West Demerara, Guyana', *Journal of Caribbean History* 22: 1 & 2 (1988), pp. 100–1.
[123] Brereton, 'Family Strategies', pp. 81–2, 91–2; Holt, *The Problem of Freedom*, p. 151.
[124] Bryan, *The Jamaican* People, p. 113; Brereton, 'Family Strategies', p. 96.
[125] I am indebted to Doug Hay for this phrase.
[126] Florencia Mallon, 'The Promise and Dilemma of Subaltern Studies: Perspectives from Latin American History', *American Historical Review* (December 1994), pp. 1491–1515.

transfer of ideas and policies among colonies. The coincidental introduction of reformatories in parts of the British Empire and the evolution of their policies clearly raise questions about the role of the Colonial Office in designing and dictating such policies, but they also raise the possibility of colonial 'contamination' from one colony to another.

Note

A version of this chapter appeared as 'Metropolitan Policies and Colonial Practices at the Boys' Reformatory in British Guiana', *Journal of Imperial and Common History*, vol. 30, no. 2 (2002). (www.tandf.co.uk/journals)

4 Discipline, reform or punish? Attitudes towards juvenile crimes and misdemeanours in the post-emancipation Caribbean, 1838–88

Sheena Boa

Introduction

During the nineteenth century, British attitudes towards children who came before the courts underwent radical changes. At the beginning of the century, children as young as seven were tried in adult courts and could be sentenced to execution. A large number of impoverished British children survived by crime, and changing legal codes effectively criminalised destitute children. Orphaned or abandoned children, who were deemed vagrants, often appeared in courts and received custodial sentences. In 1834, there were around 400 children under 12 years old, and a further 2204 between 13 and 16 years old, in prison. Some were incarcerated in the notorious hulks alongside some of the country's most dangerous men, and large numbers of children were transported to the colonies. Yet by the 1870s, children under 12 could be summarily tried by Justices of the Peace for all offences except murder, and children between 12 and 16 could elect a summary trial for certain minor offences. At the beginning of the next century, there were special juvenile courts and reform schools to deal with young offenders, and the courts no longer viewed children as small adults. These alterations were the result of both a better understanding of children and a growing reformation of the criminal justice system.[1]

---

[1] For an overview of the changing treatment of children in English courts, see, for example, Ivy Pinchbeck and Margaret Hewitt, *Children in English Society* (2 vols. London, 1969), vol. 2, pp. 351–481; Susan Magerey, 'The Invention of Juvenile Delinquency in Early Nineteenth Century England', *Labour History*, 34, 1978, pp. 11–21; Eric Hopkins, *Childhood Transformed: Working-Class Children in Nineteenth-Century England* (Manchester: Manchester University Press, 1994), pp. 193–9; Harry Hendrick, *Child Welfare, England 1872–1989* (London: Routledge, 1994), pp. 123–4.

The changing treatment of children in British courts reflects the view that children of the poor could be moulded into model citizens through their exposure to corrective habits. The courts aimed to expose destitute children to disciplines that would condition their bodies to hard work and their minds to conformity. Wayward children could also be reformed through learning habits of industry. At the same time, a conflict remained between this desire to discipline and reform 'delinquent' children and a determination to punish them. Hence, those in charge of juvenile convicts used coercion, corporal punishments and various deprivations to enforce the training, education and workloads of their charges. This chapter questions how far the changing attitudes within British society towards the treatment of juvenile offenders were applied within British Caribbean colonies. It also examines colonial and local responses to children, crime and punishment to assess how these influenced the authorities' treatment of children they considered wayward.[2]

Child prisoners after slavery

In the Caribbean, new legislation transformed criminal justice after the emancipation of the slaves. During the Apprenticeship period, Captain Pringle, a British prison inspector, conducted an investigation into the gaols and houses of correction. In his report, he recommended a total overhaul of the prison system, to enable it to adjust to the different needs of a free society. His chief concerns centred on the imposition of harsh punishments, arbitrary sentencing, unsavoury living conditions and the lack of segregation between the sexes. Although he was displeased at the general conditions of the prisons and their inmates, it is noticeable that he rarely mentioned child prisoners. Indeed he only expressed concern when he found a child of 12 chained to a man serving a life sentence. One possible reason for his lack of interest in the fate of children in the gaols in the Caribbean may have been their small numbers. In Britain, in the 1830s, there were large numbers of neglected and vagrant children in prison. In the Caribbean, most children were tied to their previous owners as apprentices or were cared for by family. Only a few free children survived as vagrants, and the control on the plantations,

---

[2] Michel Foucault, *Discipline and Punish: The Birth of the Prison,* tr. Alan Sheridan (London: Penguin, 1977), p. 138, described discipline as producing 'subjected and practised bodies, docile bodies'. This was the goal of courts and philanthropists dealing with children of the poor. They wanted children brought up in the habits of industry, to be capable, but also willing to perform arduous, manual labour.

and summary punishments inflicted on apprentices, ensured that few children faced custodial sentences in the common gaols.[3]

During Apprenticeship, child convicts shared cells with adults. The boys slept with the men, the girls with the women. Included in the child population within the gaols and houses of correction were very young children whose mothers were serving sentences. According to Pringle, the cells were disgusting. The toilet facilities consisted of open tubs which were kept in the rooms and emptied daily. In some of the gaols, particularly in Jamaica, inmates wore iron collars and chains, often weighing over three pounds. Child convicts suffered the same penalties as adults. Those sentenced to hard labour worked around nine-and-a-half hours per day, and their diet was at best meagre. In Jamaica, boys worked alongside the men in the penal gangs. In Barbados, however, boys remained with the women and worked at stone breaking within the prison walls.[4]

Pringle's report led to new rules being established for the prisons of the British West Indies. The Colonial Office became particularly concerned with the classification of prisoners and their separation into different categories. Prison officials were ordered to separate women from men, and women were given their own matron instead of remaining under the supervision of male custodians. In addition, the Colonial Office attempted to separate debtors from criminals, and those on remand from those who were already convicted. For the main part, these attempts at compartmentalising prison inmates remained unsuccessful, with the exception of the division of the sexes. Financial constraints and lack of space and facilities remained the main excuses for the intermingling of the different categories of prisoners for many years. Furthermore, in many islands, mentally ill

---

[3] The Apprenticeship period, 1834–38, was an attempt by the British Government to provide a bridge between slavery and freedom. For an overview of the period, see Swithin Wilmot, '"Not Full Free": The Ex-Slaves and the Apprenticeship System in Jamaica, 1834–38', *Jamaica Journal*, 17 (August-October 1984), pp. 2–10; Richard Frucht, 'Emancipation and Revolt in the West Indies: St. Kitts, 1834', *Science and Society* 39 (1975), pp. 199–214; Woodville Marshall, 'Apprenticeship and Labour Relations in Four Windward Islands', in David Richardson (ed.), *Abolition and its Aftermath: The Historical context, 1790–1916*, pp. 203–24 (London: Frank Cass, 1985); Sheena Boa, 'Experiences of women estate workers during the Apprenticeship period in St. Vincent, 1834 to 1838: the transition from slavery to freedom', *Women's History Review*, vol. 10, no. 3 (2001), pp. 381–407.

[4] PP, 1837–1838, vol. XL, Report of Captain J.W. Pringle on prisons in the West Indies, pp. 260–399.

people were placed in the common gaols rather than in special asylums.[5]

After emancipation, children, like other liberated slaves, had more freedom to roam. They could also face homelessness and unemployment and were no longer automatically supervised and fed by the plantation managers. As a result, the number of children who faced criminal proceedings increased.

So what constituted a young offender in the early years after emancipation? Examinations of the types of criminal proceedings involving children reveal that poverty was at the root of most of their offences. The range of prosecutions faced by children was similar to those faced by adults. Theft was a common crime committed by children, sometimes in concurrence with their parents. Children without homes or work could be picked up as vagrants. Thus, as in Britain, orphaned, abandoned or destitute children were criminalised. Some street children in the Caribbean also formed gangs and generally plagued town residents with abusive language and irritating pranks, which made them targets for arrest. New legislation also criminalised small acts of theft, and the pilfering of canes or fruits from estate land could lead to prosecution. In the early years after emancipation, as estate managers attempted to control the residency and work of labourers' families, children could also face eviction from their parents' homes and be prosecuted for trespass if they returned.[6]

Many of the serious offences relating to children involved violence. Post-emancipation society within the Caribbean contained a high

---

[5] In Jamaica, the British government's attempts to overhaul the prisons angered local legislators and they temporarily refused to do any business. See Thomas Holt, *The Problem of Freedom: Race, Labor and Politics in Jamaica and Britain, 1832–1938* (Baltimore: Johns Hopkins University Press, 1992), pp. 107–12. Governors' annual reports on the islands' prisons reveal how overcrowding and a lack of segregation remained a constant impediment to prison improvements. See, for example, PP, 1847–1848, vol. XLVI, Annual reports from Antigua, St. Vincent, St. Kitts; 1849, vol. XXXIV, reports for Jamaica, Barbados; 1852, vol. XXXI, report for Tobago. In St Vincent, the mentally ill were eventually removed from the gaol and located within the leper and pauper asylum, which created a great deal of fear on the part of the elderly paupers. CO 321/63, Robinson to Kimberley, 4 January 1883, no. 1, encl: Gore to Robinson, 28 December 1882.

[6] According to the magistrates, all the children convicted in Antigua in 1841 were vagrants. CO 7/69, Macphail to Stanley, 30 October 1841, no. 103, encl: Horsford to Macphail, 8 October 1841. Court cases printed in *The Liberal* in Barbados also revealed the convictions of children. See, for example, 1 May 1844; 9 August 1845; 19 December 1846; 22 December 1847; 13 August 1851. Acts relating to trespass can be seen in *The Liberal*, 20 January 1844; CO 7/78, FitzRoy to Stanley, 12 March 1844, Stipendiary Magistrates' reports; *The St. Vincent Chronicle and Public Gazette*, 16 April 1839.

level of aggression, within families, between employer and employee, on the streets and as part of judicial punishment. Children sometimes absorbed this violence, either as victims or as witnesses, and this could affect their behaviour. In the court proceedings, street fights and domestic violence frequently made up the majority of cases. Young boys particularly appeared to have been shaped by the hostilities that they witnessed and a few faced convictions for serious assaults. In Barbados, for example, between 1844 and 1848, two young boys were convicted of assaulting and attempting to rape girls under the age of ten. Another youth was charged with, but not convicted of, the manslaughter of another boy. York, a boy of about nine years, was actually hanged for murder. In addition, two girls were convicted with their mother for assault, and another girl was charged with infanticide. As the century progressed, the number of children facing criminal proceedings increased, and the local authorities searched for ways of dealing with them.[7]

Separate or reform?

The first attempts in the Caribbean to separate child convicts from adults took place in Antigua. Having relinquished the right to an Apprenticeship period, the Antiguan authorities were able to pass vagrancy laws similar to those in operation in England. Thus, the authorities deemed children who could not or would not find work to be vagrants. The local legislature wanted to apprentice these children for up to seven years as estate workers. However, to prevent this, Governor Colebrooke devised a special juvenile offenders' asylum.[8]

Colebrooke was very much a reformer. His vision was to create a unit where 'any disorderly habits' in the children would be corrected, 'without exposing them to the contamination of prison or withdrawing them from the protection of the magistrates'. Like reformers in England and the United States, he was concerned about the damage that was done to the young when they were placed with adult criminals. He also believed that children could and should be rehabilitated. Describing children placed in the local Houses of Correction, he wrote: 'The Hope of Reformation has hitherto been considerably diminished and in many instances their habits of Depravity more strongly confirmed.' He hoped that in the asylum, children would be kept 'usefully occupied'. They would work no more than seven hours per day in 'light agriculture', and girls would also perform laundry and sewing tasks. The chief object of

---

[7] *The Liberal*, 10 August 1844; 14 December 1844; 20 December 1848.
[8] CO 7/61, Colebrooke to Russell, 15 February 1840, no. 10.

the institution was to embody 'such discipline as shall appear conducive to their <u>Reformation,</u> to the <u>repression of crime,</u> and to the <u>engendering of industrious habits</u>'.[9]

The rules set out for this asylum were almost certainly far less punitive than those of any other place of correction in the Caribbean, England or North America at this time. There was no corporal punishment. Children who broke the rules could be placed in solitary confinement, given a reduced diet or put for no more than three hours in the stocks, but only on the orders of the Justices of the Peace or the police inspector. The superintendent and matron were to be guardians rather than jailers. They had to treat the children with 'forbearance and tolerance', ensure the children were clean and fed, and lead them at the twice-daily prayers. The children had to work on local estates, but their wages would be saved and given to their parents, or the local rector, to spend on the children on their release. They could also receive some rudimentary education.[10]

These benign rules were contrary to general British attitudes to the reformation of children. The asylum's rules came under immediate criticism from prison inspectors in England. In Britain, the first major changes to the treatment of young offenders occurred in 1838. A House of Lords enquiry into the judicial system revealed the large numbers of young people serving prison sentences. A separate institution was built at Parkhurst for young male offenders. Its aim was to prevent the contamination of the young by hardened adult criminals. Nevertheless, discipline superseded reform, and punishments included floggings, leg-irons, restricted diets and solitary confinement.[11] The Antigua institution, therefore, was far less retaliatory than the juvenile unit at Parkhurst, and prison inspectors were appalled that the children would receive their wages, seeing this as 'a bounty instead of a check on the commission of crime'. They also believed that the institution gave the children too much playtime. Juvenile offenders, they wrote, 'should be made to feel the penalties which attach to crime, ... the consequences which attend the violation of the law'.[12]

However, Colebrooke and his successor John Macphail were determined that the asylum should remain primarily a reforming institution. They both argued that the children would view wages as a reward and encouragement for working. In November 1840, the first three boys 'of

---

[9] CO 7/61, Colebrooke to Russell, 23 July 1840, no. 56.
[10] Ibid.
[11] Pinchbeck and Hewitt, *Children in English Society,* pp. 460–2.
[12] CO 7/67, Home Office Correspondence, 31 October 1840, Inspectors of Prisons to Fox Maule.

tender years' moved into the special unit. The following year, stipendiary magistrates praised the asylum, claiming that the children were 'eagerly sought after and constantly engaged ... and apparently delight in their allotted work'. In all, 52 boys stayed in the asylum during the first year, each for a maximum of three months. The largest number of boys at any one time was 19.[13]

There were far fewer girls in the asylum. Indeed, the greatest number of girls staying in the asylum at any one time was six. However, the stipendiary magistrates found the girl residents more problematical than the boys. While magistrates could state that they had had some success with some of the boys, they believed that the girls were not improving morally. One magistrate remonstrated: 'No favourable account after the release of the juvenile females, who have been inmates of the asylum has been received and it is much feared that they are not doing well.' The girls, whose ages ranged from seven to 13, had all been originally arrested for 'wandering abroad'. There were no suggestions about placing them in homes or employment after their release, and the only training that they received during their stay was in unskilled domestic duties, so it was hardly surprising that they had returned to their 'evil ways'. The limited training and employment opportunities remained a common barrier to attempts at discouraging crime among young females in both Britain and the Caribbean during the nineteenth century.[14]

Antigua's reform asylum was short-lived. In fact, it only survived until July 1843 and had little support from the legislature in Antigua. This lack of commitment can be seen from the inception of the Act. The children were never given a permanent building; rather they were housed in the back rooms of a police station. In addition, while the magistrates could see the advantages of placing children in a separate offenders' unit, they complained about the short sentences that could be imposed. When the Act expired, there were no attempts by the colonial authorities or local legislators to renew it, and children were again sent to the adult prison institutions, although now the boys were housed separately from the men. A new reformatory was eventually opened in Antigua in 1895.[15]

Colebrooke, however, retained his belief in the usefulness of rehabilitation for children. As a result of 'the success which attended the

---

[13] CO 7/63, Macphail to Russell, 19 November 1840, no. 80.
[14] CO 7/69, Macphail to Stanley, 30 October 1841, no. 103, encl: Horsford to Macphail, 8 October 1841.
[15] The asylum was abandoned in July 1843. CO 10/27, *Blue Book for Antigua, 1843*, p. 98. Mindie Lazarus-Black, *Legitimate Acts and Illegal Encounters: Law and Society in Antigua and Barbuda* (Washington: Smithsonian Institution Press, 1994), p. 114.

formation of a Juvenile Asylum at Antigua' he attempted to organise a similar separate juvenile asylum as part of his restructuring of the Barbados prison system when he assumed the governorship. Colebrooke upheld the belief that this would not only help in the reformation of the offenders, but would also stop parental neglect. However, in Barbados, boys could also receive corporal punishment. The units aimed at instilling in boys an acceptance of agricultural work, with the inmates working seven-and-a-half hours in light agriculture on nearby estates.[16]

Again, this vision of a separate reforming institution did not receive the general support of the local judiciary. Colebrooke was able to oversee the establishment of a separate house of correction for boys, but children continued to be tried in adult courts, still faced adult punishments, and remained in adult prisons. There remained some dissent between Colebrooke's notions of reform and the beliefs of the justices. On the whole, the magistrates and justices who tried child offenders in the courts saw harsh punishment and long sentences as the best deterrent for crimes. For example, one boy was sentenced to 18 months' hard labour for assault, because the justice claimed he had boasted of similar offences. Another boy, 'the most notorious of a very notorious gang of young vagabonds', received a six-month prison sentence for throwing a stone at someone who had kicked him. In the murder trial of a boy believed to be about ten or 11 years old, the justice specifically warned the jurors not to be swayed by the child's age. In addition, justices and jurors often called for flogging as a substitute for custody.[17]

Throughout this period, there was a general contradiction between the theories of separating and reforming children, and the realities of punishing them and saving money. This duality of reform and punishment for poor children stemmed from the perception that children were both victims of adult cruelty and exploitation, and a threat to social stability, morality and law and order. Legislation dealing with children therefore attempted to rescue children from harm, but also to contain them. Children were removed from the streets both for their own safety and for the protection of the nation as a whole. Therefore, while juries, prison inspectors and Colonial Office officials frequently discussed the problems of incarcerating children with adults, debtors with criminals, and habitual offenders with first-timers, financial restraints and a lack of

---

[16] CO 28/170, Colebrooke to Grey, 27 April 1849, no. 20.
[17] *The Liberal,* 10 August 1844; 20 August 1844; 14 December 1844; 19 December 1846.

real commitment to prison amelioration ensured that few reforming measures were put into practice.[18]

By the 1850s, educationalists and legislators in Britain considered the reformation of delinquent children to be a major priority. The rapid rise in urbanisation had created a vast under-class of homeless, vagrant and impoverished street children. It was estimated that over 13 000 youths under the age of 17 received prison sentences each year. In 1854, in response to agitation by reformers such as Mary Carpenter, who ran a charitable reform school for convicted children, the government passed the Youthful Offenders Act. This provided for reform schools which were set up by voluntary bodies to receive government funding. By 1858, there were more than 50 schools in operation. However, convicted children were still sent to prison for short periods before and after their spells in the reformatories, as the courts retained the principle of substituting 'reformatory treatment for retributive punishment'. Furthermore, the reformatory system was open to abuse. As the reformatories could keep the profits earned from the children's labour, children were often overworked and refused early release.[19]

In addition, in 1861, Britain introduced industrial schools. Education was now to be used to discipline and guide the children of the poor away from crime. The government-sponsored industrial schools were only for destitute, homeless or uncontrollable children, rather than criminals. Like reformatories, they sought to train children in suitable trades and give them rudimentary education. In other words, they aimed at preventing those children who were perceived as potential criminals because of their class and family background from breaking the law by instilling in them a disciplined work ethic.[20]

In some Caribbean islands there was a tradition of voluntary organisations that provided educational and medical aid, particularly to impoverished females. The Jamaican Fairfield Female Rescue Society,

---

[18] For a discussion on the dual notions of children as dangerous and in danger see Hendrick, *Child Welfare*, pp. 41–2. This conflict between rescuing and punishing can also be seen in the United States, where, from the 1820s, voluntary bodies responded to the growing numbers of impoverished, homeless immigrant children by placing them in reformatories in several of the major northern cities. These charity organisations hoped to 'subdue and conciliate' the youths who came before the courts. The organisations also ensured that these children were removed from their families, as they believed that the parents of destitute children were 'morally degenerate'. Within these institutions, the children received schooling and either worked in workshops or were apprenticed. Barry Krisberg and James Austin, *The Children of Ishmael: Critical Perspectives on Juvenile Justice* (Palo Alto, California: Mayfield), pp. 15–18.

[19] Pinchbeck and Hewitt, *Children in English Society*, pp. 477–8, 481.

[20] Hendrick, *Child Welfare*, pp. 10, 31.

for example, provided training and employment to young 'free coloured' girls during the 1830s to save them from prostitution. In other islands, private charities provided meals for destitute genteel women.[21] In Jamaica, voluntary bodies continued this tradition in response to the reformation of children. In 1857, a group of 'ladies' set up a reform school for destitute and convicted girls to save them from 'paths of sin and wickedness'. The girls learnt domestic and craft skills as well as receiving religious and moral training. Here again the emphasis was on reform. The 'ladies' wished to rescue these girls from 'idleness and vicious companions' and 'bring them to habits of regular and suitable occupation'. Unfortunately, this was predominantly domestic work, and the association found it difficult to find households willing to accept girls with such dubious pasts. In 1866, the girls' reformatory received females up to the age of 16. Little had been done to vary the work regimes of the inmates. The girls spent five hours each day washing for the public, making matchboxes, ginning cotton and cooking, cleaning and mending for themselves. They also had four hours each day at school, and three hours to eat and for recreation.[22]

The inhabitants of this reformatory included both destitute and criminal girls. In their early report, the ladies praised the progress that some of the girls made, and seemed to have a genuine belief that even the most corrupted girls with 'bad habits, violent impulses, vicious propensities, indolence, idleness and rude behaviour' could be reformed. They mentioned one girl, who had been convicted three times, who placed herself in the reformatory so she could be 'prepared to fill a useful place in society'.

By 1875, however, the educational aspirations of the reformatory had been reduced. Children received three-and-a-half hours' schooling on alternate days. The rest of their time was spent at labour or eating and resting. This may have been because a greater distinction was made between some indigent children and delinquents. In 1871, an orphanage was formed for girls. This specifically excluded any girls of 'known bad character', and offered the residents a greater variety of skills. As

---

[21] For the role of the Fairfield Female Refuge Centre, see Sheena Boa, 'Free Black and Coloured Women in a White Man's Slave Society, 1760–1834' (unpublished MPhil thesis, University of the West Indies, 1985), p. 183. See also Susan Lowes, 'They Couldn't Mash Ants': The Decline of the White and Non-White Elites in Antigua, 1834–1900', in Karen Fog Olwig (ed.), *Small Islands, Large Questions: Society, Culture and Resistance in the Post-Emancipation Caribbean* (London: Frank Cass, 1995), pp. 37–8, for charities in Antigua.

[22] CO137/343, Darling to Lytton, 31 January 1859, no. 22, encl: The first annual report of the Ladies' Industrial Association; CO 142/80, *Blue Book for Jamaica, 1866*, Report on the Girls' Reformatory, Studley Park, St. Andrews.

well as being taught the usual household chores, they could learn needlework and some were able to train to become teachers.[23]

In 1858, a separate reform school for boys opened in Jamaica. The inmates worked predominately in agriculture. Like the girls' school and the units in Antigua and Barbados, this unit housed both convicted and neglected children. Its aim also was to prepare impoverished children for a life of menial work. The boys spent most of their days at manual labour, farming, gardening and basic carpentry and tailoring. They also received some schooling. However, according to its managing committee in 1864, it was failing to improve the behaviour of the boys. Furthermore, overcrowding, bad sanitation and a lack of trained staff had resulted in the deaths of six inmates.[24]

Reformatories were eventually also set up in Barbados and Trinidad. In Barbados, a reformatory was opened in 1883, 'based on the English system'. Magistrates or justices could sentence boys for up to five years at the reformatory, or until they reached the age of 15. In Trinidad, the government introduced an industrial school in 1879 for boys and girls. In 1873, it also passed an ordinance authorising the construction of a reformatory. It was not until 1889, however, that funds were actually voted to construct a building. The delay was blamed on the two main religious bodies: the Catholic and Anglican churches refused to construct their own schools or to support a non-sectarian government-based school.[25]

Prisons

Even when the separate institutions had been reserved for young male offenders, a significant number of boys believed to be under the age of 18 ended up in the adult prisons. In 1851, for example, when the separate house of correction was first prepared to house only young offenders in Barbados, it accommodated a total of 94 black and three white boys. The town gaol held 55 black boys and one white boy under the age of 18. The following year, 111 black boys and one white boy were sent

---

[23] CO137/343, Darling to Lytton, 31 January 1859, no. 22, encl: The First Annual Report of the Ladies' Industrial Association; CO 142/89, *Blue Book for Jamaica, 1875*, Reports on the Girls' Orphan Home and Government Reform School.
[24] CO 137/388, Eyre to Cardwell, 22 March 1865, no. 57, encl: Annual Report of the Committee of Management of the Boys' Reformatory of Kingston. (I'd like to thank Diana Paton for the references to the girls' and boys' reformatories.)
[25] CO 321/61, Robinson to Derby, 29 May 1883, no. 47, encl: An act to provide for the establishment of a reformatory and industrial school; CO 295/277, Irving to Carnarvon, 7 July 1876, no. 125, Ordinance no. 4, The establishment and regulations of Industrial schools; CO 295/318, Robinson to Knutsford, 14 August 1889, no. 214.

to the juvenile unit, while 102 black and three white boys were sent to the adult prisons. In 1860, 203 black boys were sent to the juvenile unit, while 345 black and three white boys went to the adult prisons. These figures illustrate not only the significant numbers of young males in prison, but also the rapidly growing number of boys receiving custodial sentences.[26]

This was also the case in other islands. Not all convicted Jamaican children escaped prison. In 1865, for example, a total of 454 boys and 233 girls under the age of 18 were detained in the adult prisons. Furthermore, children who were considered unmanageable within the reformatories could also be placed in the common gaols and houses of correction. In Trinidad also, even after the construction of the industrial school, children continued to end up in the adult gaols. For example, in 1880, 30 boys and 15 girls were confined in the gaols, and the following year, 28 boys and 18 girls had custodial sentences in the common gaols. The magistrate claimed that the small numbers were an indication of the jurors' unwillingness to convict children, rather than an improvement in their behaviour.[27]

Children also continued to receive custodial sentences in adult prisons in many of the smaller islands because of a lack of funding to establish separate units for the small numbers of convicted children. There was, moreover, a general apathy towards the well-being of the children of the poor. In St Vincent, boys over the age of 14 were put to hard labour outside the prison in penal gangs. Females and younger boys broke stones inside the prison walls. The very young swept and cleaned the prison.[28]

It was rare for girls to obtain separate prison facilities. In Antigua, when the reformatory was disbanded in 1843, a separate facility was maintained for boys, but not for girls. This was also the case in Barbados. Legislators within the Caribbean frequently complained about the dangers of placing debtors and first-time female offenders with the more hardened female prisoners. Magistrates and prison officers claimed that women with criminal records could either shock or harm other women because they habitually used obscenities and were involved in prostitution. It would therefore seem logical that the

---

[26] There were no indications in the Barbados papers of the age limit in the juvenile prison. In Antigua and Jamaica the upper age limit was 16, so it is possible that all the under-18s in the adult institutions were 16 or 17 years old. CO 33/58, *Blue Books for Barbados, 1851, 1852,* Report on Prisons.

[27] CO 142/79, *Blue Book for Jamaica, 1865,* Report on Prisons; *Trinidad Royal Gazette,* 14 June 1882, Report of the Inspector of Prisons.

[28] CO 260/103, Mundy to Cardwell, 15 May 1865, no. 311, encl: Berkley to Mundy, 28 April 1865.

judiciary should wish young girls to be separated from such women. However, there was also a belief that women and girls could be quickly and permanently corrupted. The lack of concern for girl convicts suggests that, in the eyes of the courts, they were already irreparably damaged. According to Lionel Fraser, prison inspector for Trinidad, female prostitutes began their careers 'at an age too young to seem possible'. Writing about the problem of women swearing in the streets, he wrote: 'The profligacy of these women, and the almost childish age at which they become castaway are matters for grave consideration.'[29]

The adult prisons of the Caribbean during this period were uniformly badly run. One of the main problems, according to some legislators, was that the lack of funding had kept wages of prison officers low and therefore deterred suitable candidates from entering the prison services. Many of the gaols were poorly maintained and most were merely refurbished workhouses from the slavery era. In the first decades after abolition, many islands constructed larger new prisons in the main towns, while ignoring the state of the houses of correction and police cells in the rural areas. Furthermore, the refurbishments were frequently inadequate and overcrowding remained a primary problem throughout the period.[30]

Prisons in the nineteenth-century Caribbean must have been places of terror for many of the child inmates. The lack of discipline remained a central issue in the running of the prisons. In Barbados, for example, local legislators claimed that the inmates effectively controlled the town prison and some convicts had to be removed from the gaol to protect them from the others. One prison officer reported that prisoners had told

---

[29] CO 295/251, Longdon to Kimberley, 1 May 1870, encl: Report of the Inspector of Prisons; CO 295/278, DesVoeux to Carnarvon, 18 May 1877, no. 87, encl: Fraser to Colonial Secretary, 8 May 1877; *Trinidad Royal Gazette*, 14 June 1882, Report of the Inspector of Prisons. For a description of prostitution in Trinidad, see David Trotman, 'Women and Crime in the Late Nineteenth Century', in Hilary Beckles and Verene Shepherd (eds.), *Caribbean Freedom: Economy and Society from Emancipation to the Present* (Kingston: Ian Randle, 1993), p. 257. For attitudes to young female offenders in England and the US see Clive Emsley, *Crime and Society in England, 1750–1900* (London: Longman, 1987), pp. 67–8, and Krisberg and Austin, *Children of Ishmael*, p. 16.

[30] At one point the matron in Barbados, for example, was called 'not a fit and proper person to discharge the duties', while the work of the matron of St Vincent was called 'far from satisfactory'. For discussions on the problems within the Barbados prison systems see *The Liberal*, 20 April 1844, 12 August 1846, 15 August 1846. See also CO 260/59, 19 March 1841, no. 6, Macgregor to Russell, enclosure, 14 March 1841; Sutherland to Tyler, 14 August 1841, no. 10, Darling to Russell, enclosure, Brown to Darling, 4 August 1841; PP, 1847–1848, vol. XLVI, Annual reports from Antigua, St. Vincent, St. Kitts; 1849, vol. XXXIV, reports for Jamaica, Barbados, 1852, vol. XXXI, report for Tobago.

him that if he did not accede to their control, they would lock the door and 'beat him to a jelly'. Legislators were also concerned about the lack of respect that the inmates held for the officers. This was demonstrated by the fact that the prisoners universally called the superintendent of the prison 'Pappy'. Fights were also a common occurrence among inmates, and in 1846, in Barbados, hostilities between convicts simultaneously led to fires in both the men's and women's sections of the gaol house. In Trinidad, there was also a tradition among the female prisoners of smashing up their cells in the few days before their release.[31]

It is also possible that children faced the threat of sexual violence. While there were no discussions of sexual assaults on male offenders, there was a general belief that it was dangerous for the men to sleep in dormitories. The Jamaican prison inspector, for example, wrote:

> To crowd bad men together at night is not only to create perpetual obstacles to the maintenance of good order and discipline, but is perfectly hostile to moral improvement. ... For the moral mischief to which this nightly intercourse inevitably leads, we have no effectual antidote.[32]

It is possible that this 'moral mischief' referred to sexual activities among the male offenders. Certainly, during this period, prison reformers in Britain believed that the separation of inmates at night was crucial for their moral development. Moreover, although there were attempts to segregate men from women, in St Vincent, at least two women became pregnant during their incarceration in the local gaol. The gaoler was responsible for one of the pregnancies.[33]

Reforming the body

Michel Foucault suggested that during the nineteenth century, the European prison adapted into 'an exhausted disciplinary apparatus' with total power over the inmates. The aim was to deprive convicts of liberty, exert punishments and control, and reform them through work. Prison officials in the Caribbean frequently discussed the shortfalls in their own systems, particularly with regard to discipline and reform. They were concerned about the large number of recidivists within the prisons and their unruly behaviour, which was linked to their fears about

---

[31] *The Liberal,* 12 August 1846, 15 August 1846; CO 295/278, DesVoeux to Carnarvon, 18 May 1877, no. 87, encl: Fraser to Colonial Secretary, 8 May 1877.
[32] PP, 1849, vol. XXXIV, reports for Jamaica, p. 162.
[33] CO 321/58, Robinson to Kimberley, 27 December 1882, no. 121, encl: Gore to Robinson, 7 December 1882; *The Witness,* 4 December 1879.

the actions and the demeanour of the poor in general. Prison sentences were therefore meant to act as both a deterrent and a means of reform. By the 1850s, there was a movement away from the rational ideas of reform and the local authorities within the Caribbean began to demand a return to physical retribution and the reintroduction of control methods used during the slavery period. Reformation was still aimed at younger offenders, but an aversion developed to any forms of reformation that did not involve physical punishment.[34]

In Britain, there was a belief that the poor were physically and morally different from the middle classes. The lower classes were viewed as the 'dangerous class', who were naturally criminal and invariably indolent. Places of custody, therefore, aimed not only at containing prisoners but also at subduing them in the hope of making them more docile.

In the Caribbean, perceptions of class differences were further exacerbated by race. Thomas Holt has linked the reintroduction of corporal punishments into the prison systems of Jamaica with the strong convictions of the authorities that African-Caribbean labourers were 'degraded people', with natural criminal tendencies. As poverty increased in the Caribbean, so did the number of convictions for theft. One writer to a newspaper reported that 'nothing less than the most degrading punishment to which a human being can be subjected is likely to effect the wholesome reformation of the deprived'. After the 1850s, more corporal punishments were introduced and the treadmill, once banned in the Caribbean, was reintroduced in the belief that it would in some way train inmates to conform.[35]

Among females, reformation was linked to humiliation. Trinidad's prison inspector Lionel Fraser, for example, suggested segregating females who were convicted for swearing from others in the hope of creating a sense of shame. Prisons also attempted to break the rebellious spirit of female prisoners through solitary confinement and hard labour. Women and girls could be segregated from each other by being placed in solitary cells. Their separation from society as a whole was also intended to increase this feeling of shame. While male prisoners were often able to leave the prison yards in convict gangs to work on the roads or on plantations, females remained in the

---

[34] Foucault, *Discipline and Punish*, pp. 235–6; Trotman, 'Women and Crime', p. 256; CO 321/62, Robinson to Derby, 21 July 1883, no. 72, encl: Gaols and Prison and Criminal statistics for 1882. The report claimed that recidivism increased from 19 per cent to 39 per cent among young offenders between 1879 and 1882; Holt, *The Problem of Freedom*.
[35] Emsley, *Crime and Society in England*, p. 49; Holt, *The Problem of Freedom*, p. 287.

prison yards. Those sentenced to hard labour were employed in the mind-numbing, physically punishing labour of breaking stones.[36]

Prison officials also humiliated women by defeminising them. In most Caribbean islands, women's and girls' heads were shaved when they entered and when they left gaol. Government officials believed that this was hygienic and, more importantly, a way of curbing female criminal impulses. In Jamaica, Barbados, the Virgin Islands and Bermuda, prison officers reported that it was used as a deterrent. In the Bahamas, the police authorities reported that they used hair cropping as a threat to a woman who had been convicted 63 times. As a result she maintained 'perfect docility'. Throughout the post-emancipation period, prison officers advocated shaving the heads of recidivists or those who infringed prison discipline in order to humiliate them and expose them to the ridicule of the other inmates. Not all government officials shared this desire to humiliate female prisoners. In St Vincent, Lieutenant-Governor Rennie decided that it was unwise to degrade even criminals unnecessarily, and decided to disallow hair cropping except for second offenders. In Trinidad, the residents of Port of Spain rioted in 1849 in response to an act authorising the shaving of all prisoners' heads. This convinced the authorities that hair shaving should not be universally applied to all female prisoners.[37]

Among males, reformation was linked to work. One of the primary goals of the reformatories for boys was to turn unemployed children into cheap, productive agricultural labourers. The schooling and work regimes of the juvenile prisons concentrated primarily on plantation labour, or if that was not available, other forms of manual labour, such as road and ditch digging or stone breaking. Since the abolition of slavery, planters had attempted to find a means of retaining and controlling child labour. In Antigua, they failed to introduce an act to apprentice 'vagrant children' after abolition. In Jamaica, under the auspices of Governor Eyre, the legislature also apprenticed children believed to be vagrant for up to five years. While this act was only in force for one year, it led to rumours that slavery was about to

---

[36] CO 295/278, DesVoeux to Carnarvon, 18 May 1877, no. 87, encl: Fraser to Colonial Secretary, 8 May 1877. All women sentenced to hard labour remained within the walls of the prisons, while men could work within the towns and estates.

[37] CO 260/116, Rawson to Kimberly, 26 April 1872, no. 31, encl: Rennie to Rawson, 8 February 1872; CO 260/117, Rawson to Kimberly, 21 November 1872, no. 75, encl: Report on Cropping Women's Hair; *Royal St. Vincent Gazette,* 11 October 1849.

be reintroduced and contributed to the unrest that led to the Morant Bay rebellion.[38]

The judiciary believed that the two main paths for rehabilitating children were through hard labour and physical punishment. The language used by reformers in Britain and the authorities in the Caribbean expressed a certainty that children of the poor should be trained and accustomed to hard work. In other words, their mentalities could be manipulated through regular actions meted out on their bodies. They needed to learn habits of industry through continual exposure to labour. In fact, the main criticism of the first Antiguan reformatory was that it did not allow the children enough time to acquire these new habits. One magistrate complained that the children were 'thrown again upon the world at the very moment ... when impression for good may be just taking possession of their minds'. In Jamaica, the aims of the reform schools were to rescue children from 'idleness and vicious companions' and to bring about 'moral and social improvement to bring them to habits of regular and suitable occupation'.[39]

These sentiments were also articulated in Barbados when the reformatory was opened in 1883. William Robinson, the island's Governor, stated: 'Besides being brought under the influence of moral and religious instruction and subjected to discipline, [the child] is trained through a term of years in habits of industry.' As a result, Robinson hoped, offending children would 'turn out in the end well ordered members of the community by having developed in them those motives and aims which induce people in the humbler walks of life to settle down to work as a means of improving their condition and that of their family'. But, more portentously, he also expressed the wish that reformed children would then leave the island in search of work elsewhere, stating: 'I need not say how desirable such an emigration is.'[40]

---

[38] CO 7/69, Macphail to Stanley, 30 October 1841, no. 103, encl: Horsford to Macphail, 8 October 1841; CO 137/388, Eyre to Cardwell, 22 March 1865, no. 57, encl: Annual Report of the Committee of Management of the Boys' Reformatory of Kingston; CO 33/61, *Blue Book for Barbados, 1851,* report on prisons; CO 321/61, Robinson to Derby, 29 May 1883, no. 47, encl: An act to provide for the establishment of a reformatory and industrial school; CO 295/277, Irving to Carnarvon, 7 July 1876, no. 125, Ordinance no. 4, the establishment and regulations of Industrial schools; CO 295/318, Robinson to Knutsford, 14 August 1889, no. 214; CO 7/61, Colebrooke to Russell, 15 February 1840, no. 10; CO 137/388, Eyre to Cardwell, 27 March 1865, no. 60, encl: 28 Vic. Ap. XIX.

[39] CO 7/69, Macphail to Stanley, 30 October 1841, no. 103; CO 137/343, Darling to Lytton, 11 March 1858, no. 40.

[40] CO 321/62, Robinson to Derby, 21 July 1883, no. 72, encl: Gaols and Prisons Statistics for 1882.

Hard work, however, was not only used as a training tool for the young within Caribbean reformatories and prisons. The authorities also employed it as a punishment. Labour was closely linked to suffering within the prison systems, and prison officers attempted various methods to ensure that hard labour was both profitable to the prisons and painful to the prisoners. Thus, while the authorities deplored the reluctance of the poor to take on agricultural work, they also contributed to a negative conception of work by emphasising the degrading and disagreeable aspects of physical labour. One prison officer in Barbados, for example, claimed that hard labour was a better deterrent than the treadmill, which he described as 'idling on full diet'. Hard labour, he claimed, had 'a very decided effect on the convicts'. In particular he noted that it 'materially affected the condition of the inmates... The old convicts no longer present the sleek appearance and self-satisfied air of bygone days, but go about their work with a dogged demeanour that is very noticeable.' Similarly, in Jamaica, the prison chaplain demanded that prisoners should be 'humbled'. He suggested that 'hard, that is really painful labour' would lead to 'not only a diminution of crime, but a higher moral and social condition' among the criminal class.[41]

Throughout the history of slavery in the Caribbean, the whip symbolised the control, humiliation and subjugation of slaves. After abolition, therefore, there was a great resistance to corporal punishment by abolitionists and the free population. However, it remained the chosen form of punishment in many islands, particularly for young male offenders. Despite the associations of flogging with slavery, prison discipline and judicial punishment reverted to the use of the whip and rod. By the middle of the 1840s, juries in Barbados were calling for the introduction of flogging as a means of controlling male prisoners, and also as an alternative to custodial sentences. In St Lucia, in 1844, the views of the population and the authorities came into conflict when the courts attempted to publicly flog a middle-class 'coloured' boy for perjury. This resulted in angry riots, which forced the Lieutenant-Governor to repeal the sentence. He also vowed never to agree to public floggings again. In fact, the crowd were not demonstrating only against the use of

---

[41] CO 7/62, Colebrooke to Russell, 12 November 1840; CO 321/62, Robinson to Derby, 28 September 1883, no. 108; CO 137/388, Eyre to Cardwell, 30 March 1865, no. 69, encl: Annual Report of the Inspector of Prison; Eyre to Cardwell, 27 March 1865, no. 60; Eyre to Cardwell, 22 March 1865, no. 59.

corporal punishment: they were also stating their opposition to the public humiliation of a mixed-race, well-connected boy.[42]

In St Vincent, the legislature attempted to reintroduce the cat-o'-nine tails to punish convicted boys in 1854. Lieutenant-Governor McDowell argued that this would save the boys from custodial sentences with adult males. Governor-General Colebrooke disallowed the Act and suggested that if St Vincent could not afford to introduce a separate juvenile prison, it should consider the birch as a suitable form of punishment, as, unlike the cat, it did not scar the boys permanently. When Edward John Eyre was Lieutenant-Governor of St Vincent, he also attempted to introduce flogging to replace some punishments. He claimed that hard labour was not a sufficient deterrent. After 1868, the local legislature chose to punish boys for minor offences with flogging rather than prison. As a result, corporal punishment became common for young male offenders, often for very trivial misdemeanours. For example, in 1878, seven boys between the ages of ten and 14 were flogged. Two were flogged for throwing stones, two for throwing night-soil, two for theft, and one was flogged for threatening behaviour.[43]

Jamaica reintroduced the whip for serious offences in 1850, and in 1865, Eyre also argued for the reintroduction of corporal punishment for cases of larceny. He stated that his experience in the Caribbean had shown him that corporal punishment was the only effective means of dealing with theft. One prison inspector also stated that this would appease local residents and stop villagers from attacking thieves. The Jamaican legislature suggested a maximum 25 lashes for boys under 16 and 50 lashes for older males. The Colonial Office reduced this to 18 lashes for boys and 39 lashes for men.[44]

In the Trinidad Industrial School, boys could be beaten with a tamarind rod or given up to three months' hard labour in the common gaol if they broke the school rules or ran away. In addition, boys and

---

[42] *The Liberal,* 20 April 1844, 14 December 1844; CO 253/81, Grey to Stanley, 24 October 1844, encl: Torrens to Grey, 15 October 1844. The mass floggings after the Morant Bay rebellion express this determination to return to more vindictive forms of punishment. See Gad Heuman, *The Killing Time: The Morant Bay Rebellion in Jamaica* (London: Macmillan, 1994), pp. 134–6.

[43] CO 260/81, Colebrooke to Grey, 28 September 1854, no. 66, encl: Colebrooke to McDowell, 17 January 1854; CO 260/83, Colebrooke to Russell, 16 October 1855, no. 58, encl: An act for the further improvement of the administration of criminal justice; CO 321/23, Strahan to Hicks Beach, 6 August 1878, no. 46, encl: Dundas to Strahan, 18 July 1878.

[44] Holt, *The Problem of Freedom,* p 287; CO 137/388, Eyre to Cardwell, 22 March 1865, no. 59, encl: 28 Vic. Ch. 18, Cardwell to Eyre, no. 213, 1 June 1865; Eyre to Cardwell, 30 March 1865, no. 69, encl: Annual report from the Prison Inspector.

men in Trinidad received corporal punishment for infringements of gaol discipline. In 1879, for example, nine boys were beaten with the rod for breaching prison discipline. This suggests that among some Caribbean authorities, particularly after memories of the horrors of slavery receded and a more uncompromising attitude towards the African-Caribbean population developed, corporal punishment supplanted rehabilitation. According to Governor Rawson, the Governor-General of the Windward Islands, in 1870, prisons should be primarily a place of deterrence, not of work.[45]

The treadmill also had a history of terror and abuse within the Caribbean. The British government originally introduced it as a more humane alternative to flogging as part of the attempts to ameliorate slavery. They also viewed it as an appropriate method of punishing women. Within the Caribbean, however, it assumed the role of inflicting extreme torture. After reports of several deaths on the treadmills, as well as horrendous injuries during the Apprenticeship period, treadmills were removed from the prisons and workhouses. In 1865, Eyre reintroduced the treadmill into Jamaica as part of his strengthening of the physical control of prisoners. In St Vincent, prison officials hoped that the treadmill would deter people from choosing gaol sentences rather than paying fines. Lieutenant-Governor Rennie expressed his own opposition to the treadmill by claiming that it was 'very harsh' for black and coloured people, who were usually barefooted. He argued that it was unsuitable for the tropics and feared that it would be employed for minor offences and could be misused as a threat by plantation managers. The Colonial Office and local legislators ignored his concerns. The treadmill was the ideal mechanism for regulating the minds and bodies of convicts through steady, repetitive, physical labour. More than the shot drill and stone breaking, it combined extreme physical exertion with pointless and non-productive employment. As soon as the treadmill was constructed in St Vincent, in 1871, a local newspaper reported its disgust that a seven-year-old boy was put to work on it.[46]

---

[45] CO 300/90, *Blue Book for Trinidad* 1878, Report on Industrial School; CO 260/112, Rawson to Granville, 17 May 1870, no. 29. According to the Rules and Regulations of the Common Gaol, women could also be flogged if they broke the rules and the Governor gave his authorisation. See CO 260/103, Mundy to Cardwell, 15 May 1865, no. 311, encl: Prison Rules.

[46] Holt, *The Problem of Freedom*, 64–5, 105–7, 286; CO 260/112, Rawson to Granville, 17 May 1870, no. 29; CO 260/115, Rawson to Kimberley, 13 November 1871, no. 94, encl: Rennie to Rawson, 19 September 1871, 8 November 1871; *St. Vincent Witness*, 3 August 1871.

Conclusions

During the nineteenth century in Britain, a clear pattern of changes emerged in the treatment of delinquent children. Custodial sentences for children began to diverge from those of adults, and the treatment of juvenile criminals changed from merely punitive to reformative, through a combination of corporal punishments, work and education. The attempts to reform child-convicts within the Caribbean were at best piecemeal. On the whole, there remained a dissonance between ideals of reformation and desires to punish and degrade. The first reformatory in Antigua, with its determination to create a safe and non-violent home for destitute and convicted children and to rescue them from vice and moral contamination, was both unique and short-lived. Subsequent juvenile institutions attempted to modify children's behaviour primarily through imposing punitive labour regimes.

The treatment of prisoners in the Caribbean was influenced by European middle-class attitudes to class, race and age. The children of the Caribbean who came before the courts were perceived as threatening to the authorities because they embodied all the elements of savagery, as members of the lower classes, as African-descendent and as children. These children, many of whom were victims of poverty rather than delinquents, faced increasingly retributive and extended forms of chastisement.

Within the Caribbean, therefore, the controllers of justice often believed that the discipline and reformation of the minds of the poor could only be achieved through punishing their bodies. As a result, the courts attempted to change the habits of indigent children by subduing, beating and containing the inmates. Theories of training and control resulted in a dependence on the whip, the treadmill and penal labour to maintain prison discipline. Consequently, boy convicts suffered from the increasing reliance on corporal punishments during the second half of the nineteenth century. Lower-class girls were rarely seen as different from women. There was a perception among white males that African-Caribbean girls matured more quickly than girls in Europe. Therefore, legislators rarely provided separate facilities for young female offenders, and prisons attempted to maintain authority over females through work, humiliation and segregation.[47]

Financial restraints and a lack of commitment to social reform limited any attempts to use education as a universal means of control. In islands without separate juvenile institutions, the reformation of

---

[47] CO 295/319, Robinson to Knutsford, 11 April 1889, no. 127.

children was clearly not a priority. Without the protection of a sympathetic Governor or the interference of middle-class charity volunteers, many Caribbean children faced the full horrors of custodial sentences or the indignity of corporal punishment.

Section 2

Patterns of resistance

5 'You signed my name, but not my feet': paradoxes of peasant resistance and state control in post-revolutionary Haiti[1]

Mimi Sheller

Haiti is an unusual case in the comparative study of post-emancipation societies because its revolutionary war of 1791–1803 stands alone as the only successful case of simultaneous armed self-liberation and declaration of independence from colonial rule. The questions of control and resistance here shift to grounds quite different to those that pertained in other colonial territories, because the plantation economy and the state apparatus were prised free from white French planters and slave owners. After 1804, however, a strong class and colour divide remained between the elite freedmen who had been planters and slave owners prior to the Revolution and the majority of the population of former plantation slaves, some of whom rose through the ranks of the revolutionary army to become generals and landowners in their own right. This article will consider the specificity of ongoing forms of control and resistance in this unusual context, in contrast to other post-slavery societies where white planters and former slave owners remained in control. Given the ongoing social inequalities and political struggles in Haiti's post-independence period, what forms could control and resistance take? In a situation of successful revolutionary emancipation how would freedom be exercised?

Peasants in post-independence Haiti had an expression, 'Vous signé *nom* moi, mais vous pas signé *pieds* moi' [You signed my name, but you haven't signed my feet].[2] This notion of embodied action (walking away from a contracted place of work) superseding formal contracts signed on paper is exemplary of what we might call subaltern tactics of resistance. It shows a knowing agent who goes along with the formalities of signing a contract (perhaps in so far as it will serve the

---

[1] This piece draws in part from M. Sheller, *Democracy After Slavery: Black Publics and Peasant Radicalism in Haiti and Jamaica* (London and Oxford: Macmillan, 2000).
[2] B. Ardouin, *Etudes sur l'Histoire d'Haïti* (Paris: Dezobry, Magdeleine et Cie, 1860), vol. 10, p. 23, n.1.

purpose of getting a wage and not being arrested for 'vagrancy'), but who then asserts the freedom to leave when the time comes. Moreover, it is phrased as a direct address to a power-holder who is trying to enforce the contractual obligation; it is a public moment for the 'hidden transcript'.³ Resistance is precisely being able to work both with and against the system at the same time, to defy power even while appearing to serve it. In this case it is also a continuation of the Haitian tradition of *petit marronage*, escaping the plantation system of control as and when necessary. The success of this strategy is evident in the collapse of Haiti's plantation economy in the early nineteenth century, as I will discuss below.

The folk saying also has further resonance, however, as a commentary on the discrepancy between historical materiality (the earthy feet as 'lived experience') and the written record of history (the signature tracks left as remnants in the archives). When we write in the name of the Haitian peasantry, how much has escaped us? When does the peasant walk off the pages of the historian's archive and leave only an absence in the historical text? Marc Bloch once wrote of the task of the historian to seek out the 'traces' left in the historical record by tracking more subtle 'sources in spite of themselves'. Michel-Rolph Trouillot, however, challenges us further by calling into question any will to better historical knowledge, given the 'silencing of the past' and in particular the silencing of the Haitian revolution. However ardently the historian seeks the traces of lost facticity, Trouillot reminds us, 'facts are not created equal: the production of traces is always also the creation of silences'. Efforts to turn up facts belie the existence of the 'unthinkable', 'that which one cannot conceive of within the range of possible alternatives, that which perverts all answers because it defies the terms under which the questions were phrased'.⁴

In the terms of Western thought, Trouillot argues, the Haitian revolution was unthinkable in its time, and remains largely marginal to the main historiographic narratives of modernity, which have focused on the American and French revolutions as the measuring rods of the 'Age of Democracy'. A corollary to this is the way in which Haiti's history after the revolution has been warped and forgotten. When remembered, it is either turned into a travesty of despotic barbarism, political

---

[3] J. Scott, *Domination and the Arts of Resistance: Hidden Transcripts* (New Haven and London: Yale University Press, 1990).
[4] M. Bloch, *The Historian's Craft*, tr. P. Putnam (New York: Vintage, 1953); M.R. Trouillot, *Silencing the Past: Power and the Production of History* (Boston: Beacon Press, 1995), pp. 29, 82.

incompetence and economic decline (within Euro-American historiography), or celebrated (within Haitian and wider Caribbean historiography) as the unquestioned consolidation of a heroic anti-colonial independence. Against these trends, I want to bring back into focus the relation between the decline of planter control and the emergence of peasant agency in nineteenth-century Haiti. If we think of freedom as a continuous variable, it is clear that slave emancipation everywhere led to struggles over the liberties that planters would lose and that the formerly enslaved would gain. Even in Haiti, or perhaps *especially* in Haiti, the problem of implementing freedom remained the core social and political question.

Yet the apparent lack of any political agency, any sign of 'resistance', among the Haitian peasantry has produced a gaping silence in Haitian history. Sidney Mintz, in his introduction to James Leyburn's *The Haitian People* (1966), for example, verged on dismissing altogether the possibility of peasant political agency in Haiti. Although admitting that Haitian peasants occasionally played a political role, Mintz argues that this was exceptional; in general, he says, they are 'unable to break out of a stagnation that is economic as well as cultural', making them wholly 'apathetic'. 'Seemingly mute and invisible,' he laments, 'apparently powerless, the peasantry of Haiti remind one of Marx's famous dictum that peasants possess organization only in the sense that the potatoes in a sack of potatoes are organized'.[5] The Haitian peasantry, it would seem, is not a good candidate for exemplifying a post-slavery revolutionary (or even resistant) subaltern ideology. What happened to C.L.R. James' Black Jacobins? What can explain this apparent political apathy? Or is it a mistaken appraisal of Haitian political culture? How much do we really know about past instances of peasant political activism and resistance, especially in a field where both sources and primary research are thin on the ground? And can history ever 'sign' these 'feet', or do our very modes of asking questions make this history unthinkable?

Signs of control

What was the reality of 'freedom' for Haiti's post-revolutionary plantation labourers and 'reconstituted peasants', and what evidence do we

---

[5] S. Mintz, *Caribbean Transformations* (New York: Columbia University Press, 1989 [1974]), pp. 270, 297.

turn to in trying to reconstruct that historical reality?[6] Although the Haitian revolution succeeded in ending slavery and achieving national independence long before this was achieved in many other slave societies, it is generally argued that the real winners of the revolution were not the mass of freed slaves, but the old *mulâtre* land-owning elite (the *anciens libres*) and the new noir generals (the *nouveaux libres*) who seized the state.[7] Thus it is crucial first to recognise that the political process of revolutionary self-emancipation entailed the continuation of certain forms of control, even in Haiti. In the early decades of state-consolidation, social and political control did not actually pass to the self-liberated slaves who had achieved the 'unthinkable' revolution, but to a small elite that protected its own interests and suppressed much of the potential radicalism of the revolution. As Trouillot argues in an important essay on the 'inconvenience of freedom', the privileged group of *gens de couleur* were at first 'reluctant to admit the fact that the end of slavery signalled the slow replacement of the plantation system by a peasant-based society'. They instead 'tried to overcome the obstacle that the growing peasantry represented to their pursuit of wealth and prestige by resorting to politics and, to a lesser degree, to commerce'.[8]

Civil war from 1805 to 1820 divided the former French colony into a Republic of Haiti in the south and a Kingdom of Haiti in the north,

---

[6] Mintz defines as 'reconstituted peasantries' the slaves, indentees, maroons and other runaways who became peasants 'directly as a mode of resistance and response to the plantation system and its imposed patterns of life'; thus their very existence attests to both agency and autonomy. D. Watts, *The West Indies: Patterns of Development, Culture and Environmental Change Since 1492* (Cambridge: Cambridge University Press, 1990), p. 506.

[7] Haitian historiography commonly employs the terminology of *noir* vs. *mulâtre*, or black vs. mulatto, to describe the groups who were contending for power in the nineteenth century. See, e.g., D. Nicholls, *From Dessalines to Duvalier: Race, Colour and National Independence in Haiti*, 3d ed. (London: Macmillan Caribbean, 1996); and M.R. Trouillot, *Haiti: State Against Nation. The Origins and Legacy of Duvalierism* (New York: Monthly Review Press, 1990). I will also use these terms, but with the caveat that I understand these groupings as instances of 'racial formation' in which particular forms of distinction (based not only on phenotype, but also on ancestry, class, status, language, literacy and other markers) were used to draw *salient political boundaries.* Cf. M. Omi and H. Winant, *Racial Formation in the United States from the 1960s to the 1990s* (New York: Routledge, 1994), and M. Sheller, 'The "Haytian Fear": Racial Projects and Competing Reactions to the First Black Republic', in P. Batur-Vanderlippe and J. Feagin (eds.), *Research in Politics and Society,* vol. 6 (Greenwich, CT: JAI Press, 1999), pp. 285–303.

[8] M.R. Trouillot, 'The Inconvenience of Freedom: Free People of Color and the Political Aftermath of Slavery in Dominica and Saint-Domingue/Haiti', in F. McGlynn and S. Drescher (eds.), *The Meaning of Freedom: Economics, Politics and Culture After Slavery* (Pittsburgh and London: University of Pittsburgh Press, 1992), p. 149.

keeping both governments on a constant military footing. These initial decades of state-formation tended towards what one foreign observer paradoxically described as 'republican monarchy sustained by the bayonet'.[9] Military control was reinforced by Haiti's precarious position in a world controlled by the major slave-holding nations, all of whom refused to recognise Haitian independence and some of whom were plotting its recapture.[10] The early decades of the nineteenth century were a period of major realignment of colonial power in the Americas. The Haitian revolution sparked French territorial retreat not only in the Caribbean, but also in North America, where large territories were turned over to the British and the United States. Iberian colonial control in large parts of the Americas was also being dismantled from 1810 to 1824, and there was increasingly a realignment of external links towards British economic agents and interests.[11] These shifts in power were associated with expansions of 'Creole' power and the emergence of new American centres of gravity, as local elites redeployed colonial apparatuses of control and profit-taking towards their own interests. In Haiti too the profits of the plantation economy were momentarily tilted back into local coffers.

As soon as the French landowners and foreign occupying forces had been driven out of the island, Haitian generals seized the land of the former plantations and the reins of state power. In the northern Kingdom of Haiti, King Henry Christophe maintained the big estates intact and under the control of military men who formed a new aristocracy. In the south, the republican military traditions of the revolution

---

[9] J. Brown, *The History and Present Condition of St. Domingue*, 2 vols., (London: Frank Cass, 1972 [1837]).

[10] Though independent, Haiti was still highly vulnerable to the economic influence and military threats of France, Britain, the United States and Spain. The French persisted in plans to recapture their former colony from the end of the Napoleonic wars onward. Records from the Ministère de la Marine et des Colonies contain plans to reconquer 'Saint Domingue' by force in 1814, 1817, 1819 and 1822, in addition to more explicit attempts to negotiate French sovereignty with President Pétion in 1816 and Boyer in 1823. This culminated in the indemnification agreements of 1825 and 1838. Documents on these efforts appear in the French *Archives Nationales* [AN] CC9a.47 and AN CC9a.50–52. Although France finally recognised Haitian independence in 1838, followed shortly thereafter by Britain, it still backed Dominican independence in 1844 and secretly negotiated for exclusive use of the port of Samana. The United States did not recognise Haiti until 1863, following Abraham Lincoln's Emancipation Proclamation.

[11] S.J. Stern, 'The Decentered Center and the Expansionist Periphery: The Paradoxes of Foreign-Local Encounter', in G. Joseph, C. Legrand and R. Salvatore (eds.), *Close Encounters of Empire: Writing the Cultural History of US-Latin American Relations* (Durham and London: Duke University Press, 1998), p. 56.

were institutionalised by the constitution put into place by Dessalines in 1805, and soldiers benefited from President Pétion's distribution of land to the veterans of the wars of independence. An 1809 decree gave full title to property taken from former sugar plantations, according to military rank: 25 *carreaux* for colonels, 15 *carreaux* for battalion chiefs, ten *carreaux* for captains to second lieutenants, and five *carreaux* to non-commissioned officers and soldiers.[12] In 1814, Pétion carried out another extensive distribution of land taken from coffee estates to officers on active service. He granted 35 *carreaux* to battalion or squadron chiefs, 30 *carreaux* to captains, 25 *carreaux* to lieutenants, and 20 *carreaux* to second lieutenants; land was also distributed in smaller grants to government employees, hospital employees and members of the judicial administration, as a way of paying salaries. As one contemporary put it, Pétion had 'republicanized the soil'.[13] His land distribution achieved what Caroline Fick calls 'a stabilizing compromise between the hegemonic mulatto elite and the economically dispossessed masses'.[14]

But revolution, war and the 'flight' of ex-slaves from the plantations (despite government efforts to enforce labour) all contributed to a rapid collapse in sugar exports, which plummeted from over 141 million pounds on the eve of the French revolution in 1789 to a meagre 2.5 million pounds in 1820. At the same time, annual coffee production fell from a high of almost 77 million pounds in 1789 (when coffee exports matched white sugar exports in value) to a low of 24 million in 1822.[15] A British businessman who visited Haiti in the early 1820s described how various methods of keeping the big estates cultivated had

---

[12] R. Lacerte, 'The First Land Reform in Latin America: The Reforms of Alexander Pétion, 1809–1814', *Inter-American Economic Affairs*, 28: 4 (1975), p. 81. One *carreau* equals 1.29 hectares, or 3.33 US acres.
[13] Ibid., pp. 82–4.
[14] C. Fick, 'Black Peasants and Soldiers in the Saint-Domingue Revolution: Initial Reactions to Freedom in the South Province (1793–94)', in F. Krants (ed.), *History From Below: Studies in Popular Protest and Popular Ideology* (Oxford and New York: Basil Blackwell, 1988), p. 269.
[15] Figures from F. Knight, *The Caribbean: The Genesis of a Fragmented Nationalism*, 2d ed. (New York: Oxford University Press, 1990), p. 370. See also M.R. Trouillot, 'Coffee Planters and Coffee Slaves in the Antilles: The Impact of a Secondary Crop', in I. Berlin and P. Morgan (eds.), *Cultivation and Culture: Labor and the Shaping of Slave Life in the Americas* (Charlottesville: University of Virginia Press, 1993), p. 124; and AN CC9a.54, Communications Received at The Foreign Office Relative to Hayti, no. 18, Consul General Charles Mackenzie to the Earl of Dudley, 31 March 1828, General Table of Exports from Hayti, 1789, 1801, 1818–26.

failed since the abolition of slavery.¹⁶ First sharecropping was tried on government-owned land, with the cultivators given one-third or one-quarter of the crop. This had to be abandoned, and the next experiment was 'to purchase canes from the cultivator, who was put in possession of the land, the Government, or Owner, retaining the Mill, Boiling house, etc. in his possession, and grinding the canes purchased from the cultivator'. This too failed, because the central factories could not obtain enough canes and because the cultivators continually disputed the prices being offered. Finally, the little sugar being produced had to be paid for by wages, with men offered $3 per week and women and boys $1.50. As the unsympathetic (and pro-slavery) British Consul Charles Mackenzie reported in 1828, the plantations had been broken up and labour could not be enforced: 'The very little field labour effected is generally performed by elderly people, principally old Guinea negroes. No measure of the government can induce the young creoles to labour, or depart from their habitual licentiousness and vagrancy.'¹⁷

Control over agricultural production and export revenues became the main task of the state, providing its sole access to hard currency with which to pay off the 150 million *franc* indemnity that had been agreed with France in exchange for recognising Haiti's independence in 1825. Like the earlier rural code of Toussaint L'Ouverture, President Boyer's 1826 *Code Rural* provided for the 'protection and encouragement of agriculture' by a strict regime of rural police surveillance and regulation of work contracts and trade. Proclaiming agriculture to be the 'principal source of the prosperity of the state', the Code ordered that all citizens who were not state employees (civil or military) and were not licensed to engage in particular professions 'must cultivate the land'. As the Haitian constitutional historian Janvier noted, Boyer's code was equivalent to 'slavery without the whip'.¹⁸ Most importantly, it declared that agricultural workers were not allowed to leave the countryside and go to the towns or cities without authorisation from a Justice of the Peace, nor could their children be apprenticed in the towns. Mobility was tightly restricted by a pass system and cooperative ownership of land was outlawed. The longest section of the Code pertained to the duties of the rural police, charged with arresting vagabonds, maintaining order in

---

¹⁶ British Foreign Office, FO 35/1, Wilmot Horton to Mr Canning, 14 October 1826, enclosing Memorandum of Information from James Franklin.

¹⁷ AN CC9a.54, Document 2, Communications Received at the Foreign Office Relative to Hayti, no. 18, Charles Mackenzie to Earl of Dudley, 31 March 1828.

¹⁸ L.J. Janvier, *Les Constitutions d'Haïti (1801–1885)*, (Paris: Fardin, 1977 [1886]); and cf. J. Dayan, *Haiti, History and the Gods* (Berkeley and Los Angeles: University of California Press, 1998), p.14.

fieldwork, discipline of work-gangs, and oversight of road building. The Code also specifically outlawed collective ownership of farms and worker self-management in 'sociétés' (Art. 30).[19]

Rather than an apathetic peasantry, these Codes indicate a fluid and mobile population that was trying its best to abandon the sugar and coffee plantations. At the local level, however, resistance remained difficult. With up to 40 000 men in the army, the National Guard and the rural police, armed power not only fostered social climbing through patronage and political pacts, but also served as a brake on resistance. The soldiers and other government employees who received land grants helped to exercise control over the more numerous landless labourers, the former slaves who were now 'cultivators'. Local 'big men' also siphoned off taxes and licence fees from the small traders, mostly women, who provided the backbone of the local economy. We can also guess that men exercised control over the labour of their own family members, especially women and children.[20] So even as the Haitian state and its co-opted agents resisted the foreign powers who controlled the colonial world system (and exercised some degree of control over foreign merchants), it was also largely engaged in controlling its own population and thwarting their efforts at resistance.

Traces of resistance

Variations in post-slavery peasant autonomy in the Caribbean are generally attributed to a combination of economic, geographic and political factors that together determine the availability of land for peasant settlement.[21] It is through independent land-holding that former slaves gained a modicum of self-determination. Post-slavery peasantries 'gained a more secure foothold in the larger and more mountainous territories [like Haiti and Jamaica] ... [and] were more attenuated or constrained in smaller or flatter islands'.[22] The French colony of Saint-

---

[19] AN CC9a.54, *Code Rural d'Haïti*, 1826.
[20] For a more detailed discussion of gender inequality in nineteenth-century Haiti, see Mimi Sheller, 'Sword-bearing Citizens: Militarism and Manhood in Nineteenth Century Haiti', *Plantation Society in the Americas*, 4: 2/3 (1997): pp. 23–78.
[21] Mintz, *Caribbean Transformations*; J. Besson, 'Land, Kinship and Community in the Post-Emancipation Caribbean: A Regional View of the Leewards', in K. Olwig (ed.), *Small Islands, Large Questions: Society, Culture and Resistance in the Post-Emancipation Caribbean* (London and Portland: Frank Cass, 1995), pp. 73–99; B. Higman, 'Post-emancipation historiography in the Leeward Islands', in Olwig, op. cit., pp. 8–28; A. Stinchcombe, *Sugar Island Slavery in the Age of Enlightenment* (Princeton, NJ: Princeton University Press, 1996).
[22] Besson, 'Land, Kinship and Community', p. 73.

Domingue already had one of the most well-developed 'proto-peasantries' in the Caribbean because of its combination of early, intensive sugar plantation, large size and mountainous landscape. Its rugged interior had helped to foster both Maroon autonomy and long established traditions of land-holding kin-groups.[23] Peasant land-holding as an alternative to sugar monoculture thus became the key terrain for wresting power and some degree of self-determination from the post-slavery planters and the states they controlled throughout the Caribbean.[24] Unlike other post-emancipation peasantries, however, Haitians did not face an entrenched white planter class backed up by a distant colonial state, but new local elites who claimed to share their interests and identity.

Mobility is a key component of freedom, enabling escape from personalistic relations of domination, yet Haitian plantation workers, or 'cultivators', had few freedoms in the early days of the Republic. The 1807 'Law concerning the policing of estates and the reciprocal obligations between proprietors, farmers and cultivators' stipulated that all cultivators had to sign a work contract, and once contracted the worker could not leave the property. Disputes were to be settled in front of a Justice of the Peace (invariably a landowner); and any cultivator who provoked a 'movement' of any kind, by word or deed, would be tried for 'disturbing public order'. Written permission was needed from plantation managers to travel within a parish (checked by military patrols), and passports were needed for travel between communes.[25] The existence of such laws implies that a certain number of people were breaking their contracts, moving from place to place in search of better work or living conditions, and that some were even joining together in some kind of 'movement', labour protest, or perhaps even strike.

---

[23] Mintz, *Caribbean Transformations*, p. 241; Besson, 'Land, Kinship and Community, p 77.

[24] As argued, e.g., by Mintz, *Caribbean Transformations*; J. Besson, 'Symbolic Aspects of Land in the Caribbean: The Tenure and Transmission of Land Rights among Caribbean Peasantries', in M. Cross and A. Marks (eds.), *Peasants, Plantations, and Rural Communities in the Caribbean* (Guildford: University of Surrey and Leiden: RILA, 1979), pp. 86–116; N. Bolland, 'Systems of Domination after Slavery: the Control of Land and Labor in the British West Indies after 1838', *Comparative Studies in Society and History* 23 (1981): pp. 591–619; W. Rodney, *A History of the Guyanese Working People, 1881–1905* (Baltimore: Johns Hopkins University Press, 1981); and C. Fick, *The Making of Haiti: The Saint Domingue Revolution from Below* (Knoxville: University of Tennessee Press, 1990).

[25] 'Loi concernant la police des habitations, les obligations réciproques des propriétaires et fermiers, et des cultivateurs,' 20 avril 1807, an IV, Art. 2, in S. Linstant, *Réceuil général des Lois et Actes du Gouvernement d'Haïti* (Paris: Auguste Durand, 1851), vol. 1, pp. 307–15.

Peasant land ownership is one of the most significant measures of peasant civil rights and personal liberties in former slave societies, for with land ownership came control over everyday family decision-making, as well as some degree of economic autonomy. Although land-holding generals dominated government, they nevertheless struggled to maintain control over their plantation workforces. The most significant change in agricultural production after independence was a shift to small-scale coffee export. 'Just as the less prosperous among the whites and the freedmen of Saint Domingue had found an economic alternative in coffee,' observes Trouillot, 'so a growing number of the post-revolutionary peasants and small landowners had turned to that crop for similar reasons. It required little start-up capital, its cultivation and processing required much less labor than did sugar cane, and it sold well on the export market.'[26] Annual coffee exports stabilised at around 35 to 40 million pounds from the late 1820s to the 1840s, indicating viable production. By 1859, Haiti was the fourth largest coffee producer in the world (after Brazil, Java and Ceylon), and coffee constituted 70 per cent of its exports.[27]

In shifting into coffee cultivation, Haitian rural people appear to have built on the foundations of existing slave autonomous traditions established in what Mintz called the 'interstices' of plantation society.[28] Contrary to his image of an unorganised mass of scattered peasants, the rural working class and small *habitants* of Haiti have in fact practised their own genres of association and cooperation. Gérard Barthélémy argues that Haitian peasants developed a self-regulating culture based on egalitarianism and inter-individual reciprocity 'outside' state structures. Collective work groups, which can be traced back to the nineteenth century (such as *Sociétés de Travail, Combites, Escouades*, and *Avanjou*), shared labour outside the monetary system, worked land collectively, served as friendly societies, and in some cases elected leaders. Workers' associations – rooted in the plantation work-gangs, but looking forward to new forms of collective work based on equality, reciprocity and use of the electoral process – contained the seeds of popular political participation. Even the conservative historian Beaubrun Ardouin remarked on 'the introduction of the principle of

---

[26] Trouillot, *Haiti: State Against Nation*, p. 60.
[27] Figures are from A. Dupuy, *Haiti in the World Economy: class, race and underdevelopment since 1700* (Boulder, CO: Westview Press, 1989), p. 95. On exports in this period see also Ardouin, *Etudes sur l'Histoire d' Haïti*, vol. 9, pp. 53–4; A. Bonneau, *Haïti: ses progrès, son avenir* (Paris: E. Dentu, 1862), p. 38; Nicholls, *From Dessalines to Duvalier*, p. 69.
[28] Mintz, *Caribbean Transformations*, p. 146.

election of all the offices necessary in a rural farm, by the cultivators themselves forming associations'. Thus a form of direct democracy at the local level was founded on the republican egalitarianism of the revolutionary period, and survived throughout the post-colonial period as a major form of rural self-organisation.[29]

However, an emphasis on the development of an alternative peasant economy and way of life as the main form of resistance in post-slavery societies deflects attention from more radical political transformations, which were largely unthinkable at the time and have remained silenced in the historical narratives available today. Can we think beyond 'resistance' and begin to grasp some more positive forces of peasant agency? How did formerly enslaved 'reconstituted' peasants try to rebuild their lives in freedom? How did they work around the military state and its efforts to control them? As Stern points out, throughout Latin America there were 'repeating cycles of effort to establish a "popular" version of social identity and right that laid claim on "national" politics, identities and rights of citizenship'.[30] These efforts, seen in the notable 'cycles of liberal opening and closure, inclusionary social mobilization followed by exclusionary repression and retreat', are also evident in Haiti. Unlike the rulers of Latin American republics, however, those who ruled Haiti had a special claim to represent the interests of former slaves, the 'sons of Africa', and the 'black' people of the world. Thus in their struggles over inclusion and exclusion the identity '*noir*' became a key nexus for debates over legitimacy. As Trouillot puts it, the peasantry was 'pushed to the background, [and] remained politically marginal, while *noiriste* leaders loudly claimed power in its name by virtue of sharing the same complexion'.[31]

The Piquet Rebellion of 1844 followed closely on the heels of an important episode of liberal opening and closure in Haiti, the Liberal Revolution of 1843. This episode of peasant resistance offers evidence of the structure of political opportunities for peasants to openly contest elite control of the post-slavery state. A former member of the rural police, Jean-Jacques Acaau, led the 1844 revolt of the 'army of sufferers' affirming 'respect for the Constitution, Rights, Equality, Liberty'.[32]

---

[29] G. Barthélémy, *Le Pays en Dehors* (Port-au-Prince: H. Deschamps, 1989), pp. 93–4; and cf. H. Courlander, *The Drum and the Hoe: Life and Lore of the Haitian People* (Berkeley and Los Angeles: University of California Press, 1960).
[30] Stern, 'The Decentered Center', p. 58.
[31] Trouillot, 'The Inconvenience of Freedom', p. 165; and see Sheller, *Democracy After Slavery*.
[32] FO 35/28, Ussher to Lord Aberdeen, 2 May 1844, encl: 'Ordre du Jour' of J. Acaau, 23 April 1844.

As Leslie Manigat argues (and David Nicholls agrees), the Piquet movement 'was the fruit of the conjunction of interests between big and medium black proprietors and small peasant *parçellaires*, equally black'.[33] I have argued that the movement went beyond questions of a 'war of colour', as it has often been portrayed, in so far as it articulated a class-conscious democratic ideology.[34] However limited the success of this moment of political uprising, it is nevertheless a crucial clue to the unthinkable: it is an indicator of the freedom that might have been. This flickering ember of the democratic aspirations of the post-slavery peasantry was perhaps even a harbinger of the European movements of 1848, as some contemporaries noticed. Without romanticising it, we can nevertheless read it as a dense knot in the grain of narratives of democratisation, which usually move from Europe and North America out to 'the periphery'. What if we thought the unthinkable and followed the footsteps of peasants in their path to freedom?

The British Consul Ussher observed that Acaau 'is a man of some instruction for a negro, has great influence over his followers which he has acquired by Obeah [sic] practices, and affects the dress of a labourer'.[35] Many Haitian leaders, from Boukman to Duvalier, are said to have used the powers of Vodou in leading the masses, but the question is what kind of symbols a leader draws on, and for what purpose. The French Consul Maxime Reybaud described Acaau's manner of communicating with the people:

> The bandit Acaau came barefoot to the wayside cross of the parish, dressed in a species of canvas packing-sheet and wearing a little straw hat, and there publicly vowed not to change his clothing until the orders of 'divine Providence' were executed. Then, turning towards the negro peasants convened by the sound of the *lambi*, Acaau explained that 'divine Providence' ordered the poor people, first to chase out the mulattos, second to divide up the mulatto properties.[36]

---

[33] Cited in Nicholls, *From Dessalines to Duvalier*, p. 276 n. 68.
[34] Sheller, *Democracy After Slavery*.
[35] FO 35/28, Ussher to Lord Aberdeen, 24 May 1844. Acaau's peasant dress is also suggestive of the figure of the Vodou *lwa* related to agricultural work, Cousin Azaka, who appears as a barefoot peasant in a straw hat and protects the interests of the rural labourer (L. Hurbon, *Voodoo: Truth and Fantasy*, tr. L. Frankel [London: Thames and Hudson, 1995], pp. 79, 99).
[36] G. d'Alaux, *L'Empereur Soulouque et son Empire*, 2nd ed. (Paris: Michel Levy Frères, 1860), p. 111. D'Alaux was the nom de plume of the French consul to Haiti, Maxime Reybaud.

Standing at the crossroads of history, in his bare feet, Acaau successfully mobilised the peasantry of the south. A Methodist missionary described their rough and ready army as 'a great many men armed with sticks of different sorts of wood; they sharpened the edge, and applied poisonous gum to it, so that any wound which might not be dangerous, would through the poison become so. The sticks were from 8 to 10 feet long.'[37] But what were they fighting for?

The Piquet movement had more aims than simply the seizure of mulatto property or the imposition of black rule. Reybaud compared their ideology, in retrospect, with that of the European movements of 1848, calling it 'negro communism':

> 'Unhappy innocence' plays, for example, the same role in the proclamations of Acaau as 'the exploitation of man by man' in certain other proclamations. 'The eventuality of national education,' this other chord of Acaau's humanitarian lyre, corresponds visibly to 'free and obligatory instruction,' and in so far as he reclaims in the name of the cultivators, who are the workers down there, 'reduction in the price of foreign merchandise and augmentation in the value of their crops,' the black socialist has certainly found the clearest and most comprehensible formula for this problem of the white Acaaus: reduction of work and increase of salaries.[38]

Reybaud consoled himself that 'black communism would run aground like white communism on the extreme morcellization of property'. It is clear that the Haitian peasantry identified their enemies in class as well as colour terms. Theirs were the hybrid peasant/proletarian aims of other post-emancipation social movements in the Caribbean. Their grievances were not simply against mulatto power, but against abuses of martial law, violations of the constitution, and the subversion of democracy by President Boyer and his armed agents of control.

Tracking the bare footprints of peasant democracy across the few primary documents that remain in the archives suggests that the Piquets attempted to use democratic means of political address, publicising and justifying their claims in proclamations and in newspapers and claiming to uphold the democratic constitution of 1843. They mobilised supporters through public gatherings, with religious leaders and some spiritual content to the message. Their leaders symbolically utilised the dress and creole language of the peasantry, to show in actions the kind

---

[37] Wesleyan Methodist Missionary Society, West Indies Correspondence, Haiti, Bauduy to Secretaries, 24 May 1844.
[38] D'Alaux, *L'Empereur Soulouque*, p. 115.

of equality and participation that they were speaking about in words. The timing, form and stated grievances and demands of the Piquets all suggest a class- *and* colour-conscious movement, with democratic aims and a clear critique of landowner-merchant domination and unmitigated control of the state. They were continuing in the tradition of the anti-colonial and anti-slavery movements of the late eighteenth century, and represent the farthest 'left wing' of democratic republicanism in the Western world despite their location outside the metropolitan core.[39]

Conclusion

Like freed slaves elsewhere, the self-liberated people of Haiti also had to negotiate the terms and conditions of their freedom – not with white planters backed by a colonial state, but with land-owning generals backed by force and legitimised by a continuing foreign threat to Haiti's independence. Defensive militarisation of a weak state undermined the development of potentially democratic civil institutions in Haiti. The control of the state and its armed forces by a small elite had a strong negative impact on democratisation. The army became one of the main avenues of political inclusion, as well as a route to land ownership. Military republicanism, which initially served the necessary purpose of building a new state and citizens, became the raison d'être for a state in which there were few civil institutions to balance an overwhelmingly military power. The majority of the population had little influence over the government, and little protection from its exercise of control, whether through taxation or through armed force. Efforts to 'resist' the state via mobility and physical escape in the end contributed to further social exclusion and political silencing of the peasantry.

Thus Haitian peasants became the 'mounn andéyo', the outside people, or what Barthélemy calls 'le pays en dehors', the nation outside.[40] The peasantry condensed their experience into another pithy saying, which seems to bear some relation to the first: 'Constitusyon sé papié, bayonet sé fer' [Constitutions are paper, bayonets are iron]. While the state appears to work through paper and signatures, it is clear to the peasant that what really matters is the bayonet, which cuts straight through the niceties of citizenship written on flimsy paper, and through the bodies of those who would assert their rights as citizens. If the state's weapon of choice is the bayonet, the peasant's resistance is in the feet:

---

[39] In support of this argument cf. Stinchcombe, *Sugar Island Slavery*; and see the full argument in Sheller, *Democracy After Slavery*.
[40] Trouillot, *Haiti: State Against Nation*; cf. Nicholls, *From Dessalines to Duvalier*, pp. 245–6; Barthélemy, *Le Pays en Dehors*.

to move beyond the reach of the state is one of the few means of resistance in situations where freedom is seemingly won, yet self-determination remains elusive. Looked at on a larger stage, though, the saying also tells us something else. The revolutionary Haitian republic succeeded in escaping the colonial powers and writing a democratic constitution; yet the bayonets of France, Britain and Spain, and later the gunboats of the United States, remained turned on the renegade upstarts. It is this 'international community' which imposed its will on the Haitian government, and exercised control through demands for debt repayments and when necessary military occupation throughout the nineteenth and twentieth centuries. Today, the international economic and military context continues to have a strong influence on the failures of democracy within Haiti. Even as it 'signs its name' on the structural adjustment agreements enforced by the World Bank and the International Monetary Fund, and submits to US military interventions, Haiti's people are again using their feet to try to escape the control of violent power-holders at the local, national and international level. Haiti's hopes for resisting control by such powers remain with its 'earthy' people, who continue to search for a democratic outcome 200 years after their independence.

6 'Is this what you call free?': riots and resistance in the Anglophone Caribbean

Gad Heuman

I

On 1 August 1838, slavery came to an end in the Anglophone Caribbean. Slavery had ended in law four years previously, but the Apprenticeship System which took its place shared many of the features of formal slavery. Former slaves, now apprentices, often resisted the new system, expecting that they would be legally free rather than bound to work for their former masters for four more years. Former slaves were consequently prepared to celebrate the onset of full freedom.[1]

Reports all over the Caribbean indicated that those celebrations took place primarily in churches and chapels. On the island of Dominica, for example, the day passed quietly and a magistrate noted that 'the peasantry strictly observed the day with due solemnity…'[2] Former slaves in Barbados reacted in the same manner. The Inspector of Rural Police described the scene he witnessed on the day:

> On the 1st of August, it was most gratifying to observe the negroes, in great numbers, dressed in their best apparel, with every appearance of cheerfulness, and thankfulness, calmly and peaceably tending their steps to the churches and chapels, some of which were so filled, that numbers who could not find accommodation were content to remain without; indeed, it appeared as if with one consent they had resolved to show, that they knew how to appreciate the blessing of freedom, insomuch that the whole day carried along with it an air of solemnity which could not possibly have been anticipated by any one.

---

[1] Gad Heuman, 'Riots and Resistance in the Caribbean at the Moment of Freedom', in Howard Temperley (ed.), *After Slavery: Emancipation and its Discontents* (London: Frank Cass, 2000), pp. 135–49.

[2] CO 71/87, Colebrooke to Glenelg, 15 October 1838, no. 232, encl: report of Howard Lloyd, stipendiary magistrate, 25 September.

Observers repeatedly commented on the decorum of the people. The police in Barbados were clearly pleased that the day passed without a single breach of the peace.[3]

There were similar accounts for Jamaica. In the parish of St James, one reporter noted that all the churches and chapels in Montego Bay, the capital of the parish, were filled by midnight on 1 August. Services in the Baptist Chapel began at 3 am and continued throughout the next day. A tree was planted in front of the courthouse, where six years earlier slaves had been hanged because of their participation in a rebellion to abolish slavery. A giant illuminated canvas in front of the Baptist chapel had a series of painted scrolls, one inscribed 'LIBERTY, 1838' and another 'EQUAL LAWS AND EQUAL RIGHTS'. It also contained an image of a black hand and a white hand, 'grasped in fellowship and union' as well as the names of prominent British abolitionists, such as Clarkson, Sturge and Buxton.[4]

Yet all was not as well as it seemed. The Governor of Barbados described 'the insubordinate spirit' of some of the people on the island. Although he envisaged no real difficulties, he nonetheless stationed troops in various places in case of emergency. In Jamaica, labourers had not returned to work two weeks after the celebrations of 1 August and were holding out for better pay. In the period which followed 1838, the difficulties of working out a meaningful freedom for the ex-slaves would create serious tensions in most of the societies of the Anglophone Caribbean. There would be considerable resistance to the nature of freedom envisaged by former masters and by the colonial authorities. This became clear in the immediate aftermath of full freedom.[5]

II

In the face of emancipation, planters sought to ensure a steady and cheap supply of labour. Confronted with the possibility that ex-slaves might leave the estates, former masters turned to a variety of coercive measures to retain their labour. The most common method, known as the tenancy-at-will system, combined rents with wages and led to exorbitant charges for the rental of houses and grounds, often exceeding the wages paid to the labourers. With varying degrees of success, the

---

[3] CO 28/123, MacGregor to Glenelg, 11 August 1838, no. 214.
[4] CO 137/244, Anon. [The Negro's Friend], A Brief and Descriptive Account of the First Month of Freedom, 1838, in the Parish of Saint James, Jamaica (Falmouth Post, 1838), pp. 1–3.
[5] CO 28/123, MacGregor to Glenelg, 11 August 1838, no. 214; CO 137/231, Smith to Glenelg, 13 August 1838, no. 153.

system was used in Dominica, Nevis, Montserrat, St Lucia, Tobago, St Vincent, Antigua, Guyana, Jamaica and Barbados.[6]

For Edward Fishbourne, a magistrate in Jamaica, the rental of houses and lands was one of the most divisive issues between freed people and their former masters. During slavery, the houses and the grounds which slaves worked on their own account effectively belonged to them; indeed, they had often built their own houses. After 1 August 1838, they were obliged to pay rent for both the houses and the grounds, but the rental charges were often excessive. It was not only the rent itself which was the problem; the practice of charging each member of a family a separate rent also led to bitterness. For Fishbourne:

> Rent continues to be the cause of most of the irritation & heart-burnings which prevail throughout this parish [St George] ... Coupling the payment of rent with the application of the tenant's labour is one cause of quarrel. Charging it for every member of a family – Husbands, Wives, & Children above ten years of age – and deducting it from the labourer's weekly pay without his or her consent, prevails to a great extent, which provokes the discontent & opposition of the negroes.[7]

Lionel Smith, the Governor of Jamaica, pointed out some of the consequences of these excessive charges. He had heard of many cases in which a labourer earned 5s. a week for his work but was charged 8s. for rent, leaving him in debt to the plantation and with nothing to maintain his family.

A further problem arose when planters simply ejected their former slaves from the plantations. These 'ejectments' could arise over trivial offences. In Barbados, Betsy Cleaver, a labourer, was thrown off the plantation and had her house destroyed and her possessions thrown into the road because she had chosen to have her sugar cane processed at another estate. A magistrate in Jamaica concluded that the planters were to blame for the difficult state of labour relations after emancipation: 'what with demanding double rent, mulcting them of their pay, non payment of wages due, the daily threat of turning them off and rooting up their grounds, and of still imbibing olden prejudices, and vaunting

---

[6] Brian L. Moore, *Race, Power and Social Segmentation in Colonial Society: Guyana After Slavery, 1838–1891* (New York: Gordon and Breach, 1987), p. 39.
[7] CO 137/244, Smith to Normanby, 19 July 1839, no. 141, encl: Report of Edward Fishbourne, St. George's, 7 August.

them; that punishment alone is the impetus by which they are to be made to labour'.[8]

Freed men and women reacted to these measures, often by leaving the plantations when it was possible to do so. This was precisely what the planters had most feared. In the case of Jamaica, where there was abundant land not controlled by the estates, thousands of ex-slaves left the plantations to establish freeholds and independent villages. Thomas Holt calculated that by 1845, seven years after full emancipation, over 20 000 freeholds of less than ten acres had been registered, encompassing a population of over 60 000 people. This meant that over 20 per cent of the ex-slave population had settled on small freeholds. While many of these free people continued to work at least part-time on the estates, their freeholds provided them with a significant degree of independence from the planters. Other colonies also reported significant losses of labourers from the plantations. In Dominica, a survey of 41 estates for the six-month period after the onset of full freedom revealed a decrease in the plantation labour force of 39 per cent.[9]

While it was not possible in many cases for free people to purchase freeholds, they nonetheless made clear their views about the meaning of freedom. A magistrate in Jamaica writing about events in the western part of the island just over six months after emancipation complained about the labourers. They began work late, finished earlier than in the past, and had the idea that freedom meant they should work less than during slavery. As the magistrate put it, 'a foolish idea having got into the negroes' head that (to use his own words) he must not sell "his free" and he thinks that freedom ought at all events to produce a diminution of his manual labor, or he would be undeserving such a boon'.[10]

Other free people elsewhere in the Caribbean expressed similar ideas about labour and freedom. When a magistrate visited some of the largest estates in Dominica soon after emancipation, he asked the ex-slaves for their views. One woman said that she 'had been a slave all her life, and would not work for anybody again'. Another asked if she could go to town for a week or two and then return to work on the estate. When the magistrate told her that she needed permission, she

---

[8] CO 137/232, Smith to Glenelg, 24 September 1838, no. 182; *The Barbados Globe & Colonial Advocate*, 4 November 1839; CO 137/242, Smith to Glenelg, 23 March 1839, no. 65, encl: Report of Hamilton, Port Royal, 25 February.
[9] Thomas Holt, *The Problem of Freedom: Race, Labor, and Politics in Jamaica and Britain, 1832–1938* (Baltimore: The Johns Hopkins University Press, 1992), pp. 144, 154; Michel-Rolph Trouillot, *Peasants and Capital: Dominica in the World Economy* (Baltimore: The Johns Hopkins University Press, 1988), p. 78.
[10] CO 137/242, Smith to Glenelg, 23 March 1839, no. 65, encl: Report of Tho. Abbott, Westmoreland, 28 February.

responded, 'Is this what you call free?' Writing nearly two months after emancipation, another magistrate on the island reported that the people had done little or no work on the plantations since 1 August. According to the magistrate, the free people believed that they had two months to rest and, as they put it, 'to refresh themselves'.[11]

Some of the same people had strong views about their right to occupy their houses and grounds without paying rent. In Dominica, the ex-slaves believed that this should last until 1 October, two months after they were freed. A prominent planter in Jamaica reported that his former slaves had still not paid any rent by early January 1839, either in cash or in labour. Their view was that the Queen was about to send out a law giving them legal possession of their houses and grounds.[12] In Jamaica, a man named Richard Edwards had travelled to the Governor's residence and claimed that 'the Governor had told him he should *not* pay Rent for either his House or Grounds, although he had done no work for the Estate during four Months…'[13]

While it was possible to disabuse Edwards of the notion of a rent-free house and land, it was more difficult to persuade some ex-slaves that their freedom was permanent. Many free people believed that they could be re-enslaved. Writing to the Colonial Secretary less than two weeks after emancipation, the Governor of Barbados remarked on this point. He noted that the ex-slaves believed that 'if they turned out to labour so soon after emancipation they would forfeit their freedom, and incur a further apprenticeship of six or seven years'. Other free people thought they could be re-enslaved on a different basis. In Dominica, free people were harvesting the crops on their grounds in May 1839 in preparation for leaving their respective estates. They feared that if they were still on the estate where they had worked as apprentices on 1 August 1839, they would again be enslaved.[14]

---

[11] PP, XXXVII (107–V), Colebrooke to Glenelg, 15 October 1838, p. 390, encl. no. 2: Phillips to the President, 1 October, p. 393; CO 71/87, Colebrooke to Glenelg, 15 October 1838, no. 232, encl: report of Howard Lloyd, stipendiary magistrate, 25 September.

[12] CO 71/87, Colebrooke to Glenelg, 15 October 1838, no. 232, encl: report of Howard Lloyd, stipendiary magistrate, 25 September; PP, Part I, XXXV (158), Extract from Letter: McNeel to Seaford, 8 January 1839, p. 50.

[13] CO 137/243, Smith to Normanby, 11 May 1839, no. 99, encl: McCornock to Darling, 8 May.

[14] PP, XXXVI (107–IV), MacGregor to Glenelg, 11 August 1838, no. 214, p. 50; PP, 1839, XXXVII (107–V), Colebrooke to Glenelg, 20 May 1839, no. 38, p. 457, encl: Macphail to Colebrooke, 8 May.

Free men and women also disliked contracts of any kind, associating them with compulsory labour. In Barbados, ex-slaves were opposed to a five-day contract because they equated it with Apprenticeship, the system immediately preceding full freedom. By signing a contract, labourers felt that they would be doing the same work as apprentices and be treated similarly. There was no disputing the argument of free people in the parish of St Michael, Barbados: they wanted to take a day off whenever they chose, a feature they knew was foreign to any labour contracts.[15]

Issues of gender and labour were also highly significant to the ex-slaves. After emancipation, women often withdrew from plantation labour in large numbers. Since women had formed the majority of the field labour force during slavery, this could have dramatic effects. Swithin Wilmot has detailed the decline in the female labour force on Golden Grove Estate in Jamaica: he found that of the 137 women working on the estate up to emancipation, only 19 were at work in October, 1838. Across the island in St James parish, three-fifths of the workers on estates were women up to the end of the Apprenticeship system; less than six months into full freedom, only one-third of the labourers were women.[16]

It is likely that European ideas of gender had a role in the withdrawal of female labour from the plantations. In a proclamation issued to the free people of Jamaica a few days before 1 August 1838, the Governor emphasised the domestic responsibilities of women:

> Be honest towards all men; be kind to your wives and children; spare your wives from heavy field work as much as you can; make them attend to their duties at home, in bringing up your children, and in taking care of your stock ...[17]

---

[15] PP, XXXVI (107–IV), MacGregor to Glenelg, 20 September 1838, no 263, encl: Parry, Maxwell & Garroway to MacGregor, 17 September, p. 412; PP, XXXVII (107–VI), MacGregor to Glenelg, 23 April 1839, no. 50, encl no. 3: Memorandum of a Conversation between Acting Private Secretary and a Deputation of Labourers from St. George's Parish at Government House, 23rd April 1839, p. 614; CO 28/123, MacGregor to Glenelg, 20 September 1838, no. 263, encl: no. 3, 7 September.

[16] Swithin Wilmot, '"Females of Abandoned Character"?: Women and Protest in Jamaica, 1838–65', in Verene Shepherd, Bridget Brereton and Barbara Bailey (eds.), *Engendering History: Caribbean Women in Historical Perspective* (Kingston: Ian Randle, 1995), p. 280; PP, XXXV (272), Smith to Glenelg, 23 March 1839, no. 65, encl: Report on the actual state of the LABOURING POPULATION ... of Saint James between the abolition of the Apprenticeship System and the middle of February, 1839, p. 599.

[17] PP, XXXV, 107, Extract: Smith to Glenelg, 27 July 1838, no. 11, encl: Proclamation, p. 208.

When plantation managers subsequently complained about the absence of women on the estates, the women invariably responded that 'the Governor told us we were not to work'.[18]

Yet there were also more important factors at work. Bridget Brereton has emphasised the family strategies pursued by many ex-slaves after emancipation. Rather than working on the plantation, women chose to work in the provision grounds and in marketing their produce. This made economic sense, but it also provided a greater degree of autonomy for ex-slaves after emancipation. The free people on an estate in western Jamaica reinforced this point, when they told a magistrate

> that it was of no use being free, it was only the name 'so-so' that when it was necessary their wives would assist them, by performing light work, but they could not give their consent, to make them work always, and at all sorts of work.

Independence from the plantation meant more than just autonomy; as Brereton has argued, freedom also included 'the right to control one's own body, the right to be free of violation and abuse'. This extended to children as well: it was part of the family strategy after emancipation to keep young children out of fieldwork and, if possible, to send them to school or to use the older children in domestic production.[19]

The ex-slaves' views about gender and labour as well as about freedom led to a series of strikes and riots in the immediate aftermath of emancipation. Across the region, free men and women resisted low wages and high rents. For example, in St Lucia, one report soon after emancipation claimed that 'two-thirds of the labouring population refused to work on the estates'. There were frequent strikes on the island

---

[18] PP, Part I, XXXV (158), A Report upon the actual state of the LABOURING POPULATION, and of the SUGAR CULTIVATION, of the Parish of Trelawny, on the period intervening between the Abolition of the Apprenticeship System and the 9th of March 1839, 9 March 1839, p. 100.

[19] CO 137/232, Smith to Glenelg, 3 December 1838, no. 202, encl: Report of J.A. Harris, 3 December, Lucea; Bridget Brereton, 'Family Strategies, Gender, and the Shift to Wage Labour in the British Caribbean', in Bridget Brereton and Kevin A. Yelvington (eds.), *The Colonial Caribbean in Transition: Essays on Postemancipation Social and Cultural History* (Kingston: The Press University of the West Indies, 1999), pp. 98–9, 105. See also Mimi Sheller's article, which reinforces this point about women's resistance to labour on the plantations and describes it as 'part of a broader political strategy of strikes and labour solidarity aimed at breaking planters' power to control black families': Sheller, 'Quasheba, Mother, Queen: Black Women's Public Leadership and Political Protest in Post-Emancipation Jamaica, 1834–65', *Slavery & Abolition*, 19 (December 1998), p. 98.

and many clashes with the authorities. In Grenada, the authorities sought to eject an ex-slave from his house because he refused to accept the wages offered and also would not leave his home. But the attempt failed, as a large group of free men and women attacked the constables who sought to serve a warrant. The men and women regarded the houses as their own, 'given them by the Queen; and said, with violent oaths, they were determined to keep possession of [them]'. Writing from Tobago less than three weeks after emancipation, the Lieutenant-Governor described the reluctance of labourers to return to work for the wages on offer. He reported that 'there was as well organized a combination, from one end of the island to the other, to strike for wages as ever took place in England, but conducted with more secrecy'.[20]

High rent charges also led to violence in Jamaica. When the people on Spring Hill, a coffee estate in the parish of St George, refused to pay the rents demanded, the proprietor successfully brought the issue before the courts. When constables and then magistrates went to the estate, they were 'pelted with stones by some of the most turbulent of the party, amongst whom, however, the women were the most conspicuous'. It took a detachment of the military to arrest the ringleaders and take them to jail.[21]

The first anniversary of emancipation brought with it a different kind of threat: the fear of re-enslavement. This was a significant element in a conspiracy which came to light in Jamaica in July 1839. It arose from a rumour that 'the white and brown people were going to surround the chapel[s] on the 1st of August [the first anniversary of full freedom], and kill the black men, and make the women slaves again'.[22] Labourers in several western parishes of the island consequently purchased guns and machetes to protect themselves. They also carried out target practice and drilling exercises and, quite significantly, adopted the names of the leaders of the massive 1831 Jamaican slave rebellion in these drills.

---

[20] Michael Louis, '"An Equal Right to the Soil": The Rise of a Peasantry in St. Lucia, 1838–1900' (PhD thesis, Johns Hopkins University, 1981), p. 25; PP, XXXVI (107–IV), MacGregor to Glenelg, 18 September 1838, no. 249, p. 503, encl. A: Richard & Munn to Captain Clarke, 24 August; PP, XXXVI (107–IV), MacGregor to Glenelg, 4 September 1838, no. 242, p. 531, encl. 9: Darling to MacGregor, 18 August.

[21] PP, XXXV, 1840 (212), Smith to Normanby, 17 July 1839, no. 136, p. 7; Wilmot, '"Females of Abandoned Character"?', pp. 283–4.

[22] PP, 1840 (212) XXXV, McNeel to Smith, 23 July 1839, Evidence of Robert Murray, p. 40. The discussion of the 1839 conspiracy which follows is based on Lorna Simmonds' treatment of it: see Lorna Simmonds, '"The Spirit of Disaffection": Civil Disturbances in Jamaica, 1838–1865' (MA thesis, University of Waterloo, 1982), pp. 37–9.

The fear of re-enslavement was one of the driving forces of this conspiracy. Another was the problem of land. As Lorna Simmonds suggests, for the labourers, 'acquiring land was the true indicator that freedom had been properly achieved'.[23] Ex-slaves were therefore prepared to 'fight' for access to land. As one labourer, Edward Campbell, put it:

> the black people were going to fight in August, if the white and brown people did not deliver up the land to them...That there must be a fight to get their lands; that if the last fight [the 1831 slave rebellion] did not happen, they would not get their freedom so soon; and that everybody did not join in the last war, but now all were free, and must help in the fight that was coming.[24]

The 1831 Rebellion was the model for these ex-slaves. Moreover, just as in that rebellion, there were reports that the Queen and her forces would be on their side. There was also a suggestion that the Maroons would come to the aid of the labourers. Although no outbreak occurred, whites reportedly left the affected areas in anticipation of a rebellion.

In Barbados, labourers resorted to a different weapon: fire. At the end of 1839, a series of fires affected plantations, particularly in an eastern parish. There was little doubt that these were deliberate and also that they reflected resentment by the workers, usually against the owners of the estates and sometimes as a response to their being thrown out of their homes.[25]

Yet strikes remained a generally more potent threat. When planters in British Guiana imposed new regulations in early 1842, workers in the colony struck. For Walter Rodney, it was 'the first recorded strike in the history of the Guyanese working class'. Ex-slaves were angered by the deductions in wages and by the series of heavy penalties imposed for minor breaches of the code. Workers struck, and there was considerable civil unrest in much of British Guiana. A letter to a magistrate from labourers on a plantation summarised their views:

> During our slavery we was clothed, ration, and seported in all manner of respets. Now we are free mens (free indeed), we are to work for nothing. Then we might actually say, we becomes slaves again. We will be glad to know from the proprietors of the estates, if they are to take from us our rights all together.

---

[23] Simmonds, '"The Spirit of Disaffection"', p. 38.
[24] PP, 1840 (212) XXXV, p. 43.
[25] CO 28/133, MacGregor to Russell, 18 February 1840, no. 20, encl C, no. 1: Reports from the Inspector General of Police, Alexander Connor, 26 January.

In this case, the strike was successful; the planters withdrew their regulations and were forced to increase wages.[26]

The issues affecting free men and women in the aftermath of emancipation remained important throughout the decade after 1838. Although there were immediate difficulties in the wake of full freedom, the riots and conspiracies which broke out in the decade following emancipation revived many of the same fears about the true meaning of freedom.

III

One of the most important riots in the post-emancipation Caribbean occurred in Dominica in 1844. Many people on the island interpreted the taking of a census in that year as part of a plot to re-enslave them. Labourers in various parts of Dominica threatened census enumerators with death, and these threats escalated into attacks on property and on some of the managers of estates on the island. One observer calculated that between 1200 and 1500 people were involved in the protests, which became known as the 'Guerre Nègre'. As a result, the Privy Council on the island declared martial law and the authorities called up the militia and the 1st West India Regiment. In suppressing the protests, the militia killed four people and arrested 300 others.[27]

Harking back to fears of re-enslavement in the year following emancipation across the Caribbean, ex-slaves in Dominica were particularly concerned about the purpose of the 'taking of names'. Many of them clearly believed that they were to be re-enslaved and were therefore prepared to violently resist any attempts to do so. One freed man pointed to the example of the French Caribbean, where slavery had been reimposed in the early nineteenth century:

> I think that our freedom can be taken away from us, because it was once done in another country near to us; it was the French who gave their people free, and afterwards made them slaves again; my parents told me so when I was quite a child, and I have remembered it ever since; what is done once can be done again, and we all know that liberty is good; I don't

---

[26] Walter Rodney, *A History of the Guyanese Working People, 1881–1905* (London: Heinemann Educational Books, 1981), p. 33; CO 111/189, Light to Stanley, 13 January 1842, no. 9, encl: Letter from 'We Free Labourers of Plantation Walton Hall' to Joseph Allen, 6 January; Moore, *Race, Power and Social Segmentation*, p. 40.
[27] Russell E. Chace, Jr, 'Protest in Post-Emancipation Dominica: The "Guerre Nègre" of 1844', *The Journal of Caribbean History*, 23:2 (1989), pp. 118–23.

know but what the English will do like the French one of these days.[28]

In these circumstances, former slaves sought to destroy the census documents or take them away from the census officials. But there was no evidence of an island-wide conspiracy; the 'Guerre Nègre' broadened into a large-scale protest but one with the limited aim of refusing to comply with the census.[29]

Fears of re-enslavement were not the only problem affecting the Caribbean in the 1840s. The plantation economies of the region worsened considerably when the British government announced the equalisation of sugar duties in 1846. This resulted ultimately in the loss of protection for sugar produced in the British Caribbean and created an economic crisis for the planters. Several leading West Indian firms went bankrupt, and the Planters' Bank was forced to suspend payments in January 1848. Planters therefore sought to depress wages on the estates, often by as much as 25 per cent. However, many ex-slaves regarded this development as a first step towards the reintroduction of slavery. In Jamaica (as in Dominica four years earlier), there were rumours about how this would occur: one version had the whites and browns planning to re-enslave the blacks, while another envisaged the inhabitants of Cuba seizing blacks in Jamaica and transporting them to their island and to slavery.[30]

The Jamaican peasants and labourers were also disturbed by the planters' public outbursts. As in 1831, the planters held meetings to denounce the actions of the Home Government and again raised the possibility of annexation to the United States. This idea was given added credibility by reports in the American press which linked the distressed state of the island with the benefits of annexation.[31]

According to some officials, the response of some ex-slaves in western Jamaica was a conspiracy, aimed at expelling the whites from the island. Since the labourers and peasants believed that they would be re-enslaved on 1 August, this was the date chosen for a rebellion. Whatever the reality behind the conspiracy, it was clear that the ex-slaves were concerned about the threat of increased taxation as well as a lowering of wages on the estates. Although official reports emphasised the problem of wages and also the fear of annexation to the United

---

[28] Testimony of Saint Louis, PP, 1845, 31(146), 22 cited in Chace, 'Protest in Post-Emancipation Dominica', p. 130.
[29] Chace, 'Protest in Post-Emancipation Dominica', pp. 130–2.
[30] CO 137/299, Grey to Grey, 7 July 1848, no. 64, encl: Lyndon Howard Evelyn to Grey, 12 June 1848.
[31] Simmonds, '"The Spirit of Disaffection"', pp. 77, 80–1.

States, there was also a recognition of the 'unsettled state of the world' and the news from Europe of the uprisings there.[32]

Just as the planters came together in their denunciation of the British government, blacks involved in the conspiracy sought to create unity by using colour to appeal for support. A headman on an estate in Hanover reported being approached by several men who said, 'Mr. Brown, now you see we are all black, we must stand to our colour.'[33] There were also condemnations of brown people for helping the whites to suppress the 1831 rebellion. The 1831 rebellion as well as the Haitian Revolution continued to serve as models of protest.

One of the complaints of the blacks was directed at 'White Man's' or 'Buckra Law'. The labourers were particularly incensed at their treatment by overseers and bookkeepers on the sugar estates. In addition, as in the 1831 slave rebellion, there were reports that black Baptist leaders were leading the resistance, although the Baptist missionaries denied any involvement in any such plans.[34]

The whites took the threat of revolt seriously. Some of them moved out of the threatened districts. Although the Governor, Charles Grey, was sceptical about an outbreak, he nonetheless transferred members of the West India Regiment to strategic points in the affected areas. Grey also sent a warship to Montego Bay and to Savanna-la-Mar to calm the western part of the island. In addition, Grey issued a proclamation designed to dispel rumours of re-enslavement. The proclamation made it clear that there was no intention to revoke emancipation.[35]

While there was no general outbreak, there were localised protests in various parts of the island. Later in the year, a riot occurred in Brown's Town, St Ann, in which two people were killed and several people seriously wounded. It was followed by a riot on an estate in St Thomas-in-the-Vale that involved over 150 estate workers who resisted police seeking to execute warrants. However, the most serious outbreak during the year broke out in August on Goshen estate in St Mary.[36]

There, people on the estate reacted against high tax assessments made against them and attempts to appropriate their personal property

---

[32] CO 137/299, Grey to Grey, 22 July 1848, no. 68, encl: Rennalls to Robertson, 13 July 48; Gad Heuman, '*The Killing Time*': *The Morant Bay Rebellion in Jamaica* (London: Macmillan Caribbean, 1994), p. 39.
[33] PP, 1847/48 (685) XLIV, 11.
[34] Robert J. Stewart, *Religion and Society in Post-Emancipation Jamaica* (Knoxville: University of Tennessee Press, 1992), p. 152.
[35] Simmonds, '"The Spirit of Disaffection"', pp. 83–4.
[36] Ibid., pp. 84, 88.

because of unpaid taxes. A series of riots against the police culminated in an attack by 500 men and women against the authorities. Governor Grey, who also regarded the tax assessments as unfair, was worried about the possibility of a serious escalation in the level of violence. He had good reason to be alarmed: one of the policemen who went to Goshen estate reported hearing the people say 'that the St. James's war would be nothing to what they would commence'.[37] Although 17 years had passed since the 1831 slave rebellion, it clearly remained an important symbol.

In British Guiana, labourers were also reluctant to accept steep wage reductions and some of them feared the imposition of a system of compulsory labour. Consequently, labourers reacted by going on strike. Unlike the strike in 1842, this one affected the whole colony and lasted three months, from January to March 1848.[38]

The strike exposed some of the recent divisions in Guianese society. Since Indian and Portuguese labourers had been imported to replace former slave labour, black labourers attacked the immigrants and sought to drive them off the estates. In the case of the Portuguese, this also meant attacking their shops and property, and the Governor reported a series of such assaults resulting in considerable damage. In one case, a Portuguese shopkeeper fired at the invading crowd, killing a black labourer and wounding another. In addition, the Governor reported a number of fires on several plantations; he believed that strikers were responsible for the fires. However, the strike ended in failure for the black labourers. The planters managed to keep the plantations in operation with the help of immigrant labourers, and eventually the ex-slaves were forced to accept wage reductions of between ten and 33 per cent. As Brian Moore concluded, 'it was a bitter defeat, marked by violence ... which persisted well into the following year'.[39]

Ex-slaves in St Lucia faced similar problems to their counterparts in British Guiana and Jamaica. The fall in wages averaged 25 per cent in 1848 and a reduced money supply had the effect of lowering prices of local produce. Already finding it difficult to pay their taxes, the peasantry became inflamed at the imposition of a new tax on land in 1849. They also expressed fears of re-enslavement, and some were concerned that the necessity to pay the new taxes would result in their losing their land.

---

[37] PP, 1849 (280) XXXVII, 53.
[38] Moore, *Race, Power and Social Segmentation*, p. 41.
[39] CO 111/249, Light to Grey, 18 Jan 1848, Private; CO 111/252, Light to Grey, 4 April 1848, no. 60; Moore, *Race, Power and Social Segmentation*, p. 42.

The labourers therefore protested about the tax at a meeting of the Legislative Council. The protest turned into a riot, and troops shot dead eight people and wounded many others. There were subsequent arson attacks on plantations elsewhere on the island, an offence for which several people were indicted. A large number of people were arrested for their involvement in the riot itself.

Before the confrontation at the meeting of the Legislative Council, the rioters had assembled in front of a magistrate's office. The magistrate subsequently reported that several people spoke to him as follows:

> They told witness that they were determined not to pay the tax required of them; that it was an unjust tax, and they could not pay it... They told witness that ... they had as much right to their share of the land as himself or any other person; they said it was those in possession of the island as proprietors who ought to pay the tax, and not those who did not own the land.[40]

For the historian of this riot, Michael Louis, the protest raised issues of economic injustice and the absence of social equality. Yet for the Lieutenant-Governor, Charles Darling, it was a case of outside forces motivating the peasantry. It was the republicans of Martinique and the effects of 'evil counsels and communist ideas from the revolutions in France' which explained this action.

For Dominica, St Lucia, Jamaica and British Guiana, the riots and conspiracies of the 1840s were a response to the contradictions of emancipation, to the promise of a meaningful freedom which had not yet come. Ex-slaves were concerned about the problem of low wages, high rents, fears of re-enslavement and high taxation; they also complained about the lack of justice and the absence of equality. Their vision of freedom differed substantially from that of their former masters: as Woodville Marshall has noted, 'blacks hoped that emancipation would provide the opportunity for them to *take full control of their own lives*, to lay a completely new base for society'. Their protests in the period following full freedom underline what they sought to achieve and point to their frustrations about the nature of that freedom.[41]

---

[40] Louis, "'An Equal Right to the Soil'", p. 98.
[41] Woodville K. Marshall, "'We be wise to many more things": Blacks' Hopes and Expectations of Emancipation', in Hilary Beckles and Verene Shepherd (eds.), *Caribbean Freedom: Society and Economy from Emancipation to the Present* (Kingston: Ian Randle, 1993), pp. 18, 20.

7 Capping the volcano: riots and their suppression in post-emancipation Trinidad

David V. Trotman

Part One

Trinidad in the early nineteenth century, despite its contemporary reputation in the Anglo-Caribbean for post-independence coups, did not have behind it the kind of tradition of slave revolts or massive civil uprisings that its neighbouring fellow colonies had.[1] In fact the late development of Trinidad as a slave-based plantation economy precluded a long history of conflict and resistance typical of the other colonies. It is well known that although settled by the Spanish in 1494, the island experienced a long period of minimum agricultural development and exploitation which one historian has referred to as 'unrelieved dismalness'.[2] It was not until 1783 that there was any concentrated effort at the kind of economic development which since 1640 had been typical of the rest of the Caribbean. From then we can begin to chart the transformation of the island into the typical Caribbean plantation society, complete with all the tensions and conflicts that came with slave-based agricultural production. The transformation was rapid, as evidenced by the accelerated rise in population and economic activity between 1783 and 1838. The rumours of rebellion, the two interrupted

---

[1] See Michael Craton, *Testing the Chains: Resistance to Slavery in the British West Indies* (Ithaca, New York: Cornell University Press, 1982). For contemporary uprisings in Trinidad see Selwyn D. Ryan, *The Muslimeen Grab for Power: Race, Religion, and Revolution in Trinidad and Tobago* (Port of Spain, Trinidad, West Indies: Inprint Caribbean, 1991).

[2] See Eric Eustace Williams, *History of the People of Trinidad and Tobago* (Port-of-Spain, Trinidad: Printed by PNM Pub. Co., 1962). For other histories of Trinidad which chart this late development see James Millette, *The Genesis of Crown Colony Government: Trinidad, 1783–1810* (Curepe, Trinidad: Moko Enterprises, 1970); Donald Wood, *Trinidad in Transition — the Years after Slavery* (London: Oxford University Press, 1968); Linda A. Newson, *Aboriginal and Spanish Trinidad — a Study in Culture Contact* (London, New York, San Francisco: Academic Press, 1976); Bridget Brereton, *A History of Modern Trinidad 1783–1962* (Port of Spain, London: Heinemann, 1981).

attempts at revolt, as well as the incidents documented in the reports of the Protector of Slaves for the closing years of slavery, testify to the level of conflict and resistance in the colony.[3]

The transformation was affected, however, by the abolition of the slave trade in 1807 and the emancipation of the enslaved in 1838. This short period of slave-based exploitation in a frontier plantation economy, with all its potential for exploitation yet to be realised, brought different kinds of tensions to the post-emancipation period. Very early in its development as a plantation colony, Trinidad lacked two critical elements for successful exploitation of its potential, namely access to an unlimited source of labour via the Atlantic slave trade and the possibility of maximum control over that labour force through the well-honed techniques of slave labour exploitation. The elites of the society feared that the end of the slave trade and emancipation would bring only economic decline, social chaos and cultural degeneration.

But those were merely the tensions and anxieties felt by the plantocracy. On the other hand the recently emancipated saw the opportunities for realising freedom in a space where land seemed available in sufficient quantities to allow them to establish some measure of autonomy and independence from the plantation. These opportunities included not only work on the plantation at a market wage but also other opportunities away from the plantation and its labour regime.

The plantocracy and its allies quickly moved to undermine and frustrate these opportunities by creating a mechanism for the recruitment of imported labour, namely state-supported immigration.[4] Moreover, they created the legal mechanism for controlling that labour in the form of indentured contracts and the ordinances that made it a preferred replacement for slavery. The importation of a controlled labour force was one way of frustrating the ambitions of the recently emancipated. The state also introduced a number of other legal measures to ensure that income opportunities away from direct plantocratic control would also be severely restricted for the recently emancipated. The use of the Indentured Immigration Ordinance, the Masters and Servants Ordinance and a number of other social economy regulations served to control the labouring population in the post-emancipation

---

[3] D.V. Trotman, 'Crime and Punishment on the Plantation Frontier: Trinidad, 1800–1834' (paper presented at the Association of Caribbean Historians 32nd Annual Conference, Cayenne, Guyana, 2000).

[4] On indentured immigration see K.O. Laurence, *A Question of Labour: Indentured Immigration into Trinidad and British Guiana, 1875–1917* (New York: St. Martin's Press, 1994); Walton Look Lai, *Indentured Labor, Caribbean Sugar: Chinese and Indian Migrants to the British West Indies, 1838–1918*, Johns Hopkins Studies in Atlantic History and Culture (Baltimore: Johns Hopkins University Press, 1993).

period almost as securely as the practices of the pre-emancipation era regulated the exploitation of the labour of the enslaved. The voluminous evidence of the continuing resistance to these controls and restrictions is inscribed, if only in part, in the criminal records of the period.[5]

The move to regain control of the labour force in the post-emancipation period brought with it some other problems which added to the tensions of the time. In the slave period, Trinidad had a population composed of those drawn directly from Africa and Europe, the descendants of Africans and Europeans who had immigrated from the other nearby colonies of the Americas, and a small group of East Asians.[6] It was the French who took a backward Spanish colony in the late eighteenth century and created a budding plantation society which the British conquered and administered in the nineteenth century. Needless to say, this was done only with the unwilling but vital participation of Africans drawn from a variety of ethnic groups. In the post-emancipation period more ingredients were added to this growing cultural stew: Africans rescued from ships still involved in the Atlantic slave trade, Indians and Chinese from South and East Asia, Portuguese from Madeira, and numerous refugees from the nearby Spanish mainland joined the Spanish, Africans, French and British already on the frontier. This was a colony of the Atlantic world with all the bewildering variety of racial and ethnic origins that that entailed in the nineteenth century.

Some of them were enticed there, some were attracted there and some with little control over their final destination were merely dumped there. For all of them, though, or for the vast majority of them if not all, this new homeland, whether perceived as temporary or as permanent, offered not only economic opportunity but also a new space to which old cultural practices could be transplanted and in which new ones had to be created. The imposition of a particular cultural order, which was supportive of their economic project, was crucial for the ruling class. The satisfaction of this need entailed for them the control of the private and public cultural spaces of the working population. Therefore all cultural practices, whether imported or newly created, had to be controllable and not inimical to the grand project of producing sugar using coerced or quasi-coerced labour in their tropical version of a civilised and civilising Victorian society. The colony became in the nineteenth

---

[5] David Vincent Trotman, *Crime in Trinidad: Conflict and Control in a Plantation Society, 1838–1900* (Knoxville, TN: University of Tennessee Press, 1986); Kusha R. Haraksingh, 'Control and Resistance among Overseas Indian Workers: A Study of Labour on the Sugar Plantations of Trinidad 1875–1917', *Journal of Caribbean History* 14 (1981).

[6] On the East Asians see Barry W. Higman, 'The Chinese in Trinidad, 1806–1838', *Caribbean Studies* 12, no. 3 (1972).

century not only a battleground over the control of labour but also an arena where the validity of a number of cultural practices was vigorously contested.

At each stage of Trinidad's development the building blocks for the racial, ethnic and cultural tension and conflict that would characterise the colony then and the nation now were introduced.[7] Not only was there the potential for inter-group conflict but also, given that the groups were not necessarily homogeneous, there were also significant intra-group differences. The division in the ruling class was between a significant French Creole elite, slowly losing ground economically, and an aggressive, politically dominant but culturally marginal Anglo minority. Among the African population, although there were Creoles of either Anglo or French orientation, ethnic allegiance remained strong and potent. This was especially so among the large Yoruba and Congo contingents which arrived after slavery as part of the resettlement of liberated Africans. Moreover, increasing immigration from the other West Indian colonies had created large pockets of Afro-Creoles identified by their island allegiances. There was also the newly arrived population from the Asian sub-continent which was divided not only by caste but also by region and religion.

It was not unusual in nineteenth-century Trinidad for these various factions to erupt into battle. Ethnic, racial or cultural flags could be easily raised to recruit combatants and to mask whatever underlying economic causes for conflict there might have been in any situation. Governor Keate, commenting on the turbulent nature of the heterogeneous population, declared that he had

> known an instance of a village of independent settlers dividing itself into two parts an English and a French party and fighting for a whole day along the high road to the stoppage of all ordinary traffic and business and the terror of all peaceable persons resident in or passing through the district, and even while I am writing intelligence has been brought me of the inhabitants of the Spanish village of St. Juan's situated at about three miles from Port-of-Spain at open war with the dwellers in the eastern suburb of the Town with whom they appear to have a quarrel… Something of the same kind took place in the neighbourhood of San Fernando on Ash Wednesday, the opposing parties there being Creoles and Chinese.[8]

---

[7] On the divisions in the society see Wood, *Trinidad in Transition*, and Bridget Brereton, *Race Relations in Colonial Trinidad, 1870–1900* (Cambridge [Eng.]; New York: Cambridge University Press, 1979), esp. pp. 193–212.
[8] CO 295/204, Keate to Lytton, 10 May 1859, no. 85.

In 1848 a perceptive Governor of the island had declared that a race had been freed but a society had not been formed. For most of the nineteenth century his comment was still pertinent. Although the Anglos had sought to make the island English in law, language and religion, these persistent non-English tendencies testified to the failure to impose Anglo cultural dominance on this multi-cultural mélange. But the absence of an adequate coercive capacity made it impossible to impose cultural control on these intractable elements. For while the mechanisms for the control of labour, namely The Masters and Servants Ordinance and the Indentured Immigration Ordinances, could be used to police the labour force and govern industrial relations for the plantation economy, the popular cultural expressions of the working class, especially in the public arenas, seemed uncontrollable and potentially dangerous and therefore were cause for concern.

Of course, fear of the masses was nothing new in colonial plantation societies. Although Trinidad did not have a history of significant slave revolts, the ruling class inherited the general fears experienced by its counterparts elsewhere in the Caribbean (and wherever wealth creation depended on coerced African labour). So to the memory of Haiti of 1791, Barbados of 1816, Demerara of 1823 and Jamaica of 1831 were added the Angel Gabriel riots of 1856 in British Guiana and the Morant Bay uprising of 1865. In the aftermath of the disturbances in Jamaica, Governor Manners-Sutton acknowledged that 'interest excited here by recent events in Jamaica has been intense'. But he hastened to add that that interest was restricted to 'white inhabitants (their numbers small as a class), and some individuals (the more prominent) of mixed European and African blood, with a few Negroes, whose wealth and education has raised them above the crowd'. The Governor informed his superiors in England that neither the disturbances in Jamaica nor their suppression had caused any excitement among the non-propertied 'Negro and Coloured population', and there were ' no symptoms of active discontent, or of intended or approaching disturbances'. He further assured the Colonial Office that there were no grounds to anticipate 'any organized attack upon property, or a premeditated and systematic resistance to the law'. But he did not give an unqualified stamp of approval to the loyalty of the masses and opined that 'their credulous and impulsive character renders them peculiarly amenable to the influence of agitators'.[9]

It was not only the regional history and experience of servile and colonial revolt that informed the perceptions and consciousness of the

---

[9] CO 295/234, Governor Manners Sutton to Cardwell, Confidential, 22 January 1866.

times. Events outside the region in the ever-widening world of consolidated colonial rule were also part of the mix. The nineteenth century was the period of British imperial expansion and consolidation in Africa and Asia. These imperial incursions were ultimately successful. But at the time the contemporaries could not presume success and the incursions were met with resistance. The history of resistance is as much a part of the story as the history of conquest. Nineteenth-century Trinidad was a colony whose population was drawn from those very racial groups whose homelands were experiencing the impact of imperial expansion and resistance, and many of them were present in Trinidad as a direct or indirect result of that very expansion and its concomitant resistance. The repercussions of the Indian mutiny of 1857 were felt in Trinidad as fears were expressed that among the arriving immigrants would be 'disloyal' elements who had participated in that event.[10] African resistance to European imperial expansion in the nineteenth century, despite the use of black West Indian conscripts in that expansion, did not go unnoticed and also cast its long shadow.[11]

There is no strong evidence to illuminate for us the ways in which the non-propertied received, interpreted and reacted to these external events. The fact that there are no organised or spontaneous uprisings on record which were motivated by sentiments connected to these external events should not deter us from according the nineteenth-century masses or segments of that group a certain level of political consciousness. However slim the available evidence, it should not deter us from informed speculation; the risk is to fall into the trap of post factum arrogance which assumes that racial consciousness of the kind feared by the ruling class of the time arrived full-blown in the twentieth century. The level of consciousness of the ruling class is on record; that of the subalterns can be presumed until further research documents or dismisses it. Nor should we accept the Governor's assessment at face value and the Governor and his informants as reliable interpreters of the political consciousness of the masses. He is on safer ground with his pronouncements on the sentiments of the ruling class.

The ruling class lived in a society dependent on the exploited labour of an imported labour force and peopled by non-whites

---

[10] On the Indian mutiny see J.C. Jha, 'The Indian Mutiny-Cum-Revolt of 1857 and Trinidad (West Indies)', *Journal of Indian History*, vol. 50 no. 149 (1972), pp. 441–58; see also *Trinidad Chronicle,* 7 February 1865.
[11] On African resistance see Michael Crowder, *West African Resistance* (London: Hutchinson, 1971); see also Edward L. Cox, *Rekindling the Ancestral memory: King Ja Ja of Opobo in St. Vincent and Barbados, 1888–1891* (Barbados: UWI-Department of History, 1998).

seemingly unassimilated and whom some believed even possibly congenitally incapable of being assimilated. Segments of the ruling class always felt as if they were living on a powder keg. As Governor Keate commented,

> one only has to observe the uneasiness and anxiety which prevails, when the slightest rumour arises of disturbances in the Country Districts to feel assured of the reality of the conviction entertained that in the present stage of the social progress of the colony we are, as I have heard it, with somewhat of an exaggeration expressed, 'living on the crust of a volcano.'[12]

It was this same climate of anxiety and ever-impending crisis which saw a simple request for an interpreter to be used in a case of assault committed by a Chinese indentured immigrant turn into a comedy of errors. The request from the magistrate in Couva for an interpreter of Chinese was somehow interpreted as a request for the police to put down a mutiny among the recently arrived indentured immigrants on the Camden and Exchange estates. The Inspector-General of Police, a squad of 25 policemen, the Agent-General of Immigrants and an interpreter were rushed by special steamer from Port-of-Spain to Couva to deal with this supposed mutiny. The editorialist for the *Trinidad Chronicle* did not see much humour in the incident. The editorial applauded the prompt response of the authorities and saw it as evidence that

> the authorities at least are live to the existence of the mine which exploding under our feet, may at any moment upheave and topple down the whole of our social organization. Our proprietors and managers live in the midst of a population of strangers – of men divided from them by a deep gulf of difference of creed, language, manners and morals.[13]

In the circumstances of Trinidad this fear of the masses was a fear of non-whites, of those who it was believed could slip back into their innate condition of natural barbarity, break the barely constraining civilising bonds and attack their civilised white superiors.

Part Two

In 1849 the authorities experienced how quickly a conflagration stemming from seemingly simple causes could escalate into island-wide unrest. Since a discussion of this riot has not featured in many of the

---

[12] CO 295/204, Governor Keate to Lytton, 10 May 1859, no. 85.
[13] *Trinidad Chronicle*, 21 April 1865.

standard secondary sources on Trinidad history, a narrative of some of its details is in order.[14] An attempt to introduce new prison regulations that called for the shaving of the heads of female prisoners and which required petty debtors to wear prison dress and work at hard labour met with stiff resistance within the prison and soon spread into a two-day island-wide riot.

The proposed changes to the prison regulations were in response to the popular belief that the prison served neither as an institution of punishment nor as a place of rehabilitation. The prison was overcrowded, and the separation and classification of prisoners, then the rage in penological thinking, was impossible. According to one observation in 1840, this overcrowding made the prison more a place of amusement than one of punishment. It was reported that 'the convicted felon mixed with the untried prisoner; the sexes only separated at night'.[15] The proposed regulations classified the prisoners into eight classes to be designated by identifiable prison dress, separated those who were imprisoned with hard labour from the general population, and ordered the shaving of the heads of prisoners.

On Saturday 29 September, Lord Harris, the Governor, was informed by a country gentleman, who feared for his estate which had been threatened with arson, that there was general objection to the rules. The objection centred on the proposed treatment of the petty debtors. There appeared to be a general impression that the new rules demanded the heads of debtors be shaved, and that they were now required to wear prison dress. This was a radical change from the situation where debtors, though imprisoned, operated virtually as free citizens temporarily residing in the prison, without any of the restrictions normally associated with penal incarceration.

The Governor explained to his informant that there was a misunderstanding and the debtors had been inadvertently included in the clause that called for hard labour. Furthermore, the rules had not been finally passed and were to be discussed again at the next sitting of the Legislative Council on Monday. Harris also pointed out that although the shaving of the heads was a sanitary precaution applied to all who

---

[14] It is reported in Gertrude Carmichael, *The History of the West Indian Islands of Trinidad and Tobago* (London: Alvin Redman, 1961), pp. 254–5; Wood, *Trinidad in Transition*, pp.175–6; and Carlton Robert Ottley, *The Story of Port of Spain – from the Earliest Times to the Present Day* (Diego Martin, Trinidad: Crusoe Publications, 1977). The details are taken from the Governor's Report and the transcript of the trial in CO 295/168, Harris to Grey, 6 October 1849; CO 295/170, Harris to Grey, 5 January 1850, no.1 and enclosures; and PP 1852–53 vol. LXVII, pp. 401ff.
[15] CO 295/129, 11 January 1840, no. 3.

were imprisoned, it was not a matter of principle and could be easily altered. He encouraged his informant to pass this information on to all he should encounter in the town. He also directed the Inspector of Police to explain the situation to 'such respectable persons' as he should meet in order to allay their fears and defuse the excitement. This information may not have reached the public; or, if it did, it seems to have been ignored or disbelieved.

Notices had appeared in town on the Saturday inviting the public to a meeting at a house in Almond Walk on the Monday. The venue could not contain the crowd that attended the meeting. The butchers, who had gone on strike in order to attend, suggested that the meeting be adjourned and reconvened at the Eastern Market. The crowd broke into the market place and the meeting drew up some resolutions, which were to be presented to the Governor by a deputation of five. Governor Harris claimed that he was assured by two of the organisers of this public meeting that their intention was to inform the crowd of the situation and then to encourage them to disperse. Harris therefore assumed that this was indeed the case, since on his arrival at the Public Square in front of the Legislative Council he saw not more than a hundred persons gathered in groups which he assumed to be the remnants of the dispersed meeting at the market. He met the deputation from this meeting in the Council chamber and allowed them to read their resolutions, although in his opinion their tone was less than respectful. Harris reported that he again reassured the deputation that the rules were to be reconsidered that day and the sections viewed as objectionable were to be altered.

In the meantime, the crowd outside in the square had grown to about 5000 and some of them had entered the Council Chambers. They remained there during the preliminary deliberations of the Council. So many people had crowded the Council chambers that the Governor found the room to be insufferable. He ordered the police sergeant to remove one man who was standing behind his chair. This was done with a scuffle, at which point, according to the Governor's recollection, 'a man was seen to wave his hand to the mob below, and an attack with stones immediately commenced on the windows of the Public Buildings'. The riot had begun.

The meeting was adjourned for an hour. Troops were sent for to replace the police, who quite clearly did not have the capacity to handle the crowd. When the Council meeting resumed, the rules were discussed and the members of the deputation were instructed to inform the crowd that the rules had indeed been altered and that they should disperse. But it was apparently too late. The crowds continued to congregate and intermittently to stone the Council chambers despite the presence of the troops under Colonel Shirley. Finally, the military were ordered to clear the ground by marching past in companies in a show of force. The crowd merely stepped aside and some took the opportunity to stone the military. The Riot Act was subsequently read and the military opened fire as the crowd still refused to clear the streets. Although some pelting continued, the bulk of the crowd was dispersed, leaving two women and a man wounded, two of whom subsequently died of their wounds.

Although the crowd was dispersed, the town was still in turmoil. Lord Harris managed to get home safely but his phaeton was attacked on its return to the town. He was not in it at the time of the attack but the horses were reportedly beaten with sticks and the groom received a wound to his head. The Governor reported that on a visit to the town that night he observed 'clusters of men in the streets armed with sticks and cutlasses, who attacked every police constable and white man'. He also commented on the 'violence, scurrility, and obscenity of the language of the mob, who appeared ready for any atrocity, the women as usual being the most prominent'.

On the following day, Tuesday 2 October, it was clear that the turmoil had not been confined to the town. Several of the estates to the east of the town had been attacked and their megass houses burnt, causing property damage of about £6000. The authorities also learnt that large bodies of men armed with guns and cutlasses had marched from that area on the Monday night and had congregated in the town. In St Joseph, a group of 50 armed men, proprietors from the district of Caura, were on their way to Port-of-Spain but were intercepted by the Stipendiary Magistrate, who explained the situation and dissuaded them from proceeding to the town. In Oropouche, a crowd armed with sledgehammers and axes stormed the District Warden's house, smashed his furniture and set fire to the building. The Warden and his family barely escaped with their lives – the attackers only called off the search for the Warden when it was erroneously reported that he had been burnt in the fire.

The local police force, barely 100 in total strength, could not handle the situation. One hundred and thirty-three special constables had been hurriedly sworn in on Monday, but many of the volunteers had been injured in the skirmishes with the rioters on that same night. On Tuesday another 350 special constables were sworn in and the Governor authorised the formation of a horse patrol of 75 mounted men. These reinforcements were barely sufficient, although the horse patrol was useful in preventing a few attempts at arson in the town. With the reports of incidents in other parts of the island, Lord Harris, after consultation with Colonel Shirley, sent to Barbados for reinforcements. The arrival of HMS *Scorpion*, bringing additional troops to strengthen the local forces, reduced the threat of increased disorder and brought the situation under control. At any rate, it seemed that by Tuesday night the storm had passed, and not necessarily because of the efforts of the local police, military and volunteers. The Governor also commended the efforts of the clergy of the Anglican, Roman Catholic and other churches in 'using their endeavours to tranquilise the public mind'. But it is quite likely that the unrest had petered out on its own.

The ease with which the outburst died down and the ostensible proximate cause suggest spontaneity rather than a planned and co-ordinated effort at insurrection. Lord Harris offered the opinion that it was 'a plan not to oppose the government but to ruin the colony by burning'. We do not have a report from the meeting at the market, so we do not know precisely what was discussed, what was the popular opinion and interpretation of the situation, and why the Governor's attempts at allaying the fears of the interested parties were apparently rebuffed.

The Governor's report, despite its obvious biases, undocumented accusations and innuendoes, is still useful as the official point of view and for its perceptions of the tension points in the society. Harris saw a conspiracy behind the riots and argued that it was the result of 'a long-continued attempt to excite the passions of the people', who were being led 'to suppose that their interests were affected and injured by the acts of Government'. His explanation, which was reminiscent of most explanations of slave conspiracies and which would be very popular throughout the colonial period, was that the excitable natives were influenced and manipulated by external agents who were aided and abetted by a fifth column of disloyal residents. This accusation and innuendo was aimed at the recent arrivals from Martinique and Guadeloupe, who it was feared brought with them subversive sentiments of equality and republicanism to the loyal Creoles of Trinidad.[16] In the aftermath of the Revolution of 1848 and its repercussions in the French Caribbean colonies, these immigrants were convenient scapegoats in the context of the ongoing Anglo-French conflict in Trinidad.[17]

The Governor's explanations expressed the fears and tensions that marked the society just a decade after emancipation, and the whole affair revealed the volatility of the society. The shaving of the prisoners was only the igniting spark applied to a diverse bundle of combustible grievances. The colony was undergoing an economic crisis that was in part linked to the equalisation of sugar duties, the collapse of the West India Bank in December 1847 and the suspension of payments by the

---

[16] See, for example, *Port of Spain Gazette*, 5 October 1849.
[17] For a wider discussion of the impact of the 1848 revolutions see Miles Taylor, 'The 1848 Revolution and the British Empire', *Past and Present* no. 166 (February 2000), pp. 146–80.

Colonial Bank. This commercial crisis impacted unfavourably on all sectors of the population. The salaries of civil servants could not be paid during the last quarter of 1847 and the Treasury was empty by May of 1848. Planters found difficulty in securing loans and employers were unable to meet their wage commitments. This forced a lowering of wages with consequent hardship to the labouring population. The Governor reported that of the 210 sugar estates in cultivation at emancipation in 1838, the majority of them, at least 157, were running at a loss and many abandoned in 1848; and the Attorney-General claimed that in 1848 there were 64 petitions for insolvency.[18] There were 935 committals to prison that year, of which 312, or 33 per cent, were for the accused's failure to discharge their debts. The savings of many labourers were wiped out, and petty retail traders, shopkeepers and those hoping to escape a life of plantation labour found themselves in debt.

The consequent reduction in revenues from both import and export duties forced Governor Harris to look for ways to reduce expenditure on the civil establishment and to increase revenue. He saved £10 000 by reducing the salaries of most public servants by one-eighth. He also debated the merits of introducing a special tax on property, income, land, houses and families and a poll tax on all persons between certain ages who were resident in the colony. He agreed that a tax on property and income was unwise, not only because of the depressed state of the economy and its impact on production and income but also because there was no efficient mechanism available to handle the estimation and collection of taxes. Taxes on land were not politic or expedient, since they would have had the negative effect of checking the growth of provision cultivation, and a tax on houses and families would be an impediment to the general improvement of the former and the formation of the latter. The Governor's fiscal reorganisation finally settled on a poll tax of one dollar per year on all residents of the colony between the ages of 18 and 60, revision of the export duties and the Road Ordinance and the passage of a new Territorial Ordinance with new tax measures.[19]

The causes of the riot are deeply rooted in the financial crisis and the responses of the authorities. The crisis had created debtors of many innocent victims, and now through no fault of their own they were to be treated as petty criminals. Moreover, the Governor's suggestions seemed designed to create additional hardships. It was easy for some in this multiracial society to read the situation as one deliberately created

---

[18] On the financial crisis see Wood, *Trinidad in Transition*, pp. 121–4; and William A. Green, *British Slave Emancipation: The Sugar Colonies and the Great Experiment, 1830–1865* (London: Oxford University Press, 1976), pp. 229–44.

[19] See PP 1849 vol. 34, pp. 298ff.

by an uncaring Anglo faction personified by the aggressive anglophile Charles Warner, who was the object of negative taunts during the riot.[20] In the long run, the Governor's measures, together with interventions by the British government, allowed the colony successfully to survive the crisis.[21] But at the time this could not be seen or appreciated. In the context of the time, with its primitive means of communication, especially between government and people, information and misinformation filtered through the fears of race, colour and ethnicity which characterised this divided society could only lead to the rumours which fuelled the riot.

Part Three

The handling of the 1849 riot also revealed the weaknesses of the local forces and the incapacity of the authorities to deal with any uprising on their own. The security forces mobilised included the 100-strong police force, 483 special constables, a 75-strong specially recruited horse patrol, the 65-man deployment of the 2nd West India Regiment and the 110 troops of the 88th Regiment. But these were clearly insufficient to handle an uprising which, although focused in the capital city of Port-of-Spain, appeared to be island-wide. The uprising itself was leaderless, although 12 men and three women were subsequently arrested and charged with being ringleaders. It was also directionless, or without clearly defined aims or programme. It was a spontaneous response to a common issue, the financial crisis, but the cause, effect and solution of that issue were interpreted in different ways by groups with other and different grievances. Despite the common denominator of the financial crisis, the uprising was too diffuse to have much chances of success. Nonetheless, the authorities feared that but for the arrival of reinforcements drawn from imperial forces based in Barbados the situation could have escalated beyond their control.

The fears of possible civil unrest and racial conflict and the strategies for handling such an eventuality occupied the concerns of those responsible for law, order and internal security. Race was of course a crucial element in the discourse over security and the perceived instability of the society. This was a major concern for the remainder of the nineteenth century. The need for strong external defences against the incursions of other imperial predators, which was the concern of the pre-emancipation colonies, had generally receded in the nineteenth century. The theatre for extra-European imperial conflicts had shifted to

---

[20] See CO 295/170, no 1, pp. 7–33, encl: December Criminal Sessions.
[21] Brereton, *A History of Modern Trinidad*, pp. 82–3.

Africa, and British economic and military prowess had ensured that a kind of Pax Britannica existed in the Caribbean, and the lines settled at the Congress of Vienna and the Treaty of Amiens after the Napoleonic wars were firmly respected. The security forces could now be focused on internal concerns. Imperial forces remained stationed in Barbados and available as necessary back-up and support in the event of the failure of the resident security forces, police and regimental troops, in that order, to suppress civil unrest. These imperial forces were of important symbolic value when authorities hinted at their availability and threatened their use, and of course of practical worth when actually used in any local situation. Their presence in the region signalled to local elites that they had not been marooned or abandoned by their metropolitan supporters, and simultaneously signalled to local dissidents that the local authorities had access to the military might of the Empire.

Imperial troops resident in Trinidad consisted of troops of the British West India regiments and other British regiments who were rotated regularly. The British West India regiments had their origins in the British army's decision in 1795 to raise troops in the Caribbean, including black conscripts. After the Napoleonic wars not all of these troops were disbanded; some continued to be stationed in the various territories. The original regiments comprised free blacks and coloureds, as well as slaves specifically bought as soldiers. After 1807 the British campaign against illegal slavers also provided a source of recruits, as rescued Africans were 'encouraged' to enlist for service in the Caribbean.[22] Imperial forces in Trinidad therefore consisted of both black and white troops. In 1859, three companies of the 14th Regiment of Foot, one of the 3rd West India Regiment, and a squad of artillerymen were stationed in Trinidad – approximately 303 rank and file in all.[23] Although two companies of the 14th Regiment were to be removed to Barbados when accommodation was completed there for them, this remained the general strength and composition of the imperial forces located in Trinidad. But in the 50s and 60s these troops, especially the white contingents, were not always up to full duty strength because of poor health and a troubling death rate. Much of this was blamed on the location of the barracks and its potential to cause white soldiers to contract fevers; but in one period in 1858–59, one-third of the deaths among the white soldiers of the 41st Regiment could be accounted for

---

[22] For this see Roger Norman Buckley, *Slaves in Red Coats: The British West India Regiments, 1795–1815* (New Haven and London: Yale University Press, 1979).
[23] See Report with Blue Book for Trinidad in PP 1861, vol. XL.

by their lifestyle, in particular their proclivity for the consumption of local rum.[24]

The authorities were not comfortable with depending on black arms only for the security of the colony. When it was suggested that the white troops be removed because of the health problem, the Governor hastened to assure the Colonial Office that the sickness was temporary and there was no need to remove them even as a temporary measure. He claimed that although he had no doubt about the loyalty of the black troops in the advent of an insurrection, he believed that

> to such an extent does the confidence reposed in them depend upon their being quartered side by side with, and enjoying the support and example of, the white troops, that I feel sure the withdrawal of the latter would destroy all feelings of safety among those who are devoting their energy and intelligence to the development of the prosperity of the island...[25]

Some years later, official opinion was equally adamant about the necessity of maintaining both black and white troops, or at any rate of not having a garrison of only black troops. The Governor of the day informed the Colonial Office that

> while I do not in any way impugn the efficiency or valuable service elsewhere of Black Troops, my enquiries into the past have compelled me to adopt, without reserve, the opinion generally entertained here that a garrison composed of black troops would cause distrust and disorder, rather than afford securities for the preservation of tranquility.[26]

The black troops were seen as a necessary evil that had to be tolerated. Negative comments were made about the composition of the regiment and the source of their recruitment. It was felt that earlier recruits from Africa were more dependable and better disciplined.[27] It was claimed that in recent years the soldiers had tended to be recruited from the 'scum of the islands'. It was recommended that no more Barbadians should be admitted to the ranks, because the detachments that had been 'turbulent and disorderly' were composed of Barbadians. But it was difficult to recruit locals since 'the native coloured population is

---

[24] See CO 295/213, Keate to Newcastle, 23 July 1861, no. 112 and encl.
[25] CO 295/ 204, Keate to Lytton, 10 May 1859, no. 85.
[26] CO 295/230, 21 March 1865, Confidential.
[27] It seems that the authorities had conveniently forgotten the Army mutiny of 1837. See Thomas August, 'Rebels with a Cause: The St. Joseph Mutiny of 1837', *Slavery and Abolition* 12, no. 2 (1991).

comparatively small, is in easy circumstances being chiefly occupied in the cocoa cultivation, there is a great demand for their labour at wages exceeding the pay of soldiers and there is no pressure of population upon the means of subsistence'. The rest of the population was indentured and at any rate not deemed 'eligible in other respects'.[28]

The fears about the discipline of the black troops seemed to have been realised in Port-of-Spain in December 1860. There was some ill feeling between the black soldiers and certain sectors of the population. There is no record of whether there was animosity towards all soldiers, including the whites, or only towards the blacks, as was reported. We can only speculate on the causes of this ill feeling. The soldiers may have been behaving in the overbearing way of forces of occupation who exercised the right of plunder. It is quite possible that the soldiers may have been exploiting the many petty vendors and shopkeepers in the urban area. It is also quite likely that this foreign, all-male military squad, with some status and regular salaries but often confined to military barracks, may have run into conflict with the local town males over the attentions and affections of women. At any rate, on the night of 23 December one of these soldiers was violently assaulted by a civilian. The following night, Christmas Eve, a body of about 30 soldiers armed with sticks stood at the corner of Park and Cambridge streets and attacked all passing civilians. The assaults began at about 6 pm and continued until 10 pm. The police who were on duty and the reinforcements who were sent for were also attacked, beaten and forced to retreat. Military police were sent for, but the piquets who arrived joined their comrades in the assault on the civilians. Despite the reading of the Riot Act by the magistrate, neither the incensed civilians who started to retaliate nor the soldiers retreated from this confrontation. White troops of the 4th West India Regiment eventually forced the black troops to retreat to barracks and the police were able to disperse the civilian crowd.[29]

The commentators in the local press who were always opposed to the black troops had a field day. The *Trinidad Press* ominously advised that 'the inhabitants of this country will understand that they will have to depend upon their strong arm to protect themselves against their protectors' and warned that 'there are hundreds of men in this community who will prepare to resist that which this horde of semi-savages have sworn to execute against the inhabitants this coming carnival. We shall see.' The *Trinidad Sentinel* blamed Captain Dunlop, the white officer in charge of the black troops, for acquiescing in the indiscipline of his

---

[28] See CO 295/226, Keate to Newcastle, 7 January 1864, no. 9.
[29] See CO 295/212, Walker to Newcastle, 9 January 1861, nos. 10 and 12 and enclosures.

troops and wondered who would relieve the society 'from the presence of this band of vagabonds collected from the scum of the colonies'.[30]

The colonial authorities in London seemed unperturbed by the incident. Henry Taylor at the Colonial Office noted that that the quarrel was between 'black soldiers and the lower classes of the town, who are no doubt blacks, or at least not whites'. He argued that there was nothing in the incident to show that if the black or coloured people were to rise against the whites and the government, the West India Regiments would be found disloyal. He did not find any reason 'to apprehend disloyalty either of the Black Troops or of the Black and Coloured inhabitants of the West Indies', since 'all the riots and tumults which have taken place since emancipation have been unconnected with antipathies of race'. For him the incident corroborated the opinion 'that without white troops black troops would be rather a danger than a protection', for 'when the fire extinguisher catches fire it is a bad business'.[31] This ambivalent attitude towards the black troops would be consistent for the remainder of the century until all imperial troops were finally removed.[32]

The other plank in the strategy for internal defence against insurrection was the use of a local militia or a volunteer force. In the aftermath of Morant Bay there was much discussion about the establishment of volunteer militias. But in post-emancipation Trinidad, the creation of an armed body of citizens faced the intractable difficulties of the divisive fault-lines of the society.[33] One newspaper stated in 1865 in response to a proposal for a volunteer militia: 'Division is the besetting sin of Trinidad, and 'tis the reason we much more resemble a menagerie of wild animals, than a colony of peaceful and loyal subjects.'[34] One of these calls for the establishment of a volunteer militia came from the Naparima district. The area was a major sugar-producing district with a significant population of East Indian indentured workers and the scene

---

[30] See *Trinidad Press*, Wednesday 26 December 1860; *Trinidad Sentinel*, Thursday December 27 1860.
[31] See CO 295/212, Walker to Newcastle, 9 January 1861, no. 10, Note by Henry Taylor.
[32] For example, see CO 295/291, Governor Freeling to Kimberley, 25 October 1881, Confidential: 'I do not think it prudent, that under any circumstances, so long as European troops are stationed in the West Indies, this important Colony should be left without a detachment, the moral effect of these troops being always much greater than that of Black soldiers, however useful and well disciplined the West India Regiments may be.'
[33] There were over 25 units of volunteer troops in Trinidad between 1831 and 1834. It is not clear how many of them survived into the post-slavery period. See C.M. Kelshall, 'The Military Tradition in Trinidad' in Gerard Besson and Bridget Brereton (eds.), *The Book of Trinidad* (Port-of-Spain, Trinidad: Paria Publishing Company, 1991).
[34] *The Trinidad Chronicle*, 31 January 1865.

throughout the nineteenth century of numerous labour disputes and industrial unrest.[35] On 4 December 1865 a meeting of self-styled influential inhabitants of San Fernando and its neighbourhood recommended the formation of a volunteer cavalry corps for Naparima. They requested arms, access to an armoury and drill instruction from the government and offered to provide their own uniforms and horses.[36] It was an attempt by the planting interest to set up a vigilante-type group to deal with industrial disputes rather than civil insurrection.

But the Governor, who did a complete review of the security needs of the colony in the context of both the aftermath of Morant Bay and the suggested reduction of white troops, was not convinced of the wisdom of a volunteer militia. He was concerned that any attempts 'to establish either a militia or Volunteer Force would, in the existing state of the Colony, imperil rather than conduce to the continuance of tranquility'. He argued that the existence of militias of trained and armed sections of the population would 'excite great and general discontent, if not open and systematic resistance'. And as for volunteer corps, he was even more pointed in his objection:

> I do not believe that any volunteer corps could be raised in any part of the island which would inspire caution, or even respect, among the inhabitants of the Districts. I believe indeed that the enrollment of Volunteer corps would be regarded by the population as a challenge and a provocation... It might be argued that by the enrollment of Volunteer Corps, unity of feeling and of action would be promoted among those who are interested in, and prepared to defend, the maintenance of tranquility. On the contrary, Sir, the jealousies of colour and of creed, but especially the former would I fear acquire additional strength and activity.[37]

The Governor, relying on his observations and experiences and no doubt informed by the experiences of his predecessors, recognised that 'the existing jealousies of race, and to a lesser degree creed, constitute[d] an insuperable obstacle'. The official wisdom was clearly that militias and volunteer corps would create more problems than they would solve and, in the circumstances, would have had the effect of throwing gasoline on embers.

---

[35] On the history of the district see Michael Anthony, *Anaparima: The History of San Fernando and the Naparimas. Volume 1 1595–1900* (Trinidad, West Indies: City Corporation of San Fernando, 2001).
[36] CO 295/234, Manners-Sutton to Cardwell, 23 February 1866, no. 21.
[37] For the Governor's report see CO 295/234, Manners-Sutton to Cardwell, 22 January 1866, Confidential.

The Colonial Office did not give approval to the idea of the volunteer cavalry, although in its reply to the memorialists it deliberately omitted to disclose the Governor's specific opinion about the divisions in the colony. The authorities, both local and metropolitan, only slowly warmed to the idea of militias and volunteer corps, and only when it was quite clear that the imperial troops were to be withdrawn. By then, even the West India Committee (the planters' voice in London) could be openly bold enough to recommend 'the establishment of a Mounted Corps of 100 white men for aiding the police in the suppression of any serious disturbance' and to hope for the support of both the Governor (Robinson) and elements in the Colonial Office.[38]

But prior to this development, that is the withdrawal of the troops, the Governor had advised in 1866 that 'the real security of the internal tranquility of the Colony is the Police backed by the presence of the Queen's Troops'.[39] This was the policy that was accepted and which operated between 1866 and 1884. Successive administrations would in pursuit of this policy provide the funds and moral support for the expansion and militarisation of the police. It would be a police force partially modelled on the Royal Irish Constabulary, predominantly staffed by personnel recruited from outside Trinidad, and in particular Barbados (interesting given the earlier objection to soldiers from Barbados),[40] and increasingly focused on the eradication of those cultural practices which were demonised as the springboard for insurrection.[41] The authorities and their security forces focused on Carnival and the Hosay during the closing years of the nineteenth century.[42]

---

[38] See Trinidad Council Paper 41 of 1886: Petition for the Establishment of a Volunteer Corps in San Fernando, 15 November 1884; CO 295/319, Fowler to Knutsford, 25 October 1888, Confidential; CO 295/329, Robinson to Knutsford, 21 July 1890, no. 217; CO 295/331, West India Committee to Knutsford, 19 May 1890, pp. 225–34, and WIC to Knutsford, 29 December 1890, pp. 225–34.
[39] CO 295/234, Manners-Sutton to Cardwell, 23 February 1866, no. 21, encl: Private letter from Governor to Sir Frederick.
[40] Howard Johnson, 'Barbadian Immigrants in Trinidad, 1870–1897', *Caribbean Studies* 13, no. 3 (1973).
[41] On the development of the police and its activities in the nineteenth century see Trotman, *Crime in Trinidad*, esp. pp. 90–101; for a discussion of the militarisation of the police see Howard Johnson, 'Patterns of Policing in the Post-Emancipation British Caribbean, 1835–1895', in David M. Anderson and David Killingray (eds.), *Policing the Empire: Government, Authority and Control, 1830–1940* (Manchester: Manchester University Press, 1991).
[42] In discussions of the conflict generated by the attempt to suppress these two festivals, the 1880s have been described as years of revolt. See Anthony De Verteuil, *The Years of Revolt: Trinidad 1881–1888* (Newtown, Port-of-Spain, Trinidad, WI: Paria Pub. Co., 1984).

Part Four

The public celebrations of Carnival and Hosay expressed in horrifying ways the fears of revolt and the potential for mayhem which were the constant preoccupation of the elite.[43] The first, Carnival, was an essentially creole and secular celebration; the other, Hosay, or the Muharram, was a Muslim Indian and religious festival. But both of them brought out onto the streets masses of the working class who were deemed to be clearly intoxicated and aggressive. Participants in the Cannes Brulées segment of the carnival in the pre-dawn darkness carried lighted torches – a spectacle that sent a chill down the spine of those who recognised the potential for arson. Both festivals involved participants who were armed and engaged in ritualistic bouts of combat and demonstrations of martial ability. Many of the songs they used on the street evoked memories of a pre-imperial past, pilloried and ridiculed members of the establishment, and raised serious doubts about their loyalty to the Empire. Both the rituals of the Hosay and the masquerade performances at Carnival offended the esthetics of the elite and were graphic reminders of the non-European origins of the participants.

But what really was an even more pressing concern for the elite was the way in which both festivals had provided opportunities for participation which seemed to have transcended the ethnic and racial divisions in the society. Take Carnival, for example. The festival had its Trinidadian origins in both the traditions of the French plantocracy and the West African traditions of masking, with the former providing the opportunity for the latter to be successfully transplanted. In the post-emancipation period the festival was dominated by Afro-Creoles and Africans. The French Creole middle class had begun withdrawing in the face of what they saw as the degeneration of the festival. But they had not completely withdrawn, and some still gave at least a kind of token ideological support. Moreover, East Indian participation had been

---

[43] On Carnival see Errol Hill, *The Trinidad Carnival: Mandate for a National Theatre* (Austin and London: University of Texas Press, 1972); Bridget Brereton, 'The Trinidad Carnival', *Savacou* 11/12 (1975); Michael Anthony, *Parade of the Carnivals of Trinidad, 1839–1989* (St James, Port-of-Spain: Circle Press, 1989); John Cowley, *Carnival, Canboulay and Calypso: Traditions in the Making* (Cambridge [England]; New York, NY: Cambridge University Press, 1996); Richard D.E. Burton, *Afro-Creole: Power and Opposition at Play in the Caribbean* (Ithaca: Cornell University Press, 1997); Hollis Liverpool, *Rituals of Power and Rebellion: The Carnival Tradition in Trinidad and Tobago 1763–1962* (Chicago: Research Associates School Times Publications/Frontline Distribution Int'l Inc., 2001). For insightful commentaries on Hosay see Kelvin Singh, *Bloodstained Tombs: The Muharram Massacre 1884* (London: Macmillan Caribbean, 1988); and Neil A. Sookdeo, *Freedom, Festivals and Caste in Trinidad after Slavery: A Society in Transition* (Xlibris Corporation for Neil A. Sookdeo, 2000).

reported since the 1850s. Thus in the 1880s, despite the intra-group fighting which characterised the festival, Carnival was slowly emerging as an activity which facilitated interaction, albeit of a qualified nature, across ethnic and racial lines.

The Hosay festival was proceeding along a similar trajectory of transformation from a specifically ethnic-based celebration into one in which we can glimpse the beginnings of a proto-national festival.[44] The celebration was a religious-based practice of one segment of the Shia Muslim community. The other segment of the Muslim population, the Sunni, objected to its popularity and claimed it was a religious travesty. In 1882 there were 107 signatories to a petition that it should be banned.[45] But in nineteenth-century Trinidad many Hindus also participated in the festival. It had become in its own way a pan-Indian celebration. Moreover, the number of Africans who were observed participating had become noticeable enough to draw warning comments from those who saw this emerging inter-racial interaction as a dangerous development.

Some scholars have argued that Africans and Afro-Creoles were attracted to the festival either because as it became more secularised it resembled Carnival in its bacchanalian features, or because its use of drums as a method of musical expression resonated culturally with them. We know that many Africans and Afro-Creoles participated, but we are not sure about who and why. Perhaps some of these Africans were Muslims who were drawn to the festival for religious rather than secular reasons. One aspect of Trinidad's cultural history that has not been thoroughly explored is the extent, role and activities of African Muslims in the Trinidad population. We do know of the existence of a community of Islamic Africans during the slave period, that is, before the coming of Muslims from the Indian sub-continent.[46] We also know that other Muslim Africans came with the liberated Africans who were settled in Trinidad after emancipation. Although they came from different Islamic doctrinal traditions, it is quite conceivable that Islam may have provided the basis for non-antagonistic interaction between

---

[44] For this insightful comment see Kelvin Singh, *Bloodstained Tombs*.
[45] 'We are the Mussalmans of Trinidad. We believe in one God. We abhor all idol worship. When people drink rum and like vain fellows swing their sticks and shout Hassan and Hussain before Taziya we get much shame.' Petition of Mohammedans for discontinuance of the Taziyadari, 1 April 1882, in Trinidad Council Papers no. 26 of 1882.
[46] Carl Campbell, 'Joseph Mohammed Bath and the Free Mandingoes in Trinidad: The Question of Their Repatriation to Africa 1831–38', *Journal of African Studies* 12, no. 4 (1975); P.E. Lovejoy and D.V. Trotman, 'Creating the Community of Believers: African Muslims in Trinidad, 1790–1850' (paper presented at the Second International Conference on Slavery and Religion in the Modern World, Morocco, 2001).

segments of the African and East Indian communities in the post-emancipation period. In the tension-filled atmosphere of the post-emancipation period this participation was generalised into the spectre of Afro-Asian working class alliance.

There is very little evidence to suggest that these conflicts (and the behaviour that led to these confrontations with the police) were part of any coherent strategy of resistance to the colonial state. They were pre-political at best, and while they revealed incipient or embryonic moments of collective identity, they in no way indicated a coherent, coordinated assault on the colonial government. There is no doubt that both ethnic sections of the working class used their cultural celebrations as part of their ongoing protest over industrial issues. But the response of the colonial authorities was to criminalise both industrial negotiation and cultural celebration. Individuals reacted to what they perceived and experienced as unwarranted encroachments on their activities and defended what they saw as their right to particular forms of cultural expression and the right to unbridled secular pleasure and sacred worship. In defence of those rights they acted in common cause and in recognition of a limited collective identity. This collective identity was based on and limited by race, ethnicity, religion, place of origin, and even place of residence. The recognition of common cause leading to sustained action against a distinct enemy that transcended race, ethnicity and even locale was not easily achievable (although not impossible) in the circumstances of nineteenth-century Trinidad.

The production of both Carnival bands and Hosay tadhjias offered opportunities for the development and utilisation of social skills beyond that required merely for the display of secular artistry or religious devotion. There is no doubt that these events were occasions for drunkenness, disorderliness and other questionable social behaviour. But they also required and demonstrated levels of community organisation and mobilisation and leadership skills, as well as the sourcing and utilisation of financial resources in the planning and execution of these two secular and religious projects. These demonstrated capabilities questioned the oft-repeated stereotypes of profligacy and mindless fanaticism of which the participants in these events were accused by the ruling classes and their press.

These festivals were systematically attacked in the late nineteenth century. There had been clashes before, and the editorials in the local press as well as comments in the various Governors' dispatches record a running commentary on elite distaste and government dissatisfaction with the festivals.[47] Some scholars have correctly pointed to the

---

[47] See Liverpool, *Rituals of Power and Rebellion*; and Singh, *Bloodstained Tombs*.

economic distress of the times, which meant a reduction of wages and the lengthening of tasks for the indentured working class and unemployment and economic deprivations for the rest of the working class. The tensions of the period are of course reflected in the increase in incidents of unrest on the plantations and the increasing use of fines, imprisonment and forced extensions of indentureships to curtail that unrest. The systematic attacks on the festivals also coincided with, and provided justification for, the expansion and militarisation of the police.

It could be argued that the police force engineered the confrontations. It was seen as a test of strength by a newly expanded police force headed by an aggressive military-trained Chief of Police who assumed the role of 'domestic missionary' and was prepared to demonstrate the capacity of his Irish-led and Barbadian-dominated troops to pre-emptively strike at perceived resistance and purge the festivals of the morally objectionable behaviour of the degenerate lower orders. The Chief of Police saw it as a struggle for control of the streets and for the enhancement of the reputation of his troops. This is not to deny increasing aggressiveness on the part of the participants and their recognition of the 'political' importance of the opportunities provided by the festivals. In response to this aggression some elements of the working classes glimpsed the possibility of collective action around a common cause and a collective identity.

But neither festival could achieve anything beyond the brief moments of primitive political action expressed in the defiance of the authorities by some segments of the subaltern classes. The separation of politics and culture retarded the development of a more holistic and class-cum-ethnicity-based worldview which was crucial for the construction of any anti-colonial platform. The moral justification by the authorities was enough to undermine wider political potential and participation by isolating the creole middle classes and those concerned with respectability, even though some segments of that creole middle class understood the politics of linking the struggle over Carnival to their embryonic movement for political reform. The military might of the security forces overwhelmed the primitive military strategies of the masses. The festivals would be increasingly depoliticised and the various communities would degenerate into increased paroxysms of implosive violence and ethnic tension. It would take the emergence of organised labour and a nationalist movement to finally define the problem and confront the colonial order with its solution. In the twentieth century the festivals would be touted as emblematic of the national unity of the post-colonial state, though not without contestation over their meaning and roles.

Conclusion

The strategy for dealing with the social conflict and civil unrest generated by a multiracial and multi-ethnic plantation society was slowly developed in the nineteenth society. It involved the use of a militarised police, local militias and armed volunteer corps, backed by the presence of a patrolling British navy and marines who regularly showed the flag. The intimidatory use of the British navy and marines, ostensibly paying courtesy calls, especially at Carnival and Hosay, became a stock element of the strategy and was used well into the twentieth century. This was the only way to cap the volcano, even though it would occasionally show its potential, as in the Arouca Riot of 1891, the Water Riots of 1903 and the Labour Riots of 1937. All of the latter were themselves part of the problems inherent in the transition from emancipation.

8 Different modes of resistance by British Indian and Javanese contract labourers in Suriname?[1]

Rosemarijn Hoefte

Suriname is considered a classic Caribbean plantation colony, where slaves cultivated tropical cash crops for the European market. However, in the nineteenth century its history started to deviate from that of other colonies in the region. First, the abolition of slavery took place only in 1863, three decades later than in the British colonies and 15 years after emancipation in the French territories. As a result of this rather late abolition of slavery the state-sponsored influx of indentured labourers from Asia started much later than elsewhere in the region. In 1873, less than a month before the ten-year transition period of State Supervision[2] came to an end, the first contract labourers from British India arrived in the Surinamese capital of Paramaribo. Between 1873 and 1916, 34 400 British Indians or Hindustani[3] entered the Dutch colony.[4] In the period between 1878 and 1920, 11 623 of them (33.9 per cent) returned to their homeland.[5]

---

[1] I want to thank all participants in the workshop on control and resistance in the century after emancipation in the Caribbean (Centre for Caribbean Studies, University of Warwick, 6–7 July 2000) for their comments and suggestions. I am particularly grateful for comments made by Nigel Bolland, Gad Heuman, Mimi Sheller, David Trotman and Mary Turner.

[2] State Supervision was a mandatory apprenticeship period when the former slaves were to work for employers of their own choice under the supervision of the colonial state, hence the name.

[3] In Suriname the British Indian population is most often referred to as Hindustani, after Hindustan, the area of origin of most migrants. The (Dutch) East Indians are generally called Javanese since most of them came from Java. In this chapter I will alternate the terms British Indian/Hindustani and Javanese/East Indian.

[4] Compare this to indentured immigration from British India elsewhere in the Caribbean: British Guiana 238 909; Trinidad 143 939; Guadeloupe 42 326; Jamaica 36 420; Martinique 25 509; St Lucia 4350; Grenada 3200; St Vincent 2472. Peter van der Veer and Steven Vertovec, 'Brahmanism Abroad: On Caribbean Hinduism as an Ethnic Religion', *Ethnology* 30, 2 (1991), p. 150.

[5] Rosemarijn Hoefte, *In Place of Slavery: A Social History of British Indian and Javanese Contract Laborers in Suriname* (Gainesville: University Press of Florida, 1998), p. 63.

Second, Suriname is a unique case in the Caribbean because of the influx of not only British Indians (and much smaller groups of Chinese, Barbadians and Madeirans) but also a large group of Javanese. One of the major problems of migration from British India was that the indentureds remained British subjects who could appeal to the British Consul and thus undermine both the highest Dutch authority and the planters' search for a reliable plantation labour force. Doubts about dependence on a foreign nation for the supply of labour, as well as the growth of nationalism and the concomitant rise of an anti-emigration movement in India, also forced the Surinamese planters to look elsewhere for indentured workers. In 1890 the first migrants from Java arrived, and by the time the Second World War ended the immigration from the Netherlands East Indies, 32 956 Javanese had come to Suriname. Only 23.3 per cent (7684 individuals) returned to the Dutch East Indies between 1896 and 1939.[6]

The contract of indenture placed the immigrants on a plantation for at least five years. According to the contract, the wages of men and women were fixed, but as will be shown below, wages were a major source of conflict during the period of indenture. Fundamental to the system was the penal sanction which made neglect of duty or refusal to work punishable by gaol sentences. This penal sanction was a distinctive feature of indentured labour as compared to free labour. It gave the employer the right to press criminal charges against indentureds who broke their contract. Government officials intervened when a breach of contract occurred, and this could include drunkenness, rudeness, laziness etc. Breaking a contract was of course a civil offence, yet the contractants were subject to a criminal penalty. The locus of authority and control thus shifted partially from the planters to the state, but it was the planters who pressed charges against their workers. Therefore, the penal sanction allowed planters to impose their ideas of work discipline. Moreover, the planters restricted the geographical mobility of the indentureds by employing a pass system. In addition, a number of plantations used a truck system to keep both labourers and their money on the estates. Although the planters most frequently relied on these methods of control, rewards – the granting of passes to leave the estate or the opportunity to acquire better jobs on the plantation – were also used to discipline the labour force.

To protect the contractants against abuse of power the government established the office of (Immigration) Agent-General. The Hindustani, who until 1927 were British subjects, enjoyed in addition the protection

---

[6] Ibid.

of the British Consul. The efficacy of these officials partly depended on their influence with both planters and government officials. However, a structural problem eroding the protection of the indentureds was the discrepancy between theory and practice. In addition to language problems, cultural differences and bureaucratic inefficiency, the hybrid role of the district commissioners made it very difficult for contract labourers to obtain justice. The district commissioners were the officials most in touch with the Asian labourers. They had to inspect every plantation at least once a month. But given their many other administrative and executive duties, they could not spend enough time on the indentureds and be impartial. An additional problem was that the district commissioners had to perform a number of judicial tasks. In the event of an accusation of breach of contract by the indentured labourer, the district commissioner had to first investigate the accusation and sanction the charge before it could be taken to court. During court sessions the district commissioner was seated next to the (itinerant) judge. The district commissioner also had to see to the execution of sentences. Needless to say, this combination of functions did not make the district commissioner a model of impartiality. In short, the contract, the local labour laws, the plantation hierarchy and the state were established to regulate and control the indentureds.

This chapter focuses on the question of whether British Indian and Javanese contract workers used different means to protest against their working conditions. Secondly, the ways of resistance in Suriname are compared with those used in Asia and other plantation colonies in the Americas.

The fact that not one but two large ethnic groups entered the colony first raises the question of how the two population groups related to each other. It suffices to state here that socio-economic and cultural relations between ex-slaves and Javanese and British Indians were characterised by ethnic competition rather than the defence of communal interests. Partly this was the result of European attitudes towards non-Europeans in the colony and a policy of divide and rule. Yet, it also seems that each group held long-established stereotyped views of the others, even though it never came to major violent clashes between Afro-Surinamese and Asians.[7] The Dutch, as colonisers of the

---

[7] Ibid., p. 102. See also Bridget Brereton, *Race Relations in Colonial Trinidad, 1870–1900* (Cambridge: Cambridge University Press, 1979); Walton Look Lai, *Indentured Labor, Caribbean Sugar: Chinese and Indian Migrants to the British West Indies, 1838–1918* (Baltimore: Johns Hopkins University Press, 1993); Allen S. Ehrlich, 'Race and Ethnic Identity in Rural Jamaica: The East Indian Case', *Caribbean Quarterly* 22:1 (1976).

Netherlands East Indies, had already stereotyped the Javanese as 'submissive', 'apathetic', and 'careless regarding their material future'.[8] Archival sources indicate that the planters soon preferred the 'docile' Javanese to the British Indians, even though the latter's physical prowess was considered greater. The Javanese received preferential treatment; the Europeans seemed to fear the British Indians more.

During the time period when the immigration of both Javanese and British Indians was taking place, the management at Mariënburg, by far the largest plantation in the colony, attempted to keep a balance of Hindustani and Javanese on the estate in order to prevent domination by any group, particularly the British Indians. Hindustani, Javanese and Afro-Surinamese were lodged in ethnically separated housing divisions. Despite these deliberate attempts to divide the plantation workers along racial instead of class lines, racial conflict was less pronounced than might have been expected. Most clashes were intra-ethnic, yet there was always a danger that a relatively minor conflict could explode and imperil the plantation or government authorities. Even though inter-racial conflicts were exceptional, irritation could lead to violence.[9]

More often, however, the plantation workers expressed their opposition and frustrations about conditions on the estates through acts of non-cooperation such as 'neglect of duty' or illegal absences. However, contemporary government and plantation records, as well as newspaper articles, often neglected this type of protest and concentrated on spectacular actions and open revolt. Here I will focus first on open revolt and then on more hidden forms of resistance.

One form of individual or uncoordinated but violent resistance was, for example, the obstruction of trains on the plantation, some forms of robbery and theft,[10] the destruction of crops and/or fields, arson, and physical attacks on supervisory personnel. The latter were primarily directed against overseers and drivers, from all ethnic groups, who controlled the workers. The drivers, recruited from among the workers, were particularly unpopular among the field hands who frequently accused them of thievery by under-reporting the labourer's task work, of physical violence, and of blackmail (see also below). Often

---

[8] Hoefte, *In Place of Slavery*, p. 103.
[9] Ibid., see pp. 105–6.
[10] The targets of theft were mostly drivers, immigrants who were better off than the average field hand, or the plantation itself. This is, of course, no evidence that the perpetrators viewed thefts as a means of resistance. Their motivation makes theft an act of resistance or a criminal act. It is important, however, that the unequal distribution of wealth and the character of the plantation system made banditry a 'logical' option for the indentureds; on this topic see James C. Scott, *Weapons of the Weak: Everyday Forms of Peasant Resistance* (New Haven, Conn.: Yale University Press, 1985), p. 267.

such physical attacks resulted in injuries or even death. Ann Laura Stoler notes that on plantations in Sumatra, Netherlands East Indies, supervisory personnel were the main target of dissatisfaction too. And as in Suriname, she finds that such incidents were labelled as acts of personal revenge or as political acts of insurgency.[11]

Even though some of these attacks by individuals involved murder, they nevertheless seemed less threatening than the acts of more widespread defiance that the planters sometimes faced. Such unrest could be confined to one estate, while at other times resistance would spread to neighbouring plantations. This kind of unrest occurred during the first decades of indentured immigration in particular and later became less frequent.

To give an impression of how planters and colonial authorities viewed these protests, I will briefly review a number of incidents that took place in the period 1873–1902.[12] In 1873, the first year of indentured immigration from British India, there were mutinies on the Goudmijn, Alliance, Hooyland and De Resolutie plantations. During the period 1874–77 'the spirit among the immigrants left much to be desired', according to the colonial administration.[13] Arson and unrest at Alliance, De Resolutie and Waterloo were the major incidents. In these years it was, however, earlier immigrants from Barbados and China who rebelled. In 1879 it was the turn of the British Indians at Alliance to rise in protest. In 1884 trouble arose at Zoelen and Zorg en Hoop plantations; this incident caused the first loss of lives. The year 1891 turned out to be one of the most difficult ones for the planters to control the labour force and to convince the Governor and colonial minister that, according to them, the situation on the estates was ominous. The first problem arose during a Muslim festival at Zoelen and Geertruidenberg. A few months after this incident the director of Jagtlust plantation was killed. According to the planters, 'murder threats are of the order of the day'.[14] A labourer at Zoelen, who was convicted for leaving the plantation without a pass, threatened the British Consul, the district commissioner and two plantation directors.

The planters dreaded widespread violence, especially its collective potential. A group of planters reacted by arming their overseers with

---

[11] A.L. Stoler, *Capitalism and Confrontation in Sumatra's Plantation Belt, 1870–1979* (New Haven, Conn: Yale University Press, 1985), pp. 49–50. For similar observations on the British Caribbean see Look Lai, *Indentured Labor*, p. 142.
[12] For a fuller description see Hoefte, *In Place of Slavery*, pp. 191–4.
[13] *Koloniale Verslagen* (KVs, Colonial Reports), relevant years.
[14] Collection Stichting Suriname Museum (SSM), Paramaribo, Mariënburg records, 3 October 1891, 214.

revolvers and collectively addressing the colonial minister and the Governor concerning the 'alarming growth of resistance among the British Indian coolies'.[15] This group of some 30 owners and managers emphasised that they not only wanted to complain, but also proposed to increase the police force, to reform the judicial system and to reinstitute corporal punishment. According to the planters, the death penalty did not serve its purpose as 'a coolie does not value his life and the death penalty through hanging would, according to his belief, not prevent him from obtaining everlasting bliss; mutilation on the other hand would. Moreover, physical pain impresses him more than death.'[16] The Governor, however, was not impressed and his only concession was that the dispatch of justice was expedited. He accused the planters of overreacting to the situation, caused simply by, as he saw it, the 'usual barbarity of the Asians'.[17]

Trying to grab attention with the heading 'coolie murder mania', the managers of Mariënburg plantation listed three deadly crimes perpetrated by British Indians to illustrate their fear of the plantation labourers. After the Governor had granted a reprieve to the murderer of the director of Jagtlust, the planters listed a dozen more instances of Hindustani resistance to prove that 'Jagtlust' was not just an isolated incident, but rather a symptom of a threatening situation.

Nevertheless, it would take more than a decade before the expected great outburst of violence occurred. In June and July of 1902 violent uprisings at Alliance and Mariënburg sugar plantations took place within a few weeks of each other. A wage reduction implemented by an acting director (the director was on holiday in Europe) had caused a strike at Alliance on Saturday, 28 June.[18] One hundred British Indians and 37 Javanese left the sugar estate without permission to complain to the district commissioner of Frederiksdorp, even though Alliance fell under the jurisdiction of the district commissioner of Ephrata. In all likelihood, the protesters mistrusted this official and so bypassed him. The strikers demanded lighter tasks, higher wages, and the dismissal of a 'tyrannical' British Indian driver named Abdoolah. The district commissioner of Frederiksdorp was away for the weekend but returned on Monday. Following a meeting with the protesters, he convinced them to return to Alliance by steamboat, but not until he had taken their cutlasses from them.

---

[15] Ibid., 12 October 1891, 215.
[16] Ibid., 3 October 1891, 214.
[17] Ibid., 23 November 1891, 218.
[18] This description of events at Alliance is based on the official government version as published in KV 1903, bijlage M.

When the men arrived back at Alliance at 11 am, they encountered the district commissioner of Ephrata, accompanied by an interpreter and two policemen who were to start an investigation. The latter arrested and tied up the man they considered the leading rebel, the British Indian Jumpa Raygaroo, which caused unrest among the other workers, who started to throw missiles at the office where the district commissioner, the acting director, an overseer and the police were hiding. The district commissioner ordered the police to fire six revolver shots and to release the prisoner. The whole group tried to flee through the back door but the labourers soon found them and attacked all of them. The district commissioner of Ephrata was happy to leave the plantation alive and only with the arrival of his colleague from Frederiksdorp at 4 pm did some semblance of peace return to the estate. At 8.30 pm that same day the Attorney-General and Agent-General arrived with a detachment of army and police, but the Frederiksdorp district commissioner convinced them not to provoke the workers and to spend the night at the neighbouring estate, Nieuw Meerzorg. An investigation by the Attorney-General and the district commissioner of Frederiksdorp during the next two days indicted one Javanese and 16 Hindustani; each was sentenced to six months' hard labour on 4 October 1902. However, the strike had some success, since the owner replaced the acting director and raised wages.

Three weeks later the workers at Mariënburg rose in protest.[19] The eruption took place on 27 July, when a gang of cane cutters refused to do its task because it considered the pay inadequate. Plantation director Mavor agreed, by messenger, to increase pay slightly, but the protesters turned down this proposal. They wanted to talk to Mavor himself and marched to his office. Mavor agreed to come to the fields and three hours later he arrived on horseback to inspect the work. He promised another small rise, which the workers again rejected. They requested to see the district commissioner, and Mavor granted permission to three of them to leave the estate. When Mavor was about to leave the field, a number of Hindustani started to throw cane and to follow him. They also attacked the accompanying overseers. Mavor jumped on his horse and sped away, followed by his personnel in a train and 200 indentureds on foot. Mavor arrived at his office to call for help and then went into hiding. One of Mavor's colleagues took his horse to request police assistance. The steadily growing mass of people cut down the telephone poles to disrupt communication with the outside world and looted the office and the plantation shop. Discovering that Mavor was hiding in the

---

[19] For a more detailed description of this incident see Hoefte, *In Place of Slavery*, pp. 194–7.

factory, they invaded the building, destroying everything in their way, and killed the director.

The same district commissioner who had had to flee Alliance plantation some weeks earlier, the Attorney-General, the Agent-General, 30 policemen and an army of 126 men arrived to find peace largely restored. They arrested several British Indians along with one Javanese as the main agitators. A great number of indentureds armed with tools gathered in front of the narrow bridge connecting office and factory, calling for the release of the arrested. A lieutenant and ten soldiers could not control the crowd, and following the Attorney-General's permission they opened fire, killing 17 Hindustani and wounding 39, seven of whom later died. The volley of shots dispersed the crowd. On 31 July the labourers resumed work.

During the trial, the court needed five interpreters – Hindi, French, Sranantongo, Chinese, and Javanese – to hear the 21 Hindustani and one Javanese accused of premeditated murder and 19 witnesses. All 22 defendants denied the charge and incriminated each other. They agreed only on the arrival of Mavor and that the low wages were at the root of the tragedy. Most witnesses admitted that pay indeed had been low during the previous few years and that workers had been complaining. The overseer directly involved in the incident, however, stated that wages had not been reduced. According to him, the director had offered more to the protesting cutters because of the heaviness of the cane. The court found it impossible to single out the chief offenders and rejected the accusation of premeditated murder. It released 13 men and sentenced eight Hindustani to 12 years' hard labour.

These two cases and their aftermath demonstrate several things. First, the fact that the white elite was not always seeing eye to eye regarding the conditions on the plantations and the treatment of the workers. The colonial minister in The Hague stated bluntly that the abuses by the managements at Alliance and Mariënburg had led to the revolts. According to the official colonial report, wage questions had started the troubles. All attempts by state officials to raise the daily payments had failed. Later these authorities found out that other problems such as the preferential treatment given to some immigrant families, bad choices of overseers and inadequate control over the drivers had aggravated the unsatisfactory wage situation.

The British Consul in Suriname confirmed and elaborated on these findings. In his report to the Foreign Office in London he wrote:

> There appears to be no doubt that the late manager [Mavor] had been trying to reduce the expenditure, and among other things reduced the rate of pay for cane cutting [but there were

no official complaints to colonial authorities]. [T]here appears also, to have been much ill feeling on account of the interference with the cooly women by the deceased Manager, and because of favouritism shown to the relatives of some of these women. [...] I have also been told that the overseers were much underpaid, and that they occasionally borrowed money from the coolies, and drank with them, this, naturally, weakened their authority, and was in every way bad. This all helped to induce the very unsatisfactory state of feeling which must have existed among the coolies at Mariënburg [...] A British subject, a Scotchman, who hapened [sic] to be at Mariënburg, at the time, informed that although there were a great many Javanese in the crowd which came to demand the release of the prisoners, they all went away when the mob was ordered to disperse, consequently none of them were shot. My informant, who had nothing to do with Mariënburg, states that in his opinion it was absolutely necessary to fire on the mob, but at the same time he considered the number of shots fired excessive.[20]

Mariënburg, however, attributed the revolt to causes other than wage reductions. According to the plantation's version of the uprising, Mavor had only become the victim because he had had the courage to confront the malcontents who had been venting their rage at everyone in the plantation hierarchy. The proof that a cutback in wages had not caused the revolt came later when jobs were paid better and the mood among the immigrants did not improve at all. The plantation blamed the unrest on some 'ill-disposed' British Indians who had come from British Guiana.[21] This latter statement is rather typical: even though the authorities roundly identified low wages as a cause of problems, the planters refused to accept this explanation and instead blamed outside forces.

A second point shown by several reports on the uprisings at both Alliance and Mariënburg is that bread and butter issues – and, to a lesser degree, a quest for respect – were the root causes of the unrest. This may seem surprising, given that the work contract stipulated a fixed daily wage. Yet in effect, the indentureds often did not receive this wage. This other instance of a discrepancy between theory and practice in the so-called task system was of crucial importance. According to the contract, labourers could be paid on the basis of the number of days

---

[20] Public Record Office: Foreign Office 97, piece 884, Consul to Foreign Office, 3 December 1902.
[21] Algemeen Rijksarchief, The Hague, NHM, T 1133–9185, 1902.

worked or the number of tasks carried out. Generally, the planters preferred the second option and paid a labourer for each task he or she finished. The employers defined a task as the work an average labourer could perform in one day. The planters thus argued that they were acting according to the labour contract. Most indentureds, however, maintained that the tasks assigned were too heavy to finish in one day and, consequently, they were not able to earn the wages mentioned in the contracts. For example, as we have seen above, in the aftermath of the Mariënburg uprising, one witness claimed that the director had raised wages because the labour gang protested that the cane was too heavy, thus making it impossible to earn enough. In other words, planters, labourers and the colonial authorities, who occasionally intervened in wage disputes, employed different definitions of an 'average worker' and 'average performance'.

Non-violent resistance could take innumerable forms, from everyday actions like foot dragging to flight. All these kinds of behaviour gave strength to the stereotype of the indolent Asian. The authorities interpreted stubbornness, such as reluctance to answer questions, as well as disrespectful behaviour as threatening signs of disobedience. The Javanese in particular often seem to have resorted to *mutung* [sulking]. These forms of resistance may have been so latent or incomprehensible to supervisory personnel that they underestimated their potential.

In his study on East Asia, Michael Adas coined the term 'avoidance protest' to describe protest by 'which dissatisfied groups seek to attenuate their hardships and express their discontent through flight, sectarian withdrawal, or other activities that minimise challenges to or clashes with those whom they view as their oppressors'.[22] In Suriname especially, the Javanese resorted to flight and messianic movements.[23] The messianism centred on the return of the workers to Java. This collective homesickness, which was so characteristic of the first generations of Surinamese Javanese, was strengthened with the cult of Anton de Kom as *Ratu Adil*, righteous prince or Messiah. In 1933 De Kom, an Afro-Surinamese living in the Netherlands and active in the anti-colonial movement, arrived in Suriname, where he was regarded as a hero by Afro-Surinamese, British Indians and Javanese alike.[24]

---

[22] Michael Adas, 'From Avoidance to Confrontation: Peasant Protest in Precolonial and Colonial Southeast Asia', in Nicholas B. Dirks (ed.), *Colonialism and Culture* (Ann Arbor: University of Michigan Press, 1992), p. 89. He also considers *wayang kulit* [puppet theatre] as a (possible) form of protest because of its satirical comments and the creation of fantasy worlds, pp. 107 and 116.
[23] On messianic movements in Java see Adas, 'From Avoidance to Confrontation', p. 100, 116; Scott, *Weapons of the Weak*, p. 333.
[24] Hoefte, *In Place of Slavery*, pp. 181–2.

Interestingly, the Javanese, who thought blacks to be inferior, in particular believed 'Papa' de Kom to be a representative of Allah who would end their involuntary exile. De Kom promised all Javanese a free passage back to their homeland. Rumour had it that all plantations would close and that the ships were waiting offshore. The colonial government feared that the situation would get out of hand and arrested De Kom. Plantation authorities reported that something was brewing among the workers, which revealed itself in silence during work, reluctance to answer questions, and general rudeness and recalcitrance. A week after the arrest several thousand supporters of De Kom left the plantations without notice and marched on Paramaribo to free him. In town the military was waiting and eventually killed two people. The protesters went back to the estates, disappointed and disillusioned since their return to Java now seemed so distant. Almost no British Indians joined the march on the capital.

The most obvious form of avoidance protest is flight. Running away or marronage has a long history in Suriname as slaves escaped the plantations as early as the seventeenth century. These Maroons established themselves in the jungle in Suriname's interior, where they set up autonomous communities. The indentured labourers who fled the estates did not follow the Maroons into the rain forest, but established themselves in the coastal area along the many rivers and creeks. In 1872 the Governor of Suriname noted that desertion, often by swimming or rowing across a river, was quite common. More than 30 years later some planters claimed that the rate of desertion among Javanese indentureds was 'alarming', and in 1908 it was clear that contract labourers, particularly Javanese, had abandoned the plantations. The police rounded up Javanese runaways in camps along the Marowijne River; the colonial authorities assumed, however, that most deserters were hired by smallholders on government settlements. The planters argued that flight was a characteristic trait of contract workers who preferred stealing to working.[25] However, this wave of desertions happened to coincide with wage disputes and strikes on many plantations which were led by British Indians. Jan Breman observes that indentured workers fled the Deli plantations (Sumatra, Netherlands East Indies) in the hope of

---

[25] SSM 6 Verslag 1906; SSM 7 Mariënburg. 24 February 1908, 499. Planters in Deli, for example, reacted in the same way to desertion: it was not the conditions on the estates but the wayward behaviour of the workers that was the cause of desertion, see Jan Breman, *Koelies, planters en koloniale politiek: het arbeidsregime op de grootlandbouwondernemingen aan Sumatra's Oostkust in het begin van de twintigste eeuw* (Dordrecht, Neth.: Foris, 1987), p. 24.

settling elsewhere in 'illegal freedom'; it seems that contract workers in Suriname fled in the same hope.[26]

The most radical form of avoidance protest was suicide. In the official colonial reports from 1886 to 1920 the Agent-General officially registered 47 suicides; in 32 instances he recorded the nationality of the deceased: 22 of them were British Indian, and ten Javanese.[27]

Adas makes a sharp distinction between avoidance protest and everyday resistance like 'foot-dragging, pilfering, and grousing behind the back of the local landlord', noting that 'everyday forms of peasant response are much more limited in time span and the numbers involved *in any given occurrence*, as well as in the degree to which they challenge or disrupt the existing order'.[28] Needless to say, everyday forms of resistance are hard to detect in the sources. Some forms of everyday resistance, however, were reported. Under the labour laws indentured workers could be penalised for laziness or neglect of duty. Despite the fact that statistics in both official documents and local newspapers from this period are rather unreliable, these data do provide a useful indication of 'unlawful' behaviour by Asian contract labourers in Suriname. The percentage of British Indians convicted under the labour laws between 1885 and 1923 ranges from approximately 11 per cent to 20 per cent, with an average of 15 per cent. For Javanese contract workers the percentage of labour convictions averages 16 per cent, with a range of ten per cent to 21 per cent.[29] These statistics thus belie somewhat the argument that the Javanese were more 'docile' and 'submissive' than their Hindustani counterparts. The British/Indian investigators James McNeill and Chimmam Lal state that the Dutch nationality of the Javanese was one of the reasons why the percentage of complaints against Javanese indentured workers had always been higher than that against British Indians.[30]

More than open defiance, avoidance protest and everyday resistance were important methods of protest against the plantation system

---

[26] Breman, *Taming the Coolie Beast: Plantation Society and the Colonial Order in Southeast Asia* (Delhi: Oxford University Press, 1989), p. 148.

[27] KVs 1886–1920.

[28] Adas, 'From Avoidance to Confrontation', p. 128.

[29] KVs relevant years. Hugh Tinker, *A New System of Slavery: The Export of Indian Labour Overseas 1830–1920* (London: Oxford University Press, 1974), p. 194 gives the following data for other colonies in 1907–08: British Guiana 20 per cent; Trinidad 16 per cent; Jamaica eight per cent; Fiji 20 per cent; Mauritius three per cent.

[30] James McNeill and Chimmam Lal, *Report on the Condition of Indian Immigrants in the Four British Colonies Trinidad, British Guiana or Demerara, Jamaica and Fiji, and in the Dutch Colony of Surinam or Dutch Guiana* (London: His Majesty's Stationery Office, 1915), p. 27.

during indentureship. Expressions of resistance like foot dragging, simulation of illnesses, flight, feigned ignorance and gestures of contempt were used in Asia, yet they were also well-known phenomena in the history of resistance against slavery in the Caribbean and the US South.

Indentureship was more than a labour system, as it involved a whole new social-cultural structure. The planters and the state employed several means of coercion to ensure an adequate, dependable and regular supply of workers. The Asian indentureds had to forge their own society despite all kinds of political, social and legal constraints. Both British Indians and Javanese attempted to defy the system, but the sources suggest that the two groups generally used different means to do so. The Javanese in particular seem to have relied on such forms of avoidance protest and cultural resistance as messianism and flight, which were part of the East Asian tradition. And as the data on convictions under the labour laws indicate, the Javanese were involved in everyday forms of resistance as well. The main methods of protest by the Hindustani were also in the realm of avoidance and hidden resistance, but in contrast to the Javanese this group was more likely to demonstrate collective and open defiance.

Needless to say, the indentureds had a weak bargaining position. When all normal and largely covert forms of protest had failed and the normal networks had broken down, strikes and open rioting, with their mortal risks, were actions of last resort. And when violent actions took place, the stereotypes describing the contract labourers could change quite suddenly from 'docile' to 'barbarous'. Both were, however, two sides of the same coin: the planters and most authorities failed to recognise that the indentureds did not simply vacillate between docile submission and murderous rage because they did not notice that in between there existed an enormous grey area comprising other forms of less open resistance.

It is not surprising, then, to find that collective and open resistance flourished in the period from 1873 to 1908, when the last major strikes until the political unrest of the 1930s were recorded. This is exactly the period when the British Indian contract labourers were in the majority on the Surinamese estates. As of the five-year period 1905–09 the Javanese indentureds gained the upper hand, even though between 1910 and 1914 there was a virtual balance between Hindustani and East Indian contract workers. After 1914 the absolute and relative number of British Indians on the plantations quickly decreased.[31]

---

[31] Hoefte, *In Place of Slavery*, pp. 69–70.

There may be several reasons for the more radical nature of British Indian protest. One explanation is the cultural background of the Hindustani. Dirk Kolff points to the martial tradition in the Bhojpuri and Avadhi districts from which most migrants originated. One of the preferred pastimes of the migrants from these districts was wrestling and fencing with clubs [*gatka*]. Instead of firearms, the contract labourers now used cutlasses, cane, and other makeshift weapons.[32] A second reason for the difference in reaction between Javanese and British Indians is the nationality of the former. The Hindustani remained British subjects and enjoyed the extra protection of the British Consul, something they were apparently very conscious of and one of the reasons why they felt superior to the Javanese. Even though the efficacy of the Consul depended on his personal qualities, his presence alone seemed a deterrent to exceedingly harsh reactions by the planters and the colonial state, who both considered the British Consul a nuisance, who had no business interfering in affairs concerning indentureds.

The reactions of planters and authorities differed according to the nature of resistance. In the case of open and collective defiance, the army and police were used, if necessary, to violently suppress any unrest. As this chapter shows, the British Indians were most often the victims of this kind of reaction. In the aftermath of violence, the planters usually called for the death penalty, the reinstitution of corporal punishment and an increase in the police force. Given that generally none of these demands was met, plantation managers resorted to arming their personnel. If resistance was more covert, when it was detected, the planters would take indentureds to court, because the penal sanctions made civil breaches of contract a criminal offence. The Javanese were convicted slightly more often in court than the British Indians.

In conclusion, the behaviour of Asian indentured migrants in general and the Javanese in particular was less docile than the planters, colonial authorities, contemporary observers, and later scholars who have focused on direct, open confrontations have recognised. The contract labourers tried to shy away from open confrontation as much as possible and preferred avoidance protests and secretive everyday forms of resistance to express their dissatisfaction and undermine the system of indenture.

---

[32] D.H.A. Kolff, 'From Hindustani Diaspora to Indian Expansion: The Context of the First Phase of the Transition' (Paper presented to the workshop 'South Asian Labour', International Institute for Social History, Amsterdam, 26–27 October 1995), esp. pp. 15–17.

Section 3

Cultural conflicts

9 Afro-Cuban culture: within or outside of the nation?

Christine Ayorinde

In Cuba, the period of the abolition of slavery and emancipation coincided with the wars of independence from Spain. The island emerged as a plantation economy relatively late, well after the rest of the Caribbean. By the 1830s, it had moved from small-scale cattle and tobacco production to becoming the main sugar producer in the region. This was due to a number of factors, perhaps most importantly the fall in sugar imports from Haiti after the revolution in 1791. In contrast to other islands, the largest number of Africans was imported in the nineteenth century and despite attempts to abolish it, the trade continued well into the 1870s.

A combination of economic interests and the 'black problem' – the high proportion of Africans in the population – made the Creole elite reluctant to cut the ties to the mother country.[1] The impasse ended with the first independence war (1868–78), which began in the eastern part of the island where the economy was less dependent on either the metropole or slavery. Although the war did not result in independence, it ushered in a staged process of abolition called the *Patronato*, a form of tutelage by which former slaves became apprenticed to a master. This was intended to last until 1888, but the efforts of abolitionists and of the slaves themselves ended slavery in 1886.[2]

At the height of the slave trade, mortality rates were extremely high and it was cheaper to replace slaves than to breed them. Thus

---

The author would like to acknowledge the financial support of the AHRB and the UNESCO Nigerian Hinterland Project.

[1] In 1841 the whites formed 41.4 per cent of the population and were outnumbered by slaves, 43.4 per cent, and free blacks, 15.2 per cent: see Cuban census figures cited in Franklin Knight, *Slave Society in Cuba During the 19th Century* (Madison: University of Wisconsin, 1970), pp. 22, 86. The relatively high proportion of free blacks was due to *coartación* [self-manumission], which gave slaves the right to buy themselves in instalments. It represented a form of partial freedom, as they could live away from their master, earn their own living and acquire capital and property. The demand for labour in certain urban occupations offered some social mobility to the free black population.

[2] See Rebecca J. Scott, *Slave Emancipation in Cuba: the Transition to Free Labor 1860–1899* (Princeton, NJ: Princeton University Press, 1985), Chapter 6.

cultural and religious practices were renewed by successive waves of Africans from the continent. Economic factors overruled concern about the assimilation of the slave population. Although the importing of heathen slaves was forbidden and they received perfunctory baptism, often at the port of embarkation, the religious laxity that was characteristic of Cuban society led to no more than half-hearted catechisation of the slaves. The colonial government supported the maintenance of African ethnic differences as part of a divide-and-rule policy aimed at pre-empting pan-African rebellion against the state. Spanish pragmatism not only permitted but also encouraged practices that did not affect the exploitation of slave labour. Slaves were made to sing and dance in the belief that this would raise their spirits, boost productivity and discourage rebellion. Africans, both slave and free, congregated in the *cabildos de nación*, legally recognised mutual aid societies that were organised along ethnic lines.[3] The *cabildos* provided slaves and free blacks with a cover for conspiracy and a niche within which to preserve and recreate their cultural traditions.

By the 1880s, however, the colonial authorities changed their policy of cultural fragmentation among the black population. With abolition and moves towards independence it became expedient to prepare the Africans for citizenship. The *cabildos de nación* were regarded as anachronistic and subjected to increasing control. They began to be replaced by institutions called *sociedades de instrucción y recreo* [societies for instruction and recreation] or *sociedades de color*, which resembled the Spanish *casinos* [clubs for white immigrants].[4]

The Afro-Cuban intellectual and politician Juan Gualberto Gómez visited the remaining *cabildos de nación* in 1894 and attempted to encourage them to become centres of instruction and mutual aid instead of perpetuating the traditions of the former African slaves. As Gómez remarked: 'We are no longer Africans.' His newspaper, *La Fraternidad*, published an article entitled 'Otra vez el ñáñigo' [The ñáñigo again], which reported on a procession through Guanabacoa, at which paraders

---

[3] *Nación* = 'nation', in this case, the 'ethnic' groups into which Africans in Cuba were classified.

[4] Carmen Montejo Arrechea, *Sociedades de Instrucción y Recreo de Pardos y Morenos que existieron en Cuba colonial: período 1878–1898* (Veracruz: Instituto Veracruzano de Cultura, 1993), p. 44. Some of the *sociedades de color* were named after Catholic saints, while others had names which reflected their agenda, such as La Igualdad, El Progreso, El Adelanto [Equality, Progress, Improvement]. Some also published newspapers which generally recommended integration and the adoption of European education and culture. See Philip A. Howard, 'The Spanish colonial government's responses to the pan-nationalist agenda of the Afro-Cuban mutual aid societies, 1868–1895', *Revista Interamericana*, 22, nos. 1–2 (1992), pp. 151–67.

displayed 'their ridiculous contortions of the most recrudescent savagery'. What particularly incensed the writer was that Creole blacks, who had never seen Africa, could mount a display which worsened their existing negative public image.[5]

Members of the white elite also stressed the importance of education to prepare black Cubans for citizenship. Enrique Varona stated:

> It is incumbent upon whites in Cuba, in their position as the leading class, to win blacks over to the guiding principles of Western culture: its apparel, dances, theatre, music: it is as much in their [the whites'] interest to bring them [the blacks] closer to the scientific knowledge of natural laws as it is to drive them away from fetishism.[6]

Such statements reflected not so much a sense of altruism as fears that 'vices' associated with blacks would contaminate the rest of the population. Indeed, with the demise of the *cabildos de nación*, Afro-Cuban religious practices, hitherto associated with particular African ethnic groups, became open to Africans of other ethnicities and to Creole blacks and whites. Initiation, not descent, determined who could adopt an African cultural reference.

The period of the independence struggles also saw the forging of a vision of patriotism based on ethnic fraternity. Creole elites, hitherto excluded from political control, were forced to attempt to fuse national and racial identities as black and white Cubans fought together in the Liberation Army.[7] José Martí (1853–95), the national hero who was one

---

[5] See Montejo Arrechea, *Sociedades de Instrucción*, p. 93. Juan Gualberto Gómez (1854–1933), a mulatto born of slave parents, was educated in Paris. One of the most outstanding Afro-Cuban intellectuals of his time, he acted as the Cuban representative of the revolutionary party founded by Martí. In 1892, he founded the Directorio de las Sociedades de Color [Directorate of Societies of Colour] to unite black societies and incorporate them into the independence struggle: see Oilda Hevia Lanier, *El Directorio Central de las Sociedades Negras de Color 1886–1894* (La Habana: Editorial de Ciencias Sociales, 1996), pp. 15, 25–7.

[6] Cited in Elias Entralgo, *La liberación étnica cubana* (La Habana, 1953), p. 172. Enrique José Varona (1849–1933) was a positivist economist responsible for implementing educational reforms under the first US government of intervention from 1899 to 1902.

[7] In the independence wars the majority of the revolutionary troops and around 40 per cent of the generals and colonels were Afro-Cuban: see Louis A. Pérez, *Cuba: Between Reform and Revolution*, 2nd ed. (New York: Oxford University Press, 1995), p. 106. Some white insurgents became nervous of the black mobilisation and decided to treat with Spain, thus ending the first war (1868–78). The mulatto general Antonio Maceo was accused of hating whites and of seeking a Haitian-style victory: see Hugh Thomas, *Cuba: or the Pursuit of Freedom* (London: Eyre and Spottiswoode, 1971), pp. 264–5.

of the leaders of the independence movement, articulated this sense of a supra-racial Cuban-ness. His most frequently quoted statement is:

> Man is more than white, more than mulatto, more than black. Cuban is more than white, more than mulatto, more than black.

His views on race, unusual for a white Latin American of the time, were to become the basis for Cuba's myth of racial equality. Martí attempted to placate white Cuban fears regarding the 'black problem' after Independence. He suggested that the emancipation of the slaves by their masters during the Ten Years' War and the fact that black and white Cubans fought together heralded the ending of racial discrimination and of domestic racial warfare.[8]

The pseudo-republic

The final war of independence (1895–98) ended when the United States intervened to protect its investments. In this way Cuba exchanged dependence on Spain for American political, economic and cultural domination. The republican period, which lasted from 1902 until 1958, is often referred to as the *república mediatizada* [lit. annexed], or the pseudo- or neocolonial republic.[9]

Afro-Cubans had been able to place their own agenda within the framework of the wider national struggle during the wars of independence. With the coming of the Republic, there were expectations that their contribution to Cuba's liberation would be rewarded. A liberal republican constitution was drawn up that conferred universal male

---

[8] José Martí, *Obras completas* (La Habana: Editorial Nacional de Cuba, 1962), II, pp. 298–9; Aline Helg, *Our Rightful Share: the Afro-Cuban Struggle for Equality, 1886–1912* (Chapel Hill: University of North Carolina Press, 1995), pp. 3, 45. Diego Tejera, a follower of Martí, voiced another national myth when he asserted that slavery had been imposed on Cubans by the common enemy, Spain. He also questioned whether whites and blacks could have 'opposing ideals when history, language and religion, character, habits and customs are common to all. Could one even tell, apart from the accident of colour, that there were two races in Cuba?': *Blancos y negros* (La Habana: Imprenta 'Patria', 1900), p. 15.

[9] In 1884, the United States received 90 per cent of Cuba's exports and also provided capital for the sugar, mining and tobacco industries as well as the railways: see Marifeli Pérez-Stable, *The Cuban Revolution: Origins, Course and History* (New York: Oxford University Press, 1993), p. 15. There were two periods of direct rule, 1898–1902 and 1906–09, and also several instances of American intervention in Cuban internal affairs. The Platt Amendment, an appendix to the Cuban Constitution of 1902, which was imposed by the Americans as a condition of withdrawal, gave the United States the right to intervene militarily if order or stability (i.e., American interests) were threatened.

suffrage, stated that African former slaves were now Cubans and promised equality for all citizens. However, beneath the liberal democratic principles, old fears remained. Many of the white elite, themselves suffering from an inferiority complex vis-à-vis the Americans, felt the black population represented an obstacle to nation-building. The avenues of mobility opened to the Afro-Cubans in the wars were now blocked and the former slaves were given neither land nor new sources of employment. The drop in that population after the wars raised hopes that it would eventually disappear through *blanqueamiento* [whitening]. Racist employment practices and demographic whitening projects became a feature of successive Cuban governments. Thus, in contrast to other Spanish American former colonies, there was actually a rise in the peninsular population after independence.[10]

At the same time, the discourse of integrationism, developed during the independence struggle to organise disparate factions into a revolutionary movement, was carried over into the republican period. This sustained the notion that what held Afro-Cubans back was not their race but their lack of education or culture. The acceptance into white society of a few Afro-Cuban intellectuals and politicians, such as the mulattoes Martín Morúa Delgado[11] and Juan Gualberto Gómez, appeared to confirm this. Some prominent Afro-Cubans, while fighting for equal rights, also subscribed to the fallacy that minimising cultural differences would help to lessen discrimination against blacks. In their pursuit of assimilation, they dissociated themselves from their African forebears and strove to bring the masses up to their own level. The African-derived traditions were denigrated and linked with illiteracy. Both had to be combated by a modernising nation. In general, black Cubans made enormous strides and often outpaced their white compatriots. Unfortunately, this alone was not enough to ensure equality of opportunity.[12]

---

[10] In the 1899 census Afro-Cubans formed 33 per cent of the population. The 1902 and 1906 immigration laws restricted non-white immigration to Cuba. Between 1900 and 1929, approximately 900 000 people from Spain and the Canary Islands immigrated to Cuba. See Helg, *Our Rightful Share*, p. 104; Pérez, *Cuba*, p. 202.

[11] 1852–1910, journalist and politician. He collaborated with Martí and was a delegate to the 1901 Constitutional Assembly. In 1909 he became the first Afro-Cuban to be elected President of the Senate.

[12] Helg, *Our Rightful Share*, pp. 122, 244. In 1861, out of an Afro-Cuban population of 557 000, 600 children went to school; in 1919, out of a population of 784 000 the figure had increased to 61 000. Illiteracy levels among Afro-Cubans dropped dramatically from 72 per cent in 1899 to 55 per cent in 1907 and to 46.9 per cent in 1919. Whereas in 1880 there were only ten blacks with academic and professional qualifications, by 1907 there were 210. See Alberto Arredondo Gutiérrez, 'El negro cubano socio-económicamente considerado' (n.p. 1958 [typescript]), p. 9. Segregation in schooling was an ongoing issue as the better schools were privately run and exclusively white.

The battle between civilisation and barbarism

Despite its pseudo-scientific bias, the work of the white ethnographer Fernando Ortiz (1881–1969) was the first to acknowledge the African influence on national traits at a time when this was obscured by both the white elite and the Afro-Cuban intelligentsia. Ortiz' interest in Afro-Cuban practices was awakened while he was studying in Europe. At a visit to an exhibition at the Museo de Ultramar in Madrid he saw *ñáñigo* ritual objects which had been seized and brought to Spain. His legal training led him to plan a series of works on the *Hampa afrocubana* [Afro-Cuban underworld]. *Los negros brujos* [The Black Witchdoctors] (1906) drew on the Italian criminologist Lombroso's theory of atavism which assumed that criminals in civilised society display primitive biological characteristics. Ortiz modified the theory, seeking cultural rather than biological explanations for backwardness. He believed that the persistence of African atavisms could explain the apparent preponderance of Afro-Cubans in the criminal underworld.[13]

Like the Brazilian doctor of forensic medicine, Raimundo Nina Rodrigues, he was primarily concerned about the effect of an insufficiently de-Africanised black population on the modernising nation. Such research aimed at isolating the African cultural elements, relating them to their sources and showing how they differed from national culture in order to facilitate their elimination. Ortiz recommended the suppression of Afro-Cuban religious practices and claimed that religious atavism represented not only a threat to the population as a whole but also another form of enslavement for Afro-Cubans. Thus 'civilising' the black race was an act of altruism that would also minimise the risk of ethnic discord. Also, racial mixing, while impelling the Afro-Cuban towards progress, enabled the white lower classes to regress and explore their primitive impulses.[14]

---

[13] Ortiz, *Los negros brujos*, p. 17. Ortiz described some of the reactions to the book: 'It was generally received by whites with benevolence, but always with that complaisant and sometimes disdainful smile… Among coloured people the book only met with silence reflecting annoyance, broken by some writings of evident though sometimes restrained hostility.' Ortiz dismissed the Afro-Cuban reaction as self-denigration, conveniently disregarding the fact that his book associated blacks with a propensity for criminal activity: *Etnia y sociedad* (La Habana: Editorial de Ciencias Sociales), p. 138. One Afro-Cuban wrote to Ortiz in 1935 from abroad, complaining that a race that had fought for Cuba's freedom, and subsequently been excluded from employment, should be defamed in such a manner: see Diana Iznaga Beira, *Transculturación en Fernando Ortiz* (La Habana: Editorial de Ciencias Sociales, 1982), pp. 10–11.

[14] Ortiz, *Los negros brujos*, pp. 15, 150, 181.

The alleged battle between African 'barbarism' and Western civilisation was used to promote and justify repression when the elite became uncomfortable with Afro-Cuban challenges to the status quo. Indeed, despite the integrationist tendency, the frustration felt by some at the failure of political parties to represent their interests led to several attempts by Afro-Cubans to organise politically along racial lines. The response to these indicates the degree to which they were perceived as threatening by the establishment. The most significant was the Partido Independiente de Color (PIC) [Independent Party of Colour], founded in 1908, which demanded social reform and full equality for Afro-Cubans. Despite the fact that the PIC neither advocated separatism nor prevented whites from joining, it was denounced as racist and threatening to national unity.[15]

The party was declared illegal in 1910 and the fear of Haiti was revived when some members were imprisoned for allegedly conspiring to establish a black republic. In May 1912, an armed protest against the ban was organised in Oriente, a province where its support base was strong, and up to 4000 Afro-Cubans were massacred. The massacre was represented as a struggle between civilisation and barbarism.[16] This was in spite of the fact that while the Partido Independiente de Color did not follow the Afro-Cuban elite in attributing Afro-Cuban disadvantage solely to educational and cultural factors, neither did it privilege Afro-Cuban culture. On the contrary, *Previsión*, the party newspaper, proposed that *brujería* and traditional healing be eradicated as reminders of a servile past.[17]

Afro-Cuban choices: integrationism or separatism

The repression of 1912 discouraged further black separatist political organisation. Both the white and Afro-Cuban elites used the version of

---

[15] The PIC was the first black party in the hemisphere, preceding the Frente Negra Brasileira, which was set up in Sao Paulo in 1931: Helg, *Our Rightful Share*, p. 4.

[16] Tomás Fernández Robaina, *El negro en Cuba 1902–1958: apuntes para la historia de la lucha contra la discriminación racial* (La Habana: Editorial de Ciencias Sociales, 1990), pp. 68ff; Helg, *Our Rightful Share*, pp. 165, 218ff. Morúa Delgado presented an amendment to electoral law in February 1910, passed several months later, which proscribed the formation of racially exclusive political parties.

[17] There is, however, some degree of ambiguity as PIC material also made references to African influences in Spain and to Olorun-Olofi, the Yoruba supreme deity. In fact, a horse (associated by some with Changó) was the party's symbol. Some PIC members certainly held to Afro-Cuban traditions, for example, Lino D'Ou, the mulatto intellectual who became a congressman, was an *Abakuá* member. See Helg, *Our Rightful Share*, pp. 3, 148ff.

Cuban nationalism created in the wars of independence to stifle such movements by decrying them as unpatriotic. It left Afro-Cubans with a limited range of options. Some attempted to use what leverage they had within the mainstream political parties. It has also been suggested that the ongoing frustration of Afro-Cuban aspirations led to a flourishing of the Afro-Cuban cults, which permitted collective self-affirmation and resistance to the ideology of the white elite.[18]

In contrast to the prevailing tendency in the British Caribbean and the United States, few among the Afro-Cuban elite favoured black separatism or pan-Africanism as the strategy for achieving equality. When Marcus Garvey visited the country in 1921, most of the Afro-Cuban press denounced his race-based appeals. The director of the Club Atenas in Havana, Dr Miguel Angel Céspedes, stated that black Cubans did not share the pan-African ideal, as they had fought to create the Republic and had no other homeland. Nevertheless, by 1926, Cuba was the second largest country after the United States for UNIA (United Negro Improvement Association) activity. However, most of the branches were in the Oriente and Camagüey provinces, indicating that English-speaking Antillean migrant labourers formed a significant part of the membership. In 1928, President Machado, stating that there was no racial problem in Cuba, banned the UNIA under the Morúa Law.[19]

Du Bois' NAACP (National Association for the Advancement of Colored People), which, unlike Garvey's movement, included whites, was seen as a more appropriate model for Afro-Cubans.[20] Afro-Cuban intellectuals continued to recall the ideals of Martí in their demands for social justice, fearing the imposition of American-style segregation and Jim Crow laws. The poet Nicolás Guillén criticised North American black separatism in an article entitled 'El camino de Harlem' (1929). Contributors to the column 'Ideales de una Raza' [Ideals of a Race] echoed Martí and Juan Gualberto Gómez: Cuban blacks were, first and foremost, Cubans. As Gustavo Urrutia wrote,

> Cut off from his native land by slavery, he now has nothing in common with Africa, neither colour, language or mentality. He does not love Africa nor is he loved by the Africans and his

---

[18] Thomas, *Cuba*, p. 524; Helg, *Our Rightful Share*, pp. 246–7.
[19] Tomás Fernández Robaina, 'Marcus Garvey in Cuba: Urrutia, Cubans and Black Nationalism', in L. Brock & D. Castañeda Fuertes (eds.), *Between Race and Empire: African-Americans and Cubans Before the Cuban Revolution* (Philadelphia: Temple UP, 1998), pp. 120–8; Rupert Lewis, *Garvey: His Work and Impact* (Mona: UWI, 1988).
[20] G. Urrutia, 'Armonías', *Diario de la Marina*, 14 April 1929.

civilization does not evoke them... The black man of the Americas feels more a patriot than black.[21]

With the rise of the Cuban labour movement from the 1920s the political options of Afro-Cubans were extended, but increasingly along class rather than racial lines. The Communist Party, founded in 1925, actively recruited black members and gave them positions of leadership.[22] Although the Communist Party was the only Cuban political party to make race central to its platform, it followed the Communist International definition of blacks as a national rather than a racial minority. A resolution at the Second Communist Congress of 1934 proposed a zone of self-determination or *franja negra* [black belt] in Oriente, the region with the highest proportion of blacks. Afro-Cubans rejected the proposal, insisting that they were Cubans, not foreigners. [23]

The co-option and repression of Afro-Cuban culture

The attempts by the elite to establish Cuba as a modern, civilised nation notwithstanding, the republican period (and indeed all periods in Cuban history) saw an oscillation between the political functionalisation and suppression of African-derived cultural and religious practices. While few Afro-Cubans were able to hold political office, white candidates courted Afro-Cuban voters, one-third of the electorate, by using cultural forms such as *comparsas*, carnival parade groups which were banned in the 1910s, and symbols of their religions in rallies. Ortiz deplored the fact that political clientelism, especially in rural areas, prompted the authorities to give tacit permission for religious ceremonies, held, as during the colonial period, under the guise of innocent African pastimes.

---

[21] *Diario de la Marina*, 9 February 1930. Gustavo Urrutia (1881–1958), the Afro-Cuban architect and journalist, was one of the most important black intellectuals of the Republican period. The 'Ideales' column in the Sunday edition of the newspaper *Diario de la Marina* ran from 1928 to 1931. The column was expanded to an entire page devoted to black topics and published evidence of the progress of blacks both in and outside Cuba: Fernández Robaina, *El negro*, p. 125.

[22] Some Afro-Cuban Communist Party members and union leaders in the 1930s and 1940s, including Lazaro Peña, leader of the tobacco workers, and Aracelio Iglesias, leader of the Maritime Workers Union, were known to have practised Afro-Cuban religions.

[23] According to the 1938 census, eight *municipios* [municipalities] in Oriente province had a population that totalled 58.3 per cent black and mulatto. The national average was (allegedly) 22.4 per cent: Fernández Robaina, *El negro*, p. 136.

The Afro-Cuban intellectual Rómulo Lachatañeré was more concerned about the cynical exploitation of Afro-Cubans for political advantage.[24]

On the other side of the coin were the systematic campaigns against traditions of African origin launched at various times throughout the Republic. The first Cuban government initiated one such campaign in 1902. The press revived the ever-present fear of black peril by reporting cases of *brujería* [witchcraft] in Havana and Matanzas. These alleged that white children were being abducted and murdered for ritual purposes by practitioners of Afro-Cuban religions.[25]

In spite of the fact that few cases came to trial, all Afro-Cuban religious practices were associated with criminality. However, the existing penal code offered no legal devices to deal with the problem apart from laws relating to illicit association or criminal activity. As religious freedom was enshrined in the Constitution, the officials who appealed to Congress to declare *brujería* a crime were forced to acknowledge that Afro-Cuban practices were religions, albeit at odds with modern civilisation. This meant that their suppression could only be justified by asserting that the practices impelled practitioners to commit crimes. Repression was made to appear altruistic: as society was cleansed of the practice, believers would be enabled to ascend to successive zones of culture.[26]

The anti-*brujería* campaigns clearly reflected concern about the image of Cuba as a modernising nation. They underscored the apparent cultural distinctions between white and black Cubans, providing reassurance for a new ruling class that had an inferiority complex towards the United States. The *brujería* scare also presented prominent Afro-Cuban intellectuals of the period with a dilemma. The Afro-Cuban newspaper *El Nuevo Criollo* (1904–06) accused the mainstream press of using black *brujos* to stigmatise the whole race. However, rather than questioning the accusations, the paper attacked 'Africanisms' as

---

[24] 'The drum bothers them less when it is a question of politically courting the lower classes', Fernando Ortiz, *Los cabildos y la fiesta afrocubanos del Día de Reyes* (La Habana: Editorial de Ciencias Sociales 1992 [1921, 1920–5]), p. 22; *Los negros brujos*, pp. 149–50; Rómulo Lachatañeré, *El sistema religioso de los afrocubanos* (La Habana: Editorial de Ciencias Sociales, 1992), pp. 313–4, 402.

[25] During the colonial period, it was mainly the *Abakuá* secret society, whose members were known as *ñáñigos*, which experienced persistent official repression. The authorities appeared less concerned about the members of the other Afro-Cuban religions: Helg, *Our Rightful Share*, p. 30. One study of a number of the cases between 1904 and 1923 reveals that three of the crimes were committed by whites who dismembered the corpses in such a manner that the murders would appear to relate to *brujería*. In most of other cases the accused Afro-Cubans were released for lack of evidence: see Ernesto Alvarez Chávez, *El crimen de la niña Cecilia: la brujería en Cuba como fenómeno social (1902–25)* (La Habana: Editorial de Ciencias Sociales, 1991), pp. 27–9.

[26] Ortiz, *Los negros brujos*, p. 193. See also Rafael Roche y Monteagudo, *La policía y sus misterios*, 2nd ed. (La Habana: Impr. de la Rambla, 1914), p. 98.

barbaric and savage practices. *Previsión*, the organ of the Partido Independiente de Color, was critical of the scaremongering of the *brujería* campaigns but denounced dance and drumming as manifestations of African atavism. Afro-Cuban intellectuals did nothing to challenge the image of the black *brujo*. On the contrary, by associating themselves with Western culture and values and by making no attempt to reassert the value of the African heritage for Cuban culture, they dissociated themselves from the masses. The *raza de color* was further fragmented into 'civilised' and 'barbarian' camps.[27]

This division was highlighted by a series of articles in the newspaper *El Día*, which had invited prominent Afro-Cubans to suggest a remedy to the problem of *brujería*. Several contributors suggested it was pointless to ask *negros cultos* [educated blacks] to deal with the problem when they had no influence over the lower classes, who in fact despised them for their 'refinement'. Most correspondents emphasised that the persistence of *brujería* was a reflection of the moral and cultural atmosphere of the whole nation rather than of one race. Ramiro Neyra Lanza, the editor of *La Antorcha*, a black weekly published in Havana, pointed out:

> Neither rumba nor *brujería* are problems of the black alone, both are problems which need to be solved by all Cubans.[28]

Presenting the practices as an Afro-Cuban problem conveniently overlooked the fact that whites, not just members of the lower classes but also the rich and powerful, were also the clients and protectors of the *brujos*, 'some because they genuinely believe and others because it suits them to do so'. Thus public condemnation frequently went hand in hand with private participation. One correspondent, Amada Rosa de Cárdenas, estimated that 70 per cent of Cuban homes displayed objects relating to *brujería*.[29] Most felt that the solution was not repression but education. Unlike their counterparts in the British Caribbean or North America, the white and Afro-Cuban elites did not look to Christianity as the answer to the problem. Historically, and in contrast to other parts of Latin America, Roman Catholicism had never been the religion of the people and there was a strong anti-clerical, freethinking tradition.[30]

---

[27] Helg, *Our Rightful Share*, pp. 114–6, 135–7, 148–50, 244–5.
[28] 'El problema de la brujería tratado por los hombres de color', *El Día*, 3 September 1918, p. 1; 7 September 1918, back page.
[29] *El Día*, 25 September 1918, p. 1.
[30] Ortiz claimed that the only essential difference between Catholicism and fetishism was in the sphere of ethics, as the gods and priests of *brujería* were immoral. He also believed that an evangelical crusade would not uproot fetishism; on the contrary, the propensity to merge things might instead create a new sect: *Los negros brujos*, pp. 135, 137, 199. Lino D'Ou wrote: 'All religious rites are harmful because they lead the believer into moral slavery' [1939], *Papeles del teniente coronel Lino D'Ou* (Havana: UNEAC, 1983), p. 179.

Only after another outburst of anti-*brujo* hysteria in 1919, which led to more indiscriminate attacks on blacks and a lynching in Regla, a suburb of Havana, did Afro-Cuban intellectuals display greater solidarity with the popular classes. *La Antorcha* blamed racist editorials in the mainstream newspapers for the upsurge of violence. The elitist *sociedad de color* Club Atenas in Havana issued a manifesto accusing newspapers of using the pretext of *brujería* to justify indiscriminate attacks on blacks. This was endorsed by Afro-Cuban societies throughout the island.[31]

The scare moved eastwards in the 1920s and once again it was clear that the repression had a political motivation. This time it was directed at black migrants from other Caribbean islands such as Haiti and Jamaica who thwarted the whitening project and were believed to be introducing even more savage African practices.[32]

Afrocubanismo

Only in the 1920s did there emerge a movement that did not advocate the wholesale elimination of the African cultural heritage. The *afrocubanismo* literary and artistic movement was an attempt to co-opt Afro-Cuban forms and make them 'respectable' in order to create a national culture. This was part of a programme of national renovation that arose in response both to the increased American domination of Cuba and to the social and political fragmentation caused by a series of corrupt and incompetent governments.[33] *Afrocubanismo* also reflected external trends such as the European *vogue nègre* and the North American fashion for 'Negro' music and artistic forms. However, unlike the Harlem Renaissance and Caribbean *négritude*, it was a predominantly

---

[31] Helg, *Our Rightful Share*, pp. 242–3.

[32] Alvarez Chávez, *El crimen*, p. 33. The ban on black immigration was lifted in 1913 when President Gómez allowed the American United Fruit Company to bring in Haitian labourers. The sugar plantations had expanded eastwards to Oriente and Camagüey, zones which had the lowest populations. There was a shortage of labour and around 150 000 Jamaicans and Haitians entered over ten years (Alejandro De la Fuente, '"With all and for all": race, inequality and politics in Cuba, 1900–1930' [PhD thesis, University of Pittsburgh, 1996], pp. 63, 92–3).

[33] The search for an indigenous basis to national culture was found in other parts of Latin America and often went hand in hand with a tendency towards a reactionary romanticism which opposed modernisation. The novel *Ariel* (1900) by the Uruguayan journalist José Enrique Rodó stimulated resentment against North American cultural influence and awakened a desire for cultural affirmation, a defence of 'Latinity' and a search for national 'essences': Edwin Williamson, *The Penguin History of Latin America* (Harmondsworth: Penguin, 1992), p. 305.

white movement. Many of the writers of *negrista* poetry were white Cubans, such as Alejo Carpentier, Ramón Guirao and Emilio Ballagas. The Afro-Cuban writers who emerged included Marcelino Arozarena, Eusebia Cosme, Ignacio Villa and, of course, Nicolás Guillén, who was hailed as the national poet after the 1959 Revolution.

Guillén's work exposed the issue of racism and the undervaluing of the African component of Cuban culture. However, his poetry moved from a vindication of black culture to promoting the idea of a synthesis of Cuba's multiple heritage through *mulatez* – his term, which means 'mulattoness'. He rejected *négritude* as a divisive ideology and followed the established Cuban integrationist pattern in seeking a conciliatory rather than a divisive response to the problem of racism:

> ... the two races which emerge on the surface of the island, and which appear separate, stretch out an underwater hook like those deep bridges which secretly join two continents ... the spirit of Cuba is *mestizo*. And from the spirit to the skin the definitive colour will come to us. Some day they will say: 'Cuban colour'.[34]

The *afrocubanismo* movement followed in the tradition of Martí by extolling an elusive national unity. However, by attempting to clean up and universalise black forms, it did not remove negative attitudes towards them or the people who had produced them. A degree of cultural recognition did not go hand in hand with social equality.

Furthermore, the movement was not supported by the black middle class. Members of the Club Atenas were offended by Guillén's *Motivos del Son*, which they felt exposed the abhorrent voices of the Afro-Cuban underworld.[35] Others believed that *afrocubanismo* was a passing craze. Lachatañeré pointed out that the First World War had left the West psychologically depleted and it now looked to blacks for a strong infusion of 'cultured savagery'. European trends had inspired white Cubans to romanticise something they did not attempt to understand and which they would again condemn when it suited them to do so. According to Urrutia, it was a spectacle and a form of cultural tourism for whites and thus represented yet another form of servitude for blacks. White Cubans could both dip into the 'magical' powers of

---

[34] N. Guillén, *Obra poética, 1920–1972* (La Habana: Editorial Arte y Literatura, 1974), p. 114; Alfred Melon, *Identité nationale, idéologie, poésie et critique à Cuba (1902–1959)* (La Habana: Casa de las Américas, 1992), p. 605.
[35] Vera Kutzinski, *Sugar's Secrets: Race and the Erotics of Cuban Nationalism* (Charlottesville: University of Virginia Press, 1993), pp. 152–3; Nancy Morejón, *Nación y mestizaje en Nicolás Guillén* (La Habana: UNEAC, 1982), p. 206 n. 135.

the Afro-Cubans or pursue the modernist quest for primitive energy. In this way, a repressed culture could come to represent a repressed element of the white psyche. Much later, another Afro-Cuban intellectual, Walterio Carbonell, would observe that the conflict between the populations of Spanish and African origin appeared to diminish in the face of North American culture. Whites then adopted African music as their own and turned to the religions they had condemned.[36]

What the *afrocubanismo* movement did was acknowledge the centrality of the Afro-Cuban component of Cuban culture and also sanction its existence, albeit in an altered state. By 1940, however, the trend had passed and it had died out as a literary movement.

Cultural synthesis and the fight against racism

The *afrocubanismo* movement reflected the influence of Ortiz' pioneering work. By the 1930s he himself had abandoned his tableau of Afro-Cuban criminality and was influenced by a new set of foreign ideas, this time British and North American anthropological trends such as functionalism and culturalism, which challenged ethnocentric prejudices. In 1936, he founded the Society for Afro-Cuban Studies and the journal *Estudios Afrocubanos* (1937–40, 1945–46).

Ortiz' work moved from simply looking at the African origins of Afro-Cuban culture to the process of cultural syncretism. One important result was his theory of transculturation, which appeared in *Contrapunteo del tabaco y del azúcar* (1940). Ortiz found ethnocentric the assumption of Herskovits' theory of acculturation that the superior culture would induce the transformation of supposedly inferior cultures. Transculturation, in contrast, referred to the process whereby two cultures (in the case of Cuba, the Hispanic and the African) mutually influence each other to create something wholly new which contains elements from each.

He believed that the two would fuse to create a new culture and a community where the end product was a synthesis, a Cuban-ness in which purely racial factors would have lost their capacity for divisiveness. His cultural model was represented by a Cuban dish, the *ajiaco*:

> The characteristic thing about Cuba is that, as it is an *ajiaco*, its people are not a finished stew, but a constant process of cooking.

---

[36] Lachatañeré, *El sistema religioso*, p. 384; Gustavo Urrutia, *Cuarto (sic) charlas radiofónicas* (La Habana: n.p., 1935), pp. 6–7. Walterio Carbonell, *Crítica. Como surgió la cultura nacional* (La Habana: Editorial Yaka, 1960), pp. 25–6.

In contrast to the melting pot, each component in the mixture retains its identity. This conscious Cuban-ness, like that of Martí and others, dismissed racial categories.[37]

Nevertheless, Ortiz followed other Creole intellectuals in privileging the Hispanic component as 'our cultural trunk' and regarding African culture as an *aporte* [contribution] to Cuban culture. This ignored the fact that between 1800 and 1850, the majority of the population had been African. Ortiz also limited the Afro-Cuban contribution to three spheres: art, religion and the 'collective emotive nature'.[38] He identified the 'universal' elements in Afro-Cuban culture and compared Yoruba and *Abakuá* forms with Greco-Roman culture. This tended to imply that they were outmoded and, unlike modern European culture, had no future except as part of the national folklore.

The work of Ortiz and the influence of the *afrocubanismo* movement made some Afro-Cuban cultural forms more respectable. By the mid-1930s, Afro-Cuban music began to be performed publicly. In 1936, Ortiz organized the first public concert of Afro-Cuban religious music using consecrated *batá* drums. The following year, there was a call to reinstate the *comparsas*, which had been banned at various times in the 1910s and 1920s. This was because the growing tourist trade prompted a call for local colour.[39] The Afro-Cubans Salvador García Agüero and Angel Pinto of the Asociación Adelante declared that it was a way for the exploited masses to express themselves. A small group of Afro-Cubans dissented. They called such expressions of Africanity 'a clumsy excuse for humiliating and annoying a society whose zeal for social and cultural self-improvement is evident and undeniable'.[40]

The folklorisation of Afro-Cuban culture

One of the few among Afro-Cuban intellectuals of the period who questioned the prevailing ideology of integrationism and, even more

---

[37] Ortiz, *Etnia y sociedad* (La Habana: Editorial de Ciencias Sociales 1993), pp. 141–3, 6, 7.

[38] Ortiz, *Etnia y sociedad*, pp. 13, 15.

[39] See Rosalie Schwartz, *Pleasure Island: Tourism and Temptation in Cuba* (Lincoln and London: University of Nebraska Press, 1997), pp. 82, 87, on how Afro-Cuban culture became essential to both nationalistic and touristic image builders from the 1930s onwards. However, in the late 1940s, when Yoruba music and drums were broadcast on Radio Cadena Suaritos, this was attacked as propaganda for the 'religion of the blacks' and a cardinal forced the Minister of Communications to end the transmissions: *Gaceta de Cuba* 167 (1978), pp. 13–14.

[40] Juan Jiménez Pastrana, *Salvador García Agüero* (La Habana: Editorial de Ciencias Sociales, 1985), p. 93.

remarkably, publicly defended not only Afro-Cuban culture but also the religions, was Gustavo Urrutia. In a series of radio talks broadcast in 1935, he deplored both the failure of Martí's doctrine and the belief of *negros ilustrados* [learned blacks] that, in order to integrate, they must internalise the social and cultural codes of the dominant group. Urrutia stressed the need to overcome this tendency to despise their culture:

> Just as it is the Afro-Cuban whom they seek to embarrass and coerce because of a supposedly inherited inferiority and degrading racial defects, for this reason it is incumbent upon the Afro-Cuban to know thoroughly and to present and explain the religious, moral and artistic values of his black grandparents, which are no worse than those of his white grandparents in terms of either morality or spiritual refinement.[41]

The irony was that this tendency persisted at a time when black cultural traditions, drums, dance and ritual were revolutionising Western culture. As Urrutia pointed out, in the case of Cuba, a celebration of African culture was not an optional extra:

> The citizen of a negroid country who only knows the white branch of his people cannot consider himself perfectly educated.[42]

Of course, the problem was that those Afro-Cubans who *did* extol their racial and cultural heritage were often accused of advocating the practice of Afro-Cuban religions instead of focusing on the achievements of Afro-Cuban doctors, teachers, musicians and artists. As Urrutia's programmes broadcast music and drumming, he felt compelled to point out:

> We are neither promoting nor eradicating African *ñañiguismo* and *santería*. We are simply presenting and explaining them as religious and social phenomena that exist in our midst, that are not degrading but moral, and which cannot be uprooted from our customs and our habits by decree.[43]

Yet, in common with others of his time, Urrutia adhered to the view that as Afro-Cubans advanced culturally, manifestations of Afro-Cuban culture would gradually disappear and merely be preserved as folkloric elements. Black Cubans needed to acquire technical skills and a

---

[41] Urrutia, *Cuarto charlas*, p. 18. I am indebted to Tomás Fernández Robaina for providing me with a copy of the rare published version of these talks.
[42] Urrutia, *Cuarto charlas*, p. 19.
[43] Ibid.

university education in order to surmount the obstacle of prejudice. Urrutia drew attention to the dilemma faced by those who sought to acknowledge their African heritage while simultaneously following the path towards modernity and social ascent. Yet while recognising that Afro-Cuban culture and religion should not be allowed to hold back the masses, he felt it should not be rejected by the black intelligentsia, as it so often was.

Rómulo Lachatañeré, a contributor to Ortiz' journal *Estudios afrocubanos*, was the first Afro-Cuban intellectual to write extensively on Afro-Cuban religious practices. He was critical of the so-called anthropological studies in which black Cubans were purely a subject for speculations on criminality. These both ignored the views of Afro-Cubans themselves and misrepresented and trivialised the practices. While he acknowledged that Ortiz had made Afro-Cuban culture a legitimate area of study, his criticism certainly included Ortiz' work.[44]

Like Urrutia, he also reproached those Afro-Cubans who distanced themselves from their cultural heritage:

> The survivals of the slave past which still exist today among the Afro-Cuban population should not be regarded as an onerous burden of slavery, nor as a factor of backwardness, but as a positive and valuable element when such reminiscences express the essence of the cultures of the peoples from whom the slave was seized.[45]

But he adhered to the prevailing view that progress might demand that the cultural and religious forms survive only as folklore and believed that 'when these express the vices of those primitive societies they should be corrected in accordance with human and scientific criteria'.[46]

Ortiz' sister-in-law Lydia Cabrera (1900–91) also wrote extensively on Afro-Cuban religious forms. Like him, she developed her interest during her studies in oriental art in Paris in the late 1920s, when she was influenced by the European enthusiasm for the 'primitive'. It was only in 1954, after she had been back in Cuba for almost two decades, that her most famous work on Afro-Cuban religious practices, *El monte*, was published.[47]

---

[44] Originally from Santiago, Lachatañeré (1909–1952) was the grandson of Flor Crombet, one of the heroes of the 1868 war. *Oh, mío Yemayá* (1938) is a collection of the myths of the *orishas*, while the *Manual de santería* (1942) offers a description of the practices.
[45] Lachatañeré, *El sistema*, p. 195
[46] Lachatañeré, *El sistema*, p. 414.
[47] Her first book, *Contes negres* (1936), was published in Paris. She also translated Césaire's *Cahier d'un retour au pays natal* into Spanish (1943).

Unlike Ortiz or Lachatañeré, Cabrera did not relate her study of Afro-Cuban phenomena to their African origins. She relied extensively on informants, many of them second-generation Africans, and their collective religious memory. Cabrera was aware that living in a 'civilised' environment did not lead to a decline in Afro-Cuban religious practice:

> They still react with the same primitive mentality as their forebears in this environment of ours which is impregnated with magic to an unimaginable degree; this despite public schooling and university, or a Catholicism which perfectly accommodates their beliefs and which has not, at bottom, altered the religious ideas of the majority.[48]

Against the evolutionist theories of the time, Cabrera concluded that Cuban blacks, in spirit, were no less African than they had been in the past. She also perceived that Africanity did not only manifest itself in skin colour.[49]

Despite differences of methodology and sympathy, Ortiz, Lachatañeré and Cabrera all examined Afro-Cuban religions from an increasingly esthetic angle. This replaced the moral value judgement of Ortiz' early work.[50] The efforts of Cabrera and Lachatañeré created an Afro-Cuban literature that could be compared to classical fables or myths. Wherever possible, the mythology, music and dance were treated as arts independent of religious practice. Like the *afrocubanismo* movement, this represented a necessary compromise; it suggested ways in which Afro-Cuban culture could be made 'respectable'.[51]

Although selected components of Afro-Cuban culture began to be accepted as part of the national culture, as the Republic progressed, a question mark still hung over their ability to exist in the modern world. The political and economic conditions of Afro-Cubans did not improve significantly. The 1940 Constitution, which many felt should herald a new era, contained clauses prohibiting racial discrimination, but these were never backed by legislation. The Afro-Cuban elite continued to campaign for equal rights. A few groups promoted self-help and looked to the example of black American commercial ventures and educational

---

[48] Lydia Cabrera, *El monte* (La Habana: Ed SI-MAR, 1996), p. 11.
[49] Cabrera, *El monte*, pp. 13, 3.
[50] See Erwin Dianteill, *Le savant et le santero: naissance de l'étude scientifique des religions afro-cubaines (1906–1954)* (Paris: L'Harmattan, 1995), pp. 56ff.
[51] Ortiz had referred to this procession of selection and modification of 'African' customs such as the *comparsa*: 'Why must we lose it when we can transform it, improve it, and incorporate it, by purifying it, into our national folklore?' *Los cabildos*, p. 24.

establishments. One such was the Federación de Sociedades Negras de Cuba, which had a small and mainly urban membership.[52]

Juan René Betancourt Bencomo was one of the few Afro-Cuban intellectuals to be critical of integrationism both as an ideology and for its effect on the black psyche.[53] He pointed out that it could and usually did conceal a policy of *blanqueamiento*. He warned of the dangers facing Afro-Cubans who felt that assimilation was the route to progress, as this meant erasing themselves. Betancourt was aware that it was not lack of culture or preparation that accounted for discrimination against blacks, but simply the fact that they were black. He lamented that some had a superficial knowledge of their religion and were ashamed of it, when it was the product of a highly cultivated and cultured people.[54] What set him apart from other Afro-Cuban intellectuals, however, was that he went beyond a defence of Afro-Cuban practices to show concern about their dilution into a national whole:

> For a race like ours, which has been taken away from its geographic base and deprived of its vernacular language; without an economic foundation; despised and deceived, if it is also deprived of its religion and traditions there will be no reason to unite to fight for its destiny ... the religion which suits a people best is its own.[55]

Betancourt pointed out that something valuable would be lost if watered-down forms of the Afro-Cuban religions and traditions were used to symbolise *cubanía* at the expense of their role in providing a sense of *black* self-worth.

Conclusion

After independence, the perceived threat to the new nation of 'African barbarism' was often used to justify repressive measures of social control against Afro-Cubans. The 'otherness' of the former slave population was increasingly expressed in cultural terms, and adherence to the African heritage, despite living in a 'civilised' environment, implied not only inherent backwardness but also wilful criminality. As the twentieth

---

[52] Pedro Serviat, *El problema negro en Cuba y su solución definitiva* (La Habana: Ed. Política, 1986), pp. 129, 135–6; Fernández Robaina, *El Negro*, pp. 150–1.
[53] In January 1959, Betancourt became President of the Federación Nacional de Sociedades Negras de Cuba. Shortly afterwards, racially exclusive societies were disbanded for purposes of national unity and Betancourt, like some other Afro-Cuban middle-class spokespeople, went into exile.
[54] Betancourt Bencomo, Juan René, *Doctrina negra: La única teoría certera contra la discriminación racial en Cuba* (La Habana: P. Fernández, 1955), p. 71.
[55] Betancourt, *Doctrina negra*, p. 65.

century progressed, research into the processes of cultural syncretism opened the way for the more overt co-option of African-derived forms into the national culture. Cuban identity was proudly defined as Creole and *mestizo* or mulatto. This reflected a renewed nationalism that sought ways to differentiate Cuba from Europe and the United States.

While offering a degree of cultural recognition, a top-down appropriation involved a selection of the elements deemed appropriate. The distinction between 'high' culture and folklore, into which the Afro-Cuban forms fell, persists today. The forms themselves continued to be regarded as traditional, at odds with modernity and therefore doomed to die out, when in fact the dynamism and vitality of subaltern cultural production has ensured their successful transmission and recreation in changing social environments.

As a result of ongoing processes of cultural exchange, the Afro-Cuban heritage is not exclusively black, nor is the cultural heritage of black Cubans exclusively African. While marked off from 'white' society as a sphere of supposedly powerful mystical energies, 'African' cultural forms have provided an alternative set of cultural practices that can be activated by different sectors of the population in different ways, at different times. As a number of Afro-Cuban intellectuals pointed out during the *brujería* scare, predicating cultural allegiances on the basis of race could often prove misleading. They themselves rejected religious practices of African origin, while members of the white elite frequently participated in them.

For much of Cuba's history a critical progressive discussion of the African heritage was made impossible by the social balance of power. The 1959 Revolution carried over the discourse of integrationism, stating as before that Cuba's racial problem did not exist, this time because the Revolution had solved it. This justified curbing Afro-Cuban participation in black consciousness movements such as those that emerged in the United States and the Anglophone Caribbean in the 1960s. However, Afro-Cubans are still under-represented in certain areas, including the political leadership, and racial stereotypes prove extremely persistent. Recent research suggests that despite attempts to create a more representative and inclusive *cubanía* [Cuban-ness], esthetic patterns often exclude blacks in their determination of what is pleasing or universally relevant.[56] As at previous periods in Cuba's history, blackness can either be subsumed under a rhetoric of *mestizaje* or used as a discriminating factor, and Afro-Cubans and their cultural forms can be located both inside and outside of Cuban-ness.

---

[56] See Juan Antonio Alvarado Ramos, 'Relaciones raciales en Cuba. Notas de investigación', *Temas* (1996), pp. 37–43.

10 Reconsidering creolisation and creole societies

O. Nigel Bolland

I

The purpose of this paper[1] is to explore some of the strengths and limitations of the concepts of 'creolisation' and 'creole societies'[2] for analysing cultural changes in the Caribbean. The concept of creolisation has been widely used to analyse the process in which new cultures and societies emerged during the colonial period. Afro-Creole culture, for example, although derived from African and European[3] elements, is nevertheless distinctly Caribbean.[4] This emphasis on the originality of creole cultures emerged at a significant moment in the ideological decolonisation of the Caribbean, in the 1970s, when the analysis of the

---

[1] Among the people who have influenced and encouraged me to think along the lines of this paper I wish particularly to thank Viranjini Munasinghe, who invited me to share my early reconsiderations at a seminar of the Department of Anthropology at Cornell University in 1999. Some of these ideas were tried out at the conference at the Centre for Caribbean Studies, University of Warwick, in 2000, and further developed at the conference called (Re)Thinking Caribbean Culture at the University of the West Indies, Cave Hill, Barbados, in 2001. I wish to thank Gad Heuman and David Trotman for inviting me to the former and Aviston Downes and Richard Clarke for hosting me at the latter. I also want to thank Anton Allahar for taking the trouble to send me some valuable comments on this paper. Although many people helped me, none may be held responsible for the remaining shortcomings of this essay.

[2] I use the capital C for the proper noun Creole, referring to the individuals or the ethnic group so identified, and lower case c for the adjective creole, and for creolisation.

[3] 'African' and 'European' are terms that refer to hundreds of quite different and continually changing cultures. I acknowledge my oversimplification in using them, and terms such as 'African heritage' and 'European tradition', and I do not intend to reify or essentialise them.

[4] See E.K. Brathwaite, *The Development of Creole Society in Jamaica, 1770–1820* (Oxford: Clarendon, 1971); R.D.E. Burton, *Afro-Creole: Power, Opposition, and Play in the Caribbean* (Ithaca: Cornell University, 1997); B.L. Moore, *Cultural Power, Resistance and Pluralism: Colonial Guyana, 1838–1900* (Mona: University of the West Indies, 1995); R.M. Nettleford, *Mirror, Mirror: Identity, Race and Protest in Jamaica* (Kingston: Collins and Sangster, 1970); O. Patterson, 'Context and choice in ethnic allegiance: a theoretical framework and Caribbean case study', in N. Glazer and D.P. Moynihan (eds.), *Ethnicity Theory and Experience* (Cambridge, Mass.: Harvard University, 1975), pp. 305–49.

origins of a common culture in a 'creole community' became part of the process of nation building.

The concept of creolisation is important because it avoids both the view that enslaved Africans were stripped of their cultures and acculturated into a European culture, and also the view that evidence of the African heritage in the Caribbean lies only in 'retentions' or 'survivals'. Cultural change was not a one-way process in which colonised peoples passively absorbed the culture of the dominant Europeans, and the study of African influences should not be limited to the search for African retentions as if they are items under glass cases in a museum. The use of the concepts of creolisation and creole societies by anthropologists, historians and other scholars has successfully emphasised the active role of Caribbean peoples and the importance of African cultural traditions in shaping the new and distinctive cultures of the region. More recently, several scholars have explored the question of the creolisation of Chinese[5] and (East) Indians in the Caribbean,[6] by which is generally meant their assimilation into creole culture and society. The question must be raised as to whether the same concept that is used to describe the development of creole societies in terms of their distinctive Afro-Creole culture can be used to analyse the continuing interaction and transformation of all the different cultures in the Caribbean.

In an earlier paper[7] I argued that creolisation 'is not a homogenizing process, but rather a process of *contention*'[8] in societies that are

---

[5] C. Ho, '"Hold the chow mein, gimme soca": Creolization of the Chinese in Guyana, Trinidad and Jamaica', *Amerasia* 15:2 (1989), pp. 3–25.

[6] P. Mohammed, 'The "creolization" of Indian women in Trinidad', in S. Ryan (ed.), *Trinidad and Tobago: The Independence Experience, 1962–1987* (St. Augustine: Institute of Social and Economic Research, University of the West Indies, 1988), pp. 381–97; V. Munasinghe, *Callaloo or Tossed Salad? East Indians and the Cultural Politics of Identity in Trinidad* (Ithaca: Cornell University, 2001); S. Puri, 'Canonized hybridities, resistant hybridities: chutney soca, carnival, and the politics of nationalism', in B.J. Edmondson (ed.), *Caribbean Romances: The Politics of Regional Representation* (Charlottesville: University of Virginia, 1999), pp. 12–38; R. Reddock, 'Contestations over culture, class, gender and identity in Trinidad and Tobago: "the little tradition"', *Caribbean Quarterly* 44:1 & 2 (1998), pp. 62–80; N.M. Sampath, 'An evaluation of the "creolization"of Trinidad East Indian adolescent masculinity', in K. Yelvington (ed.), *Trinidad Ethnicity* (London: Macmillan, 1993), pp. 235–53; V.A. Shepherd, *Transients to Settlers: The Experience of Indians in Jamaica 1845–1950* (Leeds: Peepal Tree, 1994).

[7] Written for a conference at the Centre for Caribbean Studies at the University of Warwick in 1987: 'Creolization and creole societies: a cultural nationalist view of Caribbean social history', in A. Hennessy (ed.), *Intellectuals in the Twentieth Century Caribbean Vol. 1, Spectre of the New Class: the Commonwealth Caribbean* (London: Macmillan, 1992), pp. 50–79.

[8] Ibid., p. 72.

characterised by extreme social inequalities and pervasive conflicts. The concept should be used in a dialectical analysis that takes account of the social forces and formations that are related to cultural changes. In this paper that argument is my starting point.

This paper distinguishes between analytic and ideological usages of the concepts of creolisation and creole societies. M.G. Smith distinguished between the analytic and ideological functions of the concept culture.[9] Although scholars may use a concept analytically, the same concept is used in an ideological way in the culture which they study. What Smith said of the concept culture is true for the concepts 'creole' and 'creolisation', which may be used analytically in the scholarly study of cultures and societies, but are words that are used in those societies with an ideological function. We need to be aware of the problem that arises when these distinct usages of the concepts overlap.

This paper begins by comparing the dualistic and dialectical versions of creolisation that are derived from European philosophical traditions and suggests some comparisons with more 'organic' African perspectives. The paper then critiques the implications of the concept of creolisation when it is used in connection with people and cultures other than those of African and European origin. The analytic use of creolisation and creole society has been indispensable in the study of cultural change in the African diaspora. The ideological use of the concepts, however, when they are tied exclusively to Afro-Creole cultures and societies, obscures the interconnections and cultural symbiosis that exist between 'overlapping diasporas'.[10]

II

My earlier paper distinguishes between the dualistic and dialectical conceptions of creolisation. The former appears in terms of a 'black/white dichotomy', 'the juxtaposition of master and slave',[11] and the dichotomy of 'colonial' and 'creole' societies,[12] as if these categories are independent of each other. When these are conceived as if they are pairs of separate 'elements', the interaction between them is viewed mechanically and the process of creolisation appears to be simply a blending of elements borrowed from each part. The dialectical perspective, on the

---

[9] M.G. Smith, *The Plural Society of the British West Indies* (Berkeley: University of California, 1965), pp. 1–2.
[10] E. Lewis, 'To turn as on a pivot: writing African Americans into a history of overlapping diasporas', *American Historical Review* 100:3 (1995), pp. 765–87.
[11] Brathwaite, *The Development of Creole Society in Jamaica*, pp. xiv, xvi.
[12] Ibid., p. 101.

contrary, draws attention to the contradictions and conflicts that are inherent in the relationship between these elements, a relationship that actually defines the nature of the constituent parts. 'Master' and 'slave', for example, have no independent existence because each is a role defined in terms of its relationship to the other – in dialectical terms a 'unity of opposites'. Similarly, we need to understand how the socially constructed categories and identities of 'black' and 'white' were developed in relation to each other within a racial hierarchy shaped by particular historical social forces. Hence, 'whiteness' is not a kind of trait or characteristic apart from 'blackness' but is a claim of superiority over 'blackness'. Finally, colonialism, though originating from a spatially separate metropole, is not something that exists apart from the societies of the Caribbean, which are among the longest and most thoroughly colonised in history. Colonialism, far from being an 'outside influence' on creolisation,[13] is constitutive of it. The colonial system of domination and the resistant responses to that domination are two aspects of the same socio-cultural process that creates a society that is creole because it is colonial. My purpose in that earlier paper was to clarify the analysis of the process of creolisation by outlining this dialectical approach.

My argument was noted favourably by, among others, Mindie Lazarus-Black in her account of law and society in Antigua and Barbuda[14] and Richard Burton in *Afro-Creole: Power, Opposition, and Play in the Caribbean*. Burton agrees that creolisation is a process of contention and uses the dialectical approach to transcend the old argument about whether Caribbean culture is characterised chiefly by cultural loss, retention, or creation. Burton asserts that '*both* "continuity" and "creativity" are involved in creolisation'.[15] In his analysis of the central role of conflict in this process, however, Burton uses Michel de Certeau's dualistic distinction between resistance and opposition. The former is possible only when a dominated group has enough of a base of its own that it can develop a 'strategy' of resistance, whereas those who are too weak to establish such a 'space' of their own may resort only to the 'tactics' of opposition from within the system. The more complete the domination, the harder it is for any group to have the 'space', or sufficient sense of exteriority from the system, to be able to

---

[13] K. Brathwaite, 'Caliban, Ariel, and Unprospero in the conflict of creolization: a study of the slave revolt in Jamaica in 1831–32', in V. Rubin and A. Tuden (eds.), *Comparative Perspectives on Slavery in New World Plantation Societies* (New York: New York Academy of Sciences, 1977), pp. 42–3.
[14] M. Lazarus-Black, *Legitimate Acts and Illegal Encounters: Law and Society in Antigua and Barbuda* (Washington, DC: Smithsonian Institution, 1994), p. 3.
[15] Burton, *Afro-Creole*, p. 5.

resist the system as such. Burton draws attention to many forms of cultural opposition, including varieties of Afro-Christianity, calypso, carnival and cricket, in societies as diverse as Jamaica, Haiti and Trinidad. His emphasis on the politics in religion and the seriousness of 'play' helps us understand the dialectical development of Afro-Creole, and also Euro-Creole, culture.[16] In his conclusions, however, Burton appears dissatisfied with the binary opposition of resistance and opposition when he says, 'there is scarcely one cultural form discussed in this book that is not at the same time a revolt against things as they are and a form of adjustment to them, scarcely one that, even as it rebels against one form of domination ... does not contain within itself the seeds of another form of domination.'[17]

This example suggests that because dualism predominates in the European intellectual tradition the dualistic approach may creep back into the analysis of scholars who are otherwise thinking dialectically. For Descartes, who is generally considered the father of modern Western philosophy, the universe was composed of two independent, irreducible and irreconcilable components, namely mind and matter, so he then faced the problem of how these interacted. Such binary oppositions shape the hegemonic paradigms of the European intellectual tradition, but they may inhibit or distort our understanding of the cultural process of creolisation. Instead of analysing cultural contact and interaction in terms of static and irreconcilable opposites in the manner of dualism, dialectical analysis draws attention to changes in the nature of the opposing principles and forces that result from such interaction, so the cultural process is seen as open-ended and multi-directional, rather than finite and linear.[18] This more dynamic dialectical view of cultural change, which emphasises the process of creolisation more than the 'product' of creole culture and society, is similar to that of Edouard Glissant: 'If we posit *metissage* as, generally speaking, the meeting and synthesis of two differences, creolisation seems to be a limitless *metissage*, its elements diffracted and its consequences unforeseeable... Its most obvious symbol is in the Creole language, whose genius consists

---

[16] When Burton adds Meso-Creole, the 'middle culture' of the free coloured classes (p. 6), his account comes close to M.G. Smith's version of the 'three principal sections of colonial society' that were 'differentiated culturally' (*The Plural Society of the British West Indies*, p. 112).
[17] Burton, *Afro-Creole*, p. 264.
[18] Indeed, the distinction between 'dualistics' and 'dialectics' may be viewed dualistically or dialectically. Whereas the former system of reason would see this as an absolute distinction between forms of logic that are irreconcilably opposed, the latter incorporates while also transcending the former.

in always being open... Creolisation carries along then into the adventure of multilingualism and into the incredible explosion of cultures.'[19]

The tradition of dualism, like a great deal of European culture, is not so universal as is generally claimed. Some African and Asian philosophies emphasise a more holistic and organic perspective. In Chinese philosophy, for example, the cosmic principles known as *yin* and *yang* interact, like light and shadow, which suggests they are conceived as mutually constitutive rather than mutually exclusive. In Caribbean religions such as Vodou in Haiti and Orisha in Trinidad the philosophical perspective is closer to the African than to the European tradition. For example, the 'sacred' and 'profane' are viewed in European religions and philosophy as mutually exclusive spheres that should be kept separate. If profane elements occur within sacred rituals, for instance, the ritual is believed to have become defiled. By contrast, when the sacred and profane are conceived as more organically interconnected and mutually constitutive, rituals may remind the participants of this important relationship. The purpose of many Vodou rituals, for example, is to facilitate communication between the sacred and the profane, the spiritual and the worldly, and spirit possession is the ultimate achievement of flow between them. The body of the possessed devotee is the medium 'whereby the revitalizing forces of the universe flow to the community'.[20] Similarly, the belief in a divine energy force, said to reside in Damballah, the snake spirit of Fon mythology, emphasises the incessant alternation between day and night, birth and death, that characterises the eternal motion of the universe. Consequently, the essence of life is its motion – formation, transformation, deterioration – in the eternal cycle symbolised by the snake with its tail in its mouth, 'apparently swallowing itself, yet with no beginning or end'.[21] It is no coincidence that Alejo Carpentier initiated the literary phenomenon of 'magic realism' with *El reino de este mundo* in 1949, after studying Vodou in Haiti. Magic realism, contrary to the dualistic tradition, emphasises the interpenetration and unity of the fabulous and mundane aspects of the world.

The organic and dialectical development of a creole culture from diverse origins may be illustrated by a wide variety of examples of music, language, religion, or other aspects of Caribbean culture. For example, an account of a funeral, written in mid-nineteenth-century

---

[19] E. Glissant, *Poetics of Relation*, tr. B. Wing (Ann Arbor: University of Michigan, 1997), p. 34.
[20] L.G. Desmangles, *The Faces of the Gods: Vodou and Roman Catholicism in Haiti* (Chapel Hill: University of North Carolina, 1992), p. 107.
[21] G. Parrinder, *African Mythology* (London: Paul Hamlyn, 1967), p. 22.

Belize, suggests an organic cultural transformation in terms of continuities and creativity. The coexistence of African and European cultures is transformed from a mechanical juxtaposition of contrasting elements into the creation of something altogether new. This process, of course, occurred between African cultures and between European cultures, as well as between African and European cultures.

If a slave owner died, all his dependants and friends came together to be feasted; and the wife or mistress and her children prepared the house and provided provisions and plenty of ardent spirits. The corpse, dressed in its best clothes, was laid upon a bed and *waked* during the whole night. Cards, dice and backgammon, with strong drink and spiced wine, helped to beguile its watches, during which the loud laugh and the profane oath were unrestrained. In the negro yard below, 'the sheck'ka' and the drum 'proclaimed the sport, the song, the dance, and various dreem'... [of] the different African nations and Creoles, each in parties... Sometimes a tent was erected, where rum, coffee and ginger tea were dispensed to all who chose to come and make free. After a night thus spent, the corpse was carried in the morning to the churchyard, the coffin being borne by labourers, who in their progress used to run up and down the streets and lanes with their burden, knocking at some door or doors, perhaps visiting some of the friends of the deceased, professing to be impelled by him, or to be contending with the spirit who opposed the interment of the body. At length some well-known friend came forward, speaking soothingly to the dead, and calling him Brother, urging him to go home, and promised him rest and blessing. They then moved all together towards the grave, and the sheck'ka's jingle, the voice of song, and latterly, the funeral service of the Established Church were mingled together in the closing scene.[22]

The mention of 'different African nations and Creoles, each in parties' shows that people in Belize were seen to be culturally diverse in the mid-nineteenth century, some being defined as Creole as distinct from the different African and European nations, and that they formed groups and interacted with each other on the basis of those social constructions. The integration of games, strong drink, dancing and general merriment in the wake, which would be judged by most Christians as irreverent, and the custom of carrying a corpse from house to house to visit friends of the deceased, were common features of West African cultures. The bearers of the corpse were believed to be controlled by his spirit, which could reveal the source of his demise in a kind of divination, a way of giving the deceased's spirit the opportunity to disclose

---

[22] F. Crowe, *The Gospel in Central America, containing ... a History of the Baptist Mission in British Honduras* (London: Gilpin, 1850), pp. 324–5.

whether he had enemies. Such divination, which would have been familiar to most Africans in Belize, was being learned by Creoles, perhaps by white as well as black and mixed Creoles. Finally, the music in the ritual, if not synthesised, combined African and European elements, the drums and sheck'ka mingling with the Anglican funeral service. The missionary who wrote this account probably viewed this as an inappropriate mixture of sacred and profane elements, but it is unlikely that the participants in the event made such a judgement.

The celebration in this wake may reflect the participants' belief that the spirit of the deceased is being reborn in a new dimension of life, his going home to rest and blessing. In many African religions this new dimension appears in the divine and immortal form that was the spirit's primordial state before it was manifest in a passing human shape. Among Vodouissants, for example, it is believed there are two parts to a person's spirit, the eternal, cosmic life-force and the particular 'personality' of a person. However, these two aspects are organically bound together, the former becoming manifest in the latter, and the latter being an individual 'moment' of the former. 'Vodouissants do not understand their spirit as a dualism – that is, as two irreconcilable entities, one of which negates the other; rather, the two parts constitute an organic process, a dynamism which comprises divinity, authority, influence, morality, and wisdom.'[23] How can such a holistic and organic philosophy be understood in terms of the dualistic tradition of binary oppositions?

In order to understand the meanings that the participants themselves attached to their actions in an event such as the Belizean funeral we need to approximate their thoughts and philosophies. How can we understand the various relationships and patterns of change emerging in the interactions between African and Christian religions in the Caribbean unless we comprehend the philosophical orientations and propensities of the practitioners? In some instances the believers hid their real beliefs behind the permitted rituals and saints of Christianity (the 'camouflage theory') and out of this there developed associations between the two. In other cases Christian aspects were incorporated into the changing religion. In Yoruba villages in Trinidad, for example, the 'predominant Catholic religion served as a transcultural belief, in that it provided sufficient continuity in perceived religious belief to bridge partially the cultural gap and soften the dislocation caused by migration'.[24] In the case of Vodou, the relation of the diverse religious traditions from Europe and Africa is a symbiosis, meaning they 'coexist without fusing

---

[23] Desmangles, *The Faces of the Gods*, p. 68.

[24] D.V. Trotman, 'The Yoruba and Orisha worship in Trinidad and British Guiana, 1838–1870', *African Studies Review* 19:2 (1976), p. 9.

with one another',[25] both in the sense of the spatial juxtaposition of elements of both traditions and in the temporal juxtaposition of ritual observances for the *lwas* on Catholic saints' days. If, for the participants in these religions, the relations between European and African beliefs and practices are varied, flexible and organic, then we must move beyond hegemonic paradigms such as dualism in order to understand the nature of creolisation.

The hegemonic paradigms of European philosophy and science may be an obstacle when we are trying to understand the formation of Afro-Creole religions like Vodou, Santeria, Kumina, Comfa and Orisha, which are so open to influence and change, highly eclectic, and unconcerned about orthodoxy. Instead of trying to grasp the creolisation process in terms of fixed binary oppositions we should understand it as an open-ended process shaped by a dialogue of power and resistance in which shifting similarities and differences, assimilations and syncretisms, are continually renegotiated.

III

The concept of creolisation has helped to identify and analyse the dynamic social process in which Africans and their descendants contested and continue to contest their oppression in the Americas, a process that resulted in some similar features but also differences in creole cultures and societies. Creolisation, therefore, helps conceive of the 'African diaspora' in terms of a socio-historical process rather than by essentialising 'blackness'. The salience of, and also the changes and variations in, the concept of 'race' and of racial hierarchies in the Americas were themselves constructed in this socio-historical process. In fact, the social construction of 'African' or 'black', which may essentialise an identity in terms of a supposedly single or 'pure' origin, is a simplification of the very complex process which gave rise to it. Racial identity, like any other kind of identity, is both relational and historically contingent. Instead of defining the African diaspora in terms of a common 'racial essence', Stuart Hall defines it in relation to a dynamic, creolised culture: 'The diaspora experience as I intend it here is defined, not by essence or purity, but by the recognition of a necessary heterogeneity and diversity; by a conception of "identity" which lives with and through, not despite, difference; by *hybridity*. Diaspora identities are those which are constantly producing and reproducing

---

[25] Desmangles, *The Faces of the Gods*, p. 8.

themselves anew, through transformation and difference.'[26] This diaspora experience, which consisted of the unsettling and dispersion, and the pervasive exploitation, oppression and resistance of millions of Africans and their descendants in the Atlantic world, resulted in mixtures and differences both within and between creole societies.

The concept of African diaspora helps to define the context of the process of cultural exchanges, contestations, transformations and creations that is called creolisation, while the concept of creolisation helps us analyse the various experiences and cultures of different peoples of African origin in different times and places.[27] These experiences and transformations began in Sao Tome, Cape Verde and the Caribbean in the sixteenth century, with pre-echoes in the Iberian peninsula and the west coast of Africa. Successive migrations, whether forced, induced or voluntary, have not simply divided people but have also reunited them in common consciousness.[28] However, although the concept of creolisation helps us to understand the commonalities and differences within the African diaspora, it may distort our understanding of the relationships between this and other 'overlapping diasporas', such as the Indian and Chinese diasporas.

In general Caribbean usage, creole culture and identity encompass those aspects of the Caribbean that derive from African, European, or mixed African and European origins. Since the sixteenth century the word *criollo* has meant 'native' to the Caribbean but of 'Old World' origins, used as a noun or adjective referring to cattle, language, food, people, and so on. Thus, 'Creoles', who could be white, black or mixed, were simply those people who were born locally, and 'creole speech' referred to the variants of Old World languages that were developed and used by people in the Caribbean, whether they were whites, blacks or mixed. In Jamaica, for example, Edward Long wrote of 'the native white men, or Creoles of Jamaica', and distinguished between 'Creole Blacks' and Africans or 'salt-water Negroes' in 1774.[29] In some parts of the Caribbean, when referring to individuals, Creole pertains to people of African or part-African descent unless it is prefaced with a qualifier, as in 'white Creole' in Belize, or 'French Creole' in Trinidad. Creole

---

[26] S. Hall, 'Cultural identity and diaspora', in P. Williams and L. Chrisman (eds.), *Colonial Discourse and Post-Colonial Theory* (New York: Columbia University, 1994), pp. 401–2.
[27] T.C. Holt, 'Slavery and freedom in the Atlantic World: reflections on the diasporan framework', in D.C. Hine and J. McLeod (eds.), *Crossing Boundaries: Comparative History of Black People in Diaspora* (Bloomington: Indiana University, 1999), pp. 35–6.
[28] R.S. Bryce-Laporte, 'Introduction', in A.W. Bonnet and G.L. Watson (eds.), *Emerging Perspectives on the Black Diaspora* (New York: University Press of America, 1990).
[29] F.G. Cassidy, *Jamaica Talk: Three Hundred Years of the English Language in Jamaica* (London: Macmillan, 1961), pp. 161, 156.

also refers to an ethnic group sharing common cultural characteristics that distinguish it from others. In Belize, for example, to be Creole means *not* to be Mestizo, Maya or Garifuna, because the Creoles, unlike the others, are chiefly black, Creole-speaking and Protestant, while in Guyana Creole 'pertains to the black or coloured native population (called "Creoles" or "Afro-Creoles")', and local whites are called 'Anglo-' or 'Euro-Creole',[30] as distinct from the East Indians, Chinese and Portuguese who may be more or less creolised without ever becoming Creoles. In Trinidad, where similar distinctions are made, indentured Indian workers had looked down on African Trinidadians as former slaves who were also 'hopelessly polluted', according to Kusha Haraksingh,[31] but to associate with and even be seen as Creole is no longer the awful thing it once was. Sam Selvon, the Trinidadian novelist of Indian and Scottish descent, defined himself as 'completely Creolized ... meaning that you live among the people, whatever races they are, and you are a real born Trinidadian, you can't get away from it'.[32] In cases where members of a non-Creole group have become culturally assimilated, creole becomes a qualifier, as in 'creolized Chinese-Trinidadian', for example.[33] This use of creole and creolisation is identified with the authentic and national culture of the people. When creole refers in this way to a particular culture and ethnic group, and creolisation means the acculturation of others into this culture, it has a distinctly ideological quality.

Generally, when the concept creolisation is used with reference to people of Chinese, Indian, Lebanese, Portuguese and other origins, it refers to the assimilation of these ethnic groups to creole, and more specifically Afro-Creole, culture. The concept, used in this way, takes on an ideological quality when it is assumed that a process in the past resulted in the present creole culture and society to which 'newcomers' may become assimilated. When creolisation is identified solely with the creation and assimilation of Afro-Creole culture, and put at the centre of Caribbean history, indigenisation and nationalism, all 'others' become marginalised. In Trinidad, for example, the establishment of the predominantly creole cultural activities of carnival, calypso and steel bands as *national* symbols marginalised Indian Trinidadians in their own

---

[30] Moore, *Cultural Power, Resistance and Pluralism*, p. x.
[31] Quoted in S. Ryan, *The Jhandi and the Cross: The Clash of Cultures in Post-Creole Trinidad and Tobago* (St. Augustine: Institute of Social and Economic Research, University of the West Indies, 1999), p. 29.
[32] P. Nazareth, 'Interview with Sam Selvon', *World Literature Written in English* 18:2 (1979), p. 426.
[33] Ho, '"Hold the chow mein, gimme soca"', p. 21.

country. If one had to be Creole to be a true Trinidadian, then Indians and others had to become 'creolised', in the sense of becoming assimilated, in order to belong in the country where their ancestors started arriving as long ago as 1845. To see them as simply becoming assimilated, however, implies that they continue to stand outside the society, but they have been contributing to the popular culture in various ways – food, religion, music – for many years.

Chutney soca is a kind of Trinidadian music derived from Indian and Creole influences that became increasingly popular in the 1990s, but to describe it as 'merely an Indianised version of calypso' which is evidence of 'the gradual integration of the Indian population into carnival culture'[34] suggests that Indians are simply becoming assimilated, whereas they are really participating in the continuing creation of their national culture. Chutney soca is part of creole culture, so that culture can no longer be described adequately as Afro-Creole. Moreover, the commonly held view that 'influences from all the different cultures in Trinidad have mingled into one',[35] which implies that the transformation was a simple blending process that occurred in the past, suggests that the relations between the different ethnic groups are more harmonious than they really are – and that constitutes another ideological usage of the concept 'creole culture,' the ideology encapsulated in the slogan 'All o' we is one'. Shalini Puri points out that when Derek Walcott, in his Nobel Prize acceptance speech, includes Indians in Trinidad's national culture(s) by referring to Ramleela, the popular performance of the Hindu epic *Ramayana*, he 'ignores the fact that performances and funding of the Ramleela are embedded in a politics of intercultural *competition* ... of cultural struggle... Indo-Caribbean cultural production may be better understood not only in relation to a politics of cultural hybridity, but also as an assertion of ethnic identity.'[36] Intercultural relations, in other words, continue to involve a process of contention. When viewed dialectically, the present-day politics of culture between Indian and Creole Trinidadians, like that between Mestizo and Creole Belizeans, may be compared with that between Europeans and Africans in the past. In both countries one group is afraid of, or resents what it feels is already, the political and cultural domination of the other and so asserts itself in competition with the other.[37] This inter-

---

[34] P. Mason, *Bacchanal! The Carnival Culture of Trinidad* (Kingston: Ian Randle, 1998), p. 53.
[35] Ibid., p. 15.
[36] Puri, 'Canonized hybridities, resistant hybridities', p. 35.
[37] I hasten to add that I am not suggesting that any of the groups I have referred to are oppressed and exploited in the same ways that most people were oppressed and exploited under the regimes of slavery, indentured labour and colonialism.

cultural contestation is not simply a competition for resources but also a struggle for symbolic representation and respect within the 'nation'. The cultures of Trinidad, Belize, Guyana, Jamaica, Suriname and other Caribbean nations are still being formed in this continuing process of contestation.

When Afro-Creole culture and identity are placed at the national and regional centre in the Caribbean, Indians, Mestizos, Chinese and others feel that they are left the unenviable alternative of remaining distinguished by their ancestral culture and so being marginalised, or of becoming indistinguishable from Creoles in order to be accepted in their own nation. To identify and be identified as Indian in Trinidad and Guyana, for example, suggests an adherence to the culture of ancestral origin, which implies that they are less 'national' than those who are 'completely creolised'. When Brian Moore describes cultural changes among the indentured Indians and Chinese in colonial Guyana, he implies that creolisation was largely a one-way street of assimilation into Afro-Creole culture. 'Creolization, even where it did take place, was thus very incomplete', he concludes,[38] but creolisation can never be 'complete' because the development of creole culture and society can never be completed. In Belize many Creoles, who are anxious because they have recently become less numerous than Mestizos, tend to identify all Mestizos as 'Spanish' and even 'alien', whether they are new immigrants or born in Belize. The growing ethnic tensions in Belize, which are related to low-wage development strategies and the immigration of Central Americans, are the consequence of the Creoles or Afro-Belizeans feeling that they are losing 'their' country to the Mestizos.[39] Belize is in danger of becoming ethnically polarised, though politics is not so racialised there as in Trinidad and Guyana.

The identities of Creole and Indian, and of Creole and Mestizo, even when people believe they are racially determined, have been constructed in relation to each other as mutually exclusive categories that may mingle but are not supposed to mix. Even when the latter does occur, as is often the case in Trinidad, for example, the mixing of Creole and Indian produces people – called *douglas* – who are identified only as a kind of individual, not a cultural category or group equivalent to Creole or Mestizo.[40] There does not yet appear to be a *dougla* identity,

---

[38] Moore, *Cultural Power, Resistance and Pluralism*, p. 167.
[39] O. N. Bolland and M. Moberg, 'Development and national identity: creolization, immigration, and ethnic conflict in Belize', *International Journal of Comparative Race and Ethnic Studies* 2:2 (1995), pp. 1–18.
[40] D. A. Segal, '"Race" and "colour" in pre-independence Trinidad and Tobago', in K. Yelvington (ed.), *Trinidad Ethnicity* (London: Macmillan, 1993), pp. 81–115.

for example, and individuals described as *douglas* tend to become culturally assimilated into either the Creole or the Indian community.[41] Nor is there a 'white-Indian' continuum equivalent to the 'white-African' continuum that is historically important to the concept of creole, so someone like Sam Selvon could be identified only as Indian or creolised Indian.

Ironically, people of Indian ancestry appear to be faced with the same kind of restricted choice that was forced on people of African ancestry, namely to retain their ancestral culture or be acculturated into the dominant culture, because they, like the Africans before them, are not seen as co-creators of the culture. Of course, in the development of creole societies Africans who retained their culture continued to be judged by the dominant group as backward, while those who assimilated themselves culturally were never accepted as equal. But to be limited to the choice between being either 'retainers' or 'assimilators' is to be defined as passive, which excludes them from contributing to their nation's culture.[42] The concept of creolisation provided a way to understand that this was a false choice by showing that both continuity and creativity are involved when subordinated people contest culture with the dominant group. The combination of continuity *and* creativity that characterises the development of Afro-Creole culture, however, is characteristic of the development of Caribbean culture in general, and this must be conceived in such a way as to include the contributions of all people in the Caribbean, now as well as in the past. Earl Lovelace makes this point in *The Dragon Can't Dance* through the Indian, Pariag, who

---

[41] This may be changing, however. A self-defined *dougla* responded to the assumption made by Dr Kumar Mahabir that people like himself were illegitimate and prone to become social deviants by writing to the *Express*, '*Douglas* have no abnormal behavioural problems ... We have the highest degree of racial tolerance since we have no race. Don't talk for us, you of pure race. I wish in the current situation in Trinidad, with all this racist blabber, that there were more of us' (16 September 1998). Rhoda Reddock has argued that since the mid-1990s 'the population of mixed Indian and African ancestry was becoming more visible. Yet even then the voices raised were few but somewhat less tentative' ('Jahaji Bhai: the emergence of a dougla poetics in contemporary Trinidad and Tobago', in R. R. Premdas [ed.], *Identity, Ethnicity and Culture in the Caribbean* [St. Augustine: School of Continuing Studies, University of the West Indies, 1999] p. 185). The related concept of 'douglarisation' is sometimes used as a threat – 'We go douglarise the country' – by black men to the Indian fathers of Indian women, but not by Indian men to black fathers of black women (personal communication from Anton Allahar, 4 July 2001). This ideological use of 'douglarisation', meaning a biological mixing that would obliterate Indian distinctiveness, is predicated on the notion that 'blacks' and 'Indians' are 'pure' types.

[42] V. Munasinghe, 'Culture creators and culture bearers: the interface between race and ethnicity in Trinidad', *Transforming Anthropology* 6: 1 & 2 (1997), pp. 72–86.

lives in the community but has been largely invisible. He wants to belong to, or at least just to be seen by, the Creoles among whom he lives, and to contribute his music to the carnival from which he feels excluded.[43]

In short, the concepts creole and creolisation have a powerful ideological quality in their common usage. For example, people may define creolisation as a threat to Indian identity and community, or claim that Indians' adoption of creole culture is evidence of their national integration. However, to limit the alternative to the persistence of differences on the basis of retained ancestral culture or the development of national unity on the basis of acculturation obscures the fact that the development of creole culture is characterised by the persistence of differences *as well as* the creation of new phenomena. In the contested process of creolisation, as Burton argues, both continuity and creativity are involved. What is *Caribbean*, in fact, is neither the insistence on mutually exclusive and immutable ethnicities, such as 'Indian', 'Chinese', 'Mestizo' and 'Creole', nor the blending of one into the other in a general 'melting pot'.[44] What is Caribbean is the development of cultures and societies that enable people to participate at different times and in different ways in a variety of activities and identities because these need not be mutually exclusive.[45]

The more open and organic dialectical view of creolisation that I am advocating helps us to understand this, as it helps us to keep in mind that the various ways people contribute culturally depends on the distribution of power in the society. Sam Selvon was both an Indian and a Creole Trinidadian because he was, as he claimed, 'completely Creolised'. But to say he was Creole does not just mean that he was assimilated, as if he were the passive recipient of another's culture. Selvon was Creole because he contributed in his own way, out of his own cultural background and influenced by those among whom he

---

[43] Burton, in discussing the cultural dynamics revealed in Earl Lovelace's *The Dragon Can't Dance* (London: Andre Deutsch, 1979), ignores Pariag because he is outside the Afro-Creole complex, which was precisely the point Lovelace was making (op. cit., pp. 213–20).

[44] These ethnicities, and many others, such as Garifuna, Maya and Amerindian, are themselves the contingent product of Caribbean encounters. Immigrants from India who spoke different languages and were divided by religion and caste, for example, began to think of themselves as 'East Indian' through contrast with 'West Indians'. Though most people think of ethnic groups as if they are immutable categories, like species, they become identified and change through interaction with others in an open-ended process of ethnogenesis.

[45] I am not saying that this is exclusively true of the Caribbean, of course, but it has been true of the Caribbean for an unusually long time and in a particularly pervasive way.

lived, to the developing creole culture of Trinidad and the Caribbean. In this perspective, 'creoleness' is not a culture that is historically fixed, though it has been shaped by the historical circumstances and struggles of its origins. Creoleness, rather, is a culture and identity in the making, and Indians, Chinese, Portuguese, Mestizos, Javanese, Lebanese and others have been participating with other Creoles in this process for many generations. People of African descent have a key role in the history and continuing development of creolisation and creole societies, but Afro-Creole is not the whole or the end point of creole culture. The creole Caribbean has no end point.

IV

When Kenneth Ramchand, an Indian Trinidadian, introduced Anthony Winkler, a white Jamaican, as 'my fellow Creole',[46] he was claiming to share an ethnic identity that is not limited by their 'race' or nationality. This makes an ideological claim to a Caribbean identity that is related but not identical to the more specific one of Afro-Creole. Implicit in this assertion regarding creole culture and identity are some of the persistent strengths and limitations of the concepts 'creolisation' and 'creole societies'.

On the one hand, the concepts, as analytic concepts, help us to understand the relationships between cultural change and the structures and processes of social conflict in Caribbean history. By the late eighteenth and early nineteenth centuries this creative process of adaptation, transformation and synthesis had laid the groundwork of a Caribbean culture that was neither African nor European, though it grew out of the interaction between African, European and Amerindian peoples. In the Caribbean most people who participated in this process were of African descent[47] and it was largely through their struggle against the double domination of enslavement and colonialism that an Afro-Creole culture developed. By the early nineteenth century, and considerably earlier in some places, this Afro-Creole culture had emerged in the Caribbean in a socially subordinate and resistant relationship with the dominant

---

[46] At Colgate University, 28 February 2001.
[47] The proportion of Africans in the populations of individual colonies varied a great deal, however. Most of the Spanish Caribbean had a far smaller proportion of Africans because the sugar revolution came later to Cuba, San Domingo and Puerto Rico. Even in Cuba, where sugar developed earlier and on a larger scale, 'whites' were about 57 per cent of the population, slaves 23 per cent and free coloured 20 per cent at the end of the eighteenth century, at a time when people of African origin predominated in the British and French colonies.

Euro-Creole culture. The inequalities in the colonies that persisted after emancipation led to the attempt by many people of African and mixed African-European descent to become culturally assimilated to the Euro-Creole culture in order to achieve social mobility. Hence, their patterns of behaviour, beliefs, values and language, and their participation in a variety of elite and folk institutions, constituted something of a bridge between the Euro- and Afro-Creole cultures. The use of these concepts, which emphasise African traditions and the active roles of people in creating culture and asserting their identity in an oppressive context, contrasts with the imperial view of the colonies as incomplete, impure and inferior versions of their 'mother country', and is historically linked to the process of decolonisation and nation-building. These concepts, undoubtedly, have made enormous contributions to the analysis of the development of Caribbean culture.

On the other hand, when these concepts, in their common usage, are so specifically linked to the experience of people of African descent, they have a particular historical and ideological content that is problematic. The concept creolisation helps in the comparative analysis of the cultures of the African diaspora but, if creole is used synonymously with Afro-Creole, then this limits who may be considered Creole. The concept of creolisation, when used as a descriptive-empirical account of the specific socio-historical process involving people of African descent, marginalises and excludes peoples and cultures of the Caribbean who are not part of the 'Black Atlantic' community. Consequently, although the concept helps us analyse cultural conflicts, innovations and developments within the African diaspora, it may hinder the analysis of the interrelations between this and other diasporas.

Fortunately, we do not have to create a neologism in order to find a concept which encompasses *all* the cultural interactions and changes involving all the peoples of the Caribbean. In 1940, the Cuban scholar Fernando Ortiz used the term *transculturation* 'to express the highly varied phenomena that have come about in Cuba as a result of the extremely complex transmutations of culture that have taken place here... The real history of Cuba is the history of its intermeshed transculturations.'[48] Ortiz explained his preference for the new term over acculturation, which describes only a process of transition from one culture to another.

I am of the opinion that the word *transculturation* better expresses the different phases of the process of transition from one culture to another because this does not consist merely in acquiring another

---

[48] F. Ortiz, *Cuban Counterpoint: Tobacco and Sugar*, tr. H. De Onis (New York: Vintage, 1970), p. 98.

culture, which is what the English word *acculturation* really implies, but also necessarily involves the loss or uprooting of a previous culture, which could be defined as a deculturation. In addition it carries the idea of the consequent creation of new cultural phenomena.[49]

Creolisation, in its ideological usage, refers to a kind of acculturation which, as Ortiz says, describes only the loss of a previous culture and acquisition of a new one, and this does not adequately express the cultural developments that have occurred in the Caribbean during the last 150 years.

Finally, I do not believe it is helpful to think of the present as 'neo-creole' or 'post-creole',[50] because this suggests a break with the past. On the contrary, the interaction and transformation of cultures in the Caribbean continues. If the use of creolisation and creole society is limited to refer only to the development of Afro-Creole culture, however, we do need the more general concept of transculturation to encompass the conjuncture of the various Amerindian, European, African and Asian worlds in the Caribbean. Creolisation in its common usage, as distinct from its analytical function, is a more particular and ideologically loaded concept than transculturation. If we cannot escape the widespread ideological usage of the concept of creolisation, the more inclusive concept of transculturation appears to be indispensable for understanding not only Caribbean cultures but also the continuing cultural transformations of the modern world that commenced in the Caribbean crucible in 1492. When we think of the creole civilisation of the Caribbean we should be considering it in all its diversity, with its various peoples 'constantly producing and reproducing themselves anew' in an 'incredible explosion of cultures'.

---

[49] Ibid., pp. 102–103.
[50] S. Ryan, *The Jhandi and the Cross*.

11 'Married but not parsoned': attitudes to conjugality in Jamaica, 1865–1920

Brian L. Moore and Michele A. Johnson

The means by which persons in a society decide on mating patterns and family formations are important parts of that society's culture. As part of the British empire of the nineteenth century, those who attempted to guide and shape the social institutions in Jamaica sought to import the ideals of Victorian Christianity and impose them on the Jamaican people, encouraging them to take vows declaring their lifelong commitment to their mates. The ideal of Christian, monogamous marriage was accompanied by an entire ideology of what constituted morality and civility and, in as much as it provided the only 'appropriate' context within which sexual intercourse should occur, it provided the basis for the 'legitimacy' of those relationships.

For many, marriage was a key indicator of the 'improvement' of a people whose experiences during slavery had been such that it was believed they had been 'shapen in iniquity; and in sin did [their] mother[s] conceive [them]'.[1] But despite the promulgation of the ideal, and the benefits which were allegedly attendant on the state of legal marriage, the majority of the Jamaican people continued to avoid the institution and chose, instead, to live and love in non-legal relationships labelled 'concubinage', causing untold consternation to the cultural elite who encouraged them, or else tried to coerce them, into 'civilised behaviour'.

Within the Jamaican culture, there were several means by which the people constructed conjugal relationships. According to Patrick Bryan, there were two main sorts of unions: those 'founded on ... the civil, Christian or Jewish rites of marriage', and others formed through 'the pragmatic, functional marriage often referred to as "faithful concubinage"'.[2] Jean Besson, however, was more incisive in identifying two types of non-legal relationships: those established by 'consensual

---

[1] *Psalms* 51:5.
[2] Patrick Bryan, *The Jamaican People 1880–1902: Race, Class and Social Control* (London: Macmillan Caribbean, 1991; repr. Kingston: The UWI Press, 2000), p. 92.

cohabitation', and others created through 'extra-residential conjugal relations'.³ These two forms of unions, and their variants, collectively and disparagingly referred to as 'concubinage', constituted the main types of conjugal relationships in the island after emancipation. Besson regards these as 'Creole transformations of European legal marriage and social stratification based on Eurocentric respectability',⁴ and argues that they represent 'a mode of cultural resistance to the plantation system incorporating both men and women'.⁵ By her estimation, then, those persons who were labelled 'concubines' had founded a system which they controlled and which seemed to work for them.⁶ That these domestic units had their own rules, internal dynamic and, therefore, legitimacy, were ideas unrecognised by most contemporary commentators.

During the late nineteenth and early twentieth centuries, contemporary commentators repeatedly observed that the Jamaican people did not get married, and that they preferred to 'live together in sin', in 'concubinage', without the blessing of the church and the sanction of the

---

³ Jean Besson, 'Reputation & Respectability Reconsidered: A New Perspective on Afro-Caribbean Peasant Women', in Janet Momsen (ed.), *Women & Change in the Caribbean: A Pan-Caribbean Perspective* (Kingston: Ian Randle Publishers, 1993), p. 21.

⁴ Besson, 'Reputation & Respectability Reconsidered', p. 21.

⁵ Besson, 'Reputation & Respectability Reconsidered', p. 21.

⁶ In the twentieth century, the unions, families and households which were formulated along non-legal lines came under great sociological and anthropological scrutiny, which focused on discovering the reasons behind the 'difference' in Caribbean family forms. See, for instance, Melville J. Herskovits and Frances S. Herskovits, *Suriname Folk-Lore* (New York: Columbia University Press, 1936); Melville J. Herskovits and Frances S. Herskovits, *Trinidad Village* (New York: Alfred A. Knopf, 1947); Fernando Henriques, *Family and Colour in Jamaica* (London: Eyre and Spottiswoode, 1953); Fernando Henriques, 'West Indian Family Organization', *American Journal of Sociology* 55 (1949); Judith Blake, *Family Structure in Jamaica: The Social Context of Reproduction* (New York: Free Press, 1961); Edith Clarke, *My Mother Who Fathered Me* (London: George Allen and Unwin, 1957); G.E. Cumper, 'The Jamaican Family: Village and Estate', *Social and Economic Studies* 7:1 (1958); Marietta Morrissey, 'Explaining the Caribbean Family: Gender Ideologies and Gender Relations', in Christine Barrow (ed.), *Caribbean Portraits: Essays on Gender Ideologies and Identities* (Kingston: Ian Randle Publishers, 1998), p. 81; M.G. Smith, *Kinship and Community in Carriacou* (New Haven: Yale University Press, 1962); Raymond T. Smith, 'The Family in the Caribbean', in Vera Rubin (ed.), *Caribbean Studies: A Symposium* (Seattle, Washington: University of Washington Press, 2nd ed., 1960); Raymond T. Smith, 'Hierarchy and the Dual Marriage System in West Indian Society', in J.F. Collier and S.J. Yanagisako (eds.), *Gender and Kinship: Essays Toward a Unified Analysis* (Palo Alto, CA: Stanford University Press, 1987); Raymond T. Smith, 'The Matrifocal Family', in J. Goody (ed.), *The Character of Kinship* (Cambridge: Cambridge University Press, 1973).

law.[7] As they put it themselves, they were 'married but not parsoned', so that '[legal] marriage is the exception, and living in a state of uncleanness the rule'.[8] This 'base and barefaced uncleanness of the people' did not meet with the approval of the clergy who inveighed against it both from the pulpit and in their daily visitations to their houses.[9] Yet, in spite of their efforts, the marriage rates were generally below those in Britain, Europe and the white empire, although they were on a par with those in Trinidad and Barbados.[10] As can be gleaned from Table 1, the rate rose from 3.7 per thousand of population in 1879–80 (when statistical recording began) to a peak of 7.4 in 1907–08 (the year of the great earthquake), then back down to an all-time low of 3.0 in 1914–16 (during the First World War).

Table 1: Legal marriages in Jamaica 1879–1920

Year	Number	Rate Per Thousand
1879–1880	2101	3.7
1880–1881	n/a	n/a
1881–1882	2368	4.0
1882–1883	2869	4.9
1883–1884	2953	5.0
1884–1885	2995	5.0
1885–1886	2390	3.9
1886–1887	2551	4.4

---

[7] See, for instance, William Pringle Livingstone, *Black Jamaica: A Study in Evolution* (London: Sampson Low, Marston and Co., 1899), pp. 113–4, 210–5; Bessie Pullen-Burry, *Jamaica As It Is, 1903* (London: T. Fisher Unwin, 1903), pp. 16–17; Herbert G. De Lisser, *Twentieth Century Jamaica* (Kingston: The Jamaica Times, 1913), p. 96; Winifred James, *The Mulberry Tree* (London: Chapman and Hall, 1913), p. 103; *Reports and Statistics of the Moravian Church in Jamaica* (Carisbrook), 1912, JA 5/5/Periodicals; Mary White, *Friends Jamaica Mission* (Port Antonio), 1915–16, JA 5/8/2/431.

[8] Livingstone, *Black Jamaica*, p. 114.

[9] Stephen Sutton to General Secretaries, 8 July 1868, MMS Box 200 [mf# 2418]. See also Arthur Bourne to General Secretaries, 7 November 1877, MMS Box 201 [mf# 2468], and the Annual Report of the Jamaica Baptist Union in the *75th Report of the Baptist Missionary Society* 1867.

[10] The comparative rates in 1878–79 were, for England and Wales 7.6 per 1000, Scotland 6.5, France 7.5, Italy 7.1, Spain (1870) 6.2, Australian colonies 7.3, New Zealand 7.4, Ontario (Canada) 8.0; and for those WI colonies on record: St Vincent (1872–76) 6.3, Grenada (1871–78) 5.6, Dominica (1871–75) 6.9, while Barbados (1872–77) was just 3.7, and Trinidad (1871–75) 3.8. Figures for the UK in early 1892–93 were: England and Wales 7.35 and Scotland 7.05. Only Ireland had comparably low rates: 4.7 in 1878 and 1893. See the Registrar General's Returns for 1879–80, 1882–83 and 1894–95 in the *Department Reports* of those years.

Table 1: Legal marriages in Jamaica 1879–1920 (continued)

Year	Number	Rate Per Thousand
1887–1888	3353	5.4
1888–1889	3387	5.4
1889–1890	3397	5.3
1890–1891	3560	5.5
1891–1892	3405	5.2
1892–1893	3349	5.1
1893–1894	3734	5.5
1894–1895	3629	5.3
1895–1896	3242	5.6
1896–1897	3026	4.3
1897–1898	2661	3.7
1898–1899	3362	4.6
1899–1900	3767	5.0
1900–1901	3221	4.2
1901–1902	3202	4.1
1902–1903	3601	4.6
1903–1904	3576	4.5
1904–1905	2880	3.6
1905–1906	3116	3.8
1906–1907	5507	6.6
1907–1908	6251	7.4
1908–1909	3526	4.1
1909–1910	3543	4.1
1910–1911	3340	4.0
1911–1912	3607	4.2
1912–1913	3218	3.7
1913–1914	2683	3.1
1914–1915	2721	3.0
1915–1916	2677	3.0
1916	2964	3.3
1917	2966	3.3
1918	2776	3.1
1919	3305	3.7
1920	4124	4.8

Sources: Reports of the Registrar General.

Despite the overall low marriage rates in the period, there were intervals of 'improvement' that provided encouragement to the elites, some of whom were inclined to think that a small 'moral' and cultural revolution was in the making.[11] W.P. Livingstone, editor of the *Gleaner*, was most effusive about this impression:

> It is noticed that those irregularly related are more sensitive as to their position, and readier to listen to argument on the subject. An appreciation of right relations is spreading, and although the number of marriages is not rising in proportion to the population, there is a better knowledge of all that the ceremony involves. It means, in addition to the legal advantages, elevation in the social scale, respectability, and the possession of all the privileges connected with the Church. These are the simple objects of negro ambition, and ... along with economic prosperity they will act more and more as a magnet to draw them into a proper conjugal condition.[12]

The benefits that marriage was supposed to offer to its adherents were clear, and any people who made a claim to and a pretence of civilisation were bound to uphold the institution as an ideal. If this were the case, then according to the statistics, the Jamaican people were decidedly 'uncivilised'.

As far as the contemporaries were concerned, the people were sending mixed signals which were difficult to interpret, and none of the social advantages mentioned by Livingstone seemed to influence their behaviour unduly. That the marriage rate should have peaked in 1907, the year of the devastating earthquake, to reach parity with the leading European countries, could have seemed at first glance to signify that the people did recognise that they had indeed been living in sin, and that God had visited them with a terrible vengeance as a censure. If so, this was only a partial, though not unimportant, explanation. The Registrar General's statistics showed that the upward trend had begun in the last quarter of 1906, *before* the earthquake, although it did peak in the second and third quarters of 1907, *after* that catastrophe.[13] Those rates

---

[11] See Richard Harding to E. Hoole, 22 October 1867, MMS Box 200 [mf# 2413]); George Lockett to W.B. Boyce, 21 October 1871, MMS Box 200 [mf# 2438]); *Friends Jamaica Mission* VI:2 (February 1898), JA 5/8/78/5906; VII:7 (July 1899), JA 5/8/78/5917; VIII:1 (January 1900), JA 5/8/78/5944); and *Reports and Statistics of the Moravian Church in Jamaica*, Carisbrook, 1912, JA 5/5/Periodicals.

[12] Livingstone, *Black Jamaica*, pp. 214–5.

[13] The number of marriages rose sharply from 798 in the third (June) quarter of 1906 to 924 in the fourth (September) quarter. In the quarter coinciding with the January 1907 earthquake, the figure rose to 988, and then suddenly leapfrogged to 2797 in the second (March) quarter of 1907 and 2319 in the following (June 1907) quarter, before declining to a still relatively high level of 1278 in the first quarter of 1908. See the Registrar General's Report for 1907–08. See also the editorial in *Daily Gleaner*, 12 May 1909.

declined steadily thereafter, and in fact if anything they went to the other extreme during the First World War.

According to Bryan, several explanations have been advanced to explain the universal reluctance to marry, 'ranging from black moral turpitude, to white example, to the breakdown of African family practices, and to the low self-esteem of the black population'.[14] On the basis of the contemporary discussions, however, there seem to have been essentially two schools of thought seeking to explain the failure, unwillingness or refusal of the people to get legally married. One held that the costs, which included the Governor's licence, the marriage officer's fee and all the ingredients considered essential for a 'proper wedding' (trousseau and feast), were a major deterrent. 'It matters not how many years a couple have lived together when at last they marry, the rule is – a great display so far as dress and feasting are concerned.'[15] Livingstone considered this to be the result of their desire to emulate the whites; and because they were unable to afford the costs, they simply cohabited.[16]

According to this body of thought, despite the absence of the sanction of the church or the law, the conjugal pair had no intention of separating. Having cohabited for some time, they saw no very great necessity to marry. In their case, it was also claimed that the marriage ceremony was connected with some feeling of shame,[17] especially since it entailed the prior reading of banns, which, as Anglican priest C.H. Coles put it, called attention to their improper relation.[18] So they never got married at all. H.G. De Lisser, on the other hand, argued that 'the simple truth is that no disgrace attaches to members of the labouring and peasant class who do not choose to get married'.[19] This suggests that the people had their own criteria of what constituted unacceptable moral behaviour, and despite the efforts of the authorities and the clergy, cohabitation was not one of them.

But 'shacking up' did not mean rejection of the 'ideal' of marriage, and many couples resolved to find the money and conform to 'accept-

---

[14] Bryan, *The Jamaican People 1880–1902*, p. 100. There is no indication as to who advanced these explanations, or whether they were contemporary or 'modern'.
[15] *Friends Jamaica Mission* VIII:1 (January 1900), JA 5/8/78/5944; *Friends Jamaica Mission* VI:2 (February 1898), JA 5/8/78/5906; also Bryan, *The Jamaican People 1880–1902*, p. 100.
[16] Livingstone, *Black Jamaica*, pp. 114, 210–1.
[17] Letter by 'An old minister', *Daily Gleaner*, 5 June 1885.
[18] Letter by C.H. Coles, *Jamaica Times*, 20 July 1901.
[19] De Lisser, *Twentieth Century Jamaica*, p. 96; Martha Warren Beckwith, *Black Roadways: A Study of Jamaican Folklore* (Chapel Hill: University of North Carolina Press, 1928), p. 63; and letter of Friends' missionary M.S. Mickle (Hector's River), 4 April 1919, JA 5/8/1/82.

able' convention, however long that took. 'Half a lifetime frequently passes away before the intention is realised, and it is no uncommon thing to witness a marriage where the bridesmaids are the grown-up daughters of the family.' In one case, the couple had lived together for 35 years before getting married[20] – clear testimony of the stability of some of these unions. This also brings into sharp focus the place of marriage in the realm of 'correct' and 'appropriate' behaviour that the populace was aware of and perhaps even hankered after (for all of its alleged benefits) but that they did not *practise*, for one reason or another. Marriage may, in fact, have been taken with such seriousness and viewed with such solemnity that there was great hesitation about entering into it, particularly given its irrevocability under the law.

This links with the other main contemporary school, which argued that the people's failure to 'tie the knot' was related to the unwillingness of the parties to be bound for life to any one person regardless ('for better or for worse'). The stereotyped version was that marriage 'was opposed to the whole bent of their nature... They loved freedom and licence, and were not sufficiently trustful to place their lives permanently in each other's keeping.'[21] De Lisser noted that many men did not want to be tied to one woman because, apart from the responsibility of marriage, they were aware that they might not get on very well with their wives.[22] Livingstone observed a reluctance in some men of the artisan class who, while inclined to marry and settle down, did not want to be tied to a woman of the same class 'because of her lack of training and domestic qualities'. In fact he attributed the failure of many unions to this want of Victorian female domesticity.[23]

But such disinclination was by no means a male prerogative. Women seemed to entertain even clearer notions about the disadvantages of marriage, and many felt no shame about cohabiting with a man out of wedlock. Bryan argues that in keeping with the pattern of female subordination in Victorian marriage, there was a concern among women that 'formal marriage would lead to a reduction of female independence'.[24] Hence one woman reportedly said: 'If we love each other, what need is there of marrying? If we don't, we are able to leave each other.'[25] Women seemed far more reluctant to bind themselves for life to men

---

[20] Livingstone, *Black Jamaica*, pp. 114, 210–1.
[21] Livingstone, *Black Jamaica*, pp. 113–4; *Daily Gleaner*, 16 October 1905.
[22] De Lisser, *Twentieth Century Jamaica*, p. 96.
[23] Livingstone, *Black Jamaica*, p. 213. For a discussion of the 'appropriate roles for women, see Barbara Welter, 'The Cult of True Womanhood: 1820–1860', *American Quarterly* XVIII:2 (Summer 1966): p. 152.
[24] Bryan, *The Jamaican People 1880*–1902, p. 100.
[25] James, *The Mulberry Tree*, pp. 103–4.

who might turn out to be lazy, good-for-nothing and a burden requiring support along with the children. They preferred a relationship which could, if necessary, give them their freedom at any time. 'Me get tired of him, sah, and he get tired of me,' was a common refrain.[26] They claimed that as long as they were not married, the man worked for them, and if he did not they were free to get rid of him and have one who would. But once they got married, it was generally understood that the woman would have to maintain/keep him, and sooner or later there might follow sexual promiscuity, neglect and/or desertion on his part.[27] In fact, Bessie Pullen-Burry asserted that desertion was most dreaded by black women,[28] although some commentators like Livingstone believed that the dissolution of non-legal unions was effected with consummate casualness.[29]

The church considered marriage a permanent institution of God, prescribed by holy scripture, and it lost no opportunity to instruct its followers 'to avoid fornication, [and] let every man have his own wife, and let every woman have her own husband'.[30] Livingstone, however, reflected the Jamaican reality when he opined that as long as unions remained 'temporary' (open-ended) they could be lasting. 'When casual, necessity for mutual kindness and forbearance establishes a condition that is the best guarantee of permanence.' But if made legal and indissoluble, the risk was that they would become intolerable and cease by virtue of one of the parties leaving the other.[31] This situation prompted Winifred James to express the radical view that whites, 'who call it morality to tie together two comparative strangers so hideously bound or else wade in the mud to get free', could learn many lessons from the blacks in their domestic relationship.[32] The black Jamaican population had constructed a viable alternative culture in which the insecurity of cohabitation engendered better relationships that featured more negotiation than the legal marriages of their middle- and upper-class counterparts. At the same time, the possibility of uncomplicated severance acted as a check on inappropriate behaviour.

As was so often the case in other aspects of the creole culture, this disinclination to marry was not confined to the poorer classes. Some

---

[26] Pullen-Burry, *Jamaica As It Is*, pp. 16–17.
[27] James, *The Mulberry Tree*, pp. 103–4.
[28] Pullen-Burry, *Jamaica As It Is*, pp. 16–17.
[29] Livingstone, *Black Jamaica*, p. 214.
[30] See I Corinthians 6:18–19, 7:2; also Acts of the Apostles 15:20, 29; Romans 1:29; I Corinthians 5:1; I Corinthians 6:13; Galatians 5:19; Ephesians 5:3; I Thessalonians 4:3, Jude 1:7 and Hebrews 13:4 among other biblical references.
[31] Livingstone, *Black Jamaica*, p. 213.
[32] James, *The Mulberry Tree*, pp. 103–4.

among the middle and upper classes who portrayed themselves as the preservers of 'correct' British culture had reasons for their own hesitation to be tied, for ever, to one person. A letter by 'Simplicite, Symitric, et Solidite' to the *Gleaner* in 1899 suggested that middle-class young men preferred 'celibacy' to marriage for several reasons: scarcity of remunerative employment, an unwillingness to drag an innocent woman into sharing their distress, fear of marital failure and unhappiness, and a refusal to follow in the iniquitous footsteps of their ancestors.[33] Whether they did remain celibate is open to doubt.

Towards the turn of the twentieth century the emergence of the so-called 'new woman' among the middle classes brought new attitudes, and challenges to the prevailing ideas. This new breed of womankind was not considered sufficiently 'feminine' to make attractive marriage partners.[34] In any case, the 'new woman' was also reputed to be instinctively disinclined to marry:

> These women are bent on pleasure at any cost and the subject of marriage is as distant from their ideals as the North is from the South pole; consequently to propose marriage to such women would certainly end in zero, because their natures being of such a masculine turn would fall within the meaning of the well known truism, "two bulls cannot reign in one pen."[35]

'Young Woman', aged 20, seemed to epitomise the 'new woman'. She vehemently contested the prevailing notion 'that the be-all and end-all of a woman's life should be to please man! How is it that we never hear of men being educated so as to be our companions? Where, pray, are we to find men to suit us? Why should things continue thus?'[36] Nor were women 'ripe cherries ready to fall into the matrimonial basket the moment an opportunity offers'.[37] She felt that marriage worked to women's disadvantage, no matter how educated they were.[38]

Marriage to her was synonymous with children, a thought she found unsettling at best: 'Since babies invariably give much trouble in coming into the world, and in some cases cause loss of life, I shall ever hold that marriage is a handicap.'[39] 'A Married Woman' endorsed this 'heresy'. On

---

[33] Letter titled 'Why our Young Men do not Marry?', in *Daily Gleaner*, 11 February 1899; also letter by 'Bachelor', *Daily Gleaner*, 18 October 1904.
[34] Letter titled 'Why our Young Men do not Marry?', in *Daily Gleaner*, 11 February 1899.
[35] Ibid.
[36] Letter by 'Young Woman', *Daily Gleaner*, 18 October 1904.
[37] Letter by 'Young Woman', *Daily Gleaner*, 24 October 1904.
[38] Letter by 'Young Woman', *Daily Gleaner*, 18 October 1904.
[39] Letters by 'Young Woman', *Daily Gleaner*, 18 and 31 October 1904.

the basis of her experience she could categorically state that the work of a married woman with children was never done, and at times she was cut off from forms of amusement for many months of the year:

> There is no denying the fact that marriage is a handicap, and the young men and women of to-day know it. They are afraid of venturing on the unknown waters and so steer clear of matrimony. We cannot expect every young woman to like all the phases of the married life, and who can say whether the old maids of twenty and thirty years ago did not object to marriage on account of over-refinement.[40]

Although emanating from a small minority of elite women, heretical ideas like these, which openly challenged the 'sacred' institution of 'holy' matrimony, the nuclear family and the overarching patriarchal system which they bolstered, aroused hostile reaction not only from men, but also from women. Twenty-one-year-old male 'Amor' argued that the 'so hard to please' – this tendency of over-refinement and ostentation' attitude shared by 'most young women' was responsible for the failure of many relationships and 'the chief factor of creating the "Old Maid"'. Marriage for him was not based on material considerations; it was a spiritual 'union of two souls by invisible links that man cannot sever; links that make "a man leave his father and his mother and cleave unto his wife."' Children are not a compulsory sequel, but they are optional and desirable, depending on the married parties.' Besides, 'man' had not found a substitute for marriage.[41] It is ironic that although living in a society with a viable option to legal marriage, 'Amor' was nevertheless socially blind to it. He would/could not see that the alternative system of non-legal marriage might answer some of the concerns that reluctant parties had about the institution.[42]

Women also joined the chorus of criticism of 'Young Woman' on account of her attitude to marriage and to children. 'Some Of It' was scathing:

> Those women who prefer a method of worldliness and selfishness to the affection of "children" are devoid of much, so do well to remain "single" – poor would be the man with such a wife or mother for his children ... no sensible mother

---

[40] Letter by 'A Married Woman', *Daily Gleaner*, 7 November 1904.
[41] Letters by 'Amor', *Daily Gleaner*, 24 October and 1 November 1904.
[42] Letters by 'Amor', *Daily Gleaner*, 24 October and 1 November 1904; 'Experience', *Daily Gleaner*, 2 November 1904; and S.R. Brathwaite, *Daily Gleaner*, 27 October 1904. The female responses are embodied in letters by 'Young Woman', *Daily Gleaner*, 31 October 1904; and 'A Married Woman', *Daily Gleaner*, 7 November 1904.

could allow love and devotion to her children to interfere with her duty and sociability to their father. Then also, no home-loving or *wise* husband would be so ungenerous and unsympathetic as to deprive her of his presence which she needs to cheer her on, after the day's labour of love.[43]

Eloise DaCosta asserted that it was only 'the common everyday woman who can have no conception of marriage in its most sacred and holy ties',[44] while 'A Mother' thought that 'marriage calls a woman to a higher sphere of usefulness'.[45]

Within a society built on the precepts of racial difference and deference, race also presented a substantial obstacle to marriage. Whereas there were sexual relationships between whites and blacks, marriages were rare. Quaker missionary Naomi George Swift observed that while it was not uncommon for white and black to live together, it was rare for them ever to marry, for fear on the part of the white man of ostracism by fellow whites. A good example was an Englishman named Jones who lived with a black woman in Manchioneal for about eight to ten years and had four illegitimate mulatto children by her. Their marriage in November 1890 was an aberration and caused quite a stir in the community; as Swift put it, 'it will make the English hate him for marrying her... I think eternal punishment has been staring him in the face and to escape he has felt that he must either give up his wife and children, or bear humiliation in the sight of all the prejudiced [sic] whites.'[46] What was at issue was the 'legitimacy' that he offered his black 'concubine' and their 'bastards'. Such episodes unmasked an underlying hypocrisy in Jamaican society which permitted the campaign for moral 'upliftment' to be sacrificed on the altar of racism.

Bryan labels these intimate relationships between individuals from the different races/classes 'elite concubinage', and claims that they were qualitatively different from those practised by the peasants. Relying on Gardner's assertion that gentlemen in Jamaican society in the 1870s had 'concubines' as an 'all but universal appendage',[47] he argues that the 'arrangement' was usually between a white or coloured male and a coloured or black woman who maintained his house (usually in the position of 'housekeeper') and who made way for a white wife when the 'right time' arrived. These unbalanced relationships did not compare

---

[43] Letters by 'Some Of It', *Daily Gleaner*, 27 October and 2 November 1904.
[44] Letters by Eloise A. DaCosta, *Daily Gleaner*, 25 October and 7 November 1904.
[45] Letter by 'A Mother', *Daily Gleaner*, 24 October 1904.
[46] Naomi George (Swift), 4 November 1890, JA 5/8/10/941.
[47] William James Gardner, *History of Jamaica From Its Discovery by Christopher Columbus to the Year 1872* (London: E. Stock, 1873), p. 377.

well, in his eyes, with those among the peasants or working class where 'men and women ... were economic partners in day to day survival'.⁴⁸ In a situation where women provided labour on the sugar, coffee and banana estates of the island, worked on their own provision grounds and dominated the marketing networks that linked the island's agriculturally productive areas with the main residential centres, women, he claims, entered into relationships of 'partnership rather than domination'. Further, he agrees with Livingstone that the economic contributions that women made to their unions gave them 'a certain power ... over the men', and at the same time removed them from the 'prevailing concept of femininity, domesticity, the woman's role as mother...'⁴⁹

What Bryan does *not* take cognisance of is the fact that in most cases these economic realities meant neither a lessening of male authority (within the larger patriarchal structures) nor a suspension of the Victorian ideal of true womanhood. His argument becomes even more questionable in the case of non-cohabiting unions – what Besson called 'extra-residential conjugal relations', where women and their children constituted the primary unit, men 'visited', and women were assumed to be 'in charge' of their own households. But even in these 'woman-headed households', which are a focus of the interest in the region's alleged 'matrifocality', assumptions like Bryan's have been questioned and even overturned. According to Morrissey, there is no reason to think that because men might not have resided with their companions, their influence over 'their' women was slight. Male authority in such households was to some extent perpetuated by the 'emotional and social contributions' of men; and even where it may have been questioned or apparently lacking, it was in fact 'embodied in the patriarchal family [that was] often an ideal' which the community, as a whole, aspired to.⁵⁰ Rather than creating households of partnership, therefore, the prevailing economic reality of women contributing significantly to their households did not materially alter male authority, which was reinforced by the overarching ideological constructions of patriarchy in the wider society.

---

⁴⁸ Bryan, *The Jamaican People 1880–1902*, p. 97.
⁴⁹ Bryan, *The Jamaican People 1880–1902*, pp. 97–8.
⁵⁰ Morrissey, 'Explaining the Caribbean Family', p. 82; see also Joycelin Massiah, *Women and Heads of Household in the Caribbean: Family Structure and Feminine Status* (Paris: UNESCO, 1983); Raymond T. Smith, *The Negro Family in British Guiana: Family Structure and Social Status in Villages* (New York: Grove Press, 1956).

Controlling 'concubinage'

During the nineteenth century and into the twentieth, the colonial authorities made several attempts to curb the Jamaican penchant for living in non-legal unions, claiming that 'concubinage' contributed to the destruction of the country's moral fibre. The use of the law in this effort pointed to the mindset of those who sought to 'improve' the society by legislating morality. Until 1879, the law gave power to an authorised clergyman to conduct a legal marriage ceremony after the publication of banns, and without the necessity for any witness to be present. The separation of church and state by the disestablishment of the Anglican Church in 1870 meant that it was obligatory that this arrangement be changed. For, as the *Gleaner* observed, it produced a curious anomaly 'that while the State visited with the heaviest penalties the children of unmarried parents, it left the regulation of the conditions under which marriage could be performed entirely in the hands of a variety of conflicting bodies, over none of which had it any control'.[51] Hence in 1879 a new law placed marriage under the full control of the state. A Superintendent Registrar was appointed in each parish, who was responsible for publishing Notices of Marriage and who could also conduct civil marriage. Marriage officers were also to be appointed by the Governor, and each wedding required two independent witnesses. A licence fee of £10 was imposed.[52]

This, however, did not go down well with the Anglican Church, which duly protested: first on the grounds that the new law was fundamentally unchristian and did not recognise marriage as a divine institution, but instead dealt with it as a civil contract. This was especially because it required that certain civil declarations should be made before the religious ceremony was performed. This, they argued, introduced a secular tone to marriage which would reduce its importance in the minds of the people. They also felt that the law needlessly multiplied obstructions and imposed restraints, not least the burdensome licence fee and the restricted hours in which marriages could be performed (10 am to 4 pm), rather than facilitated and encouraged marriage. And they objected to its provision (Article 8) which seemed to restrict marriage officers to functioning only in the parish in which they officiated.[53]

---

[51] *Daily Gleaner*, 29 October 1879.
[52] CO 137/489, Musgrave to Hicks Beach, 2 April 1879, no. 101, and encl: Report of the Attorney General, 31 March 1879. The new law was no. 15 of 1879.
[53] Church of England Scrapbook no. 2, IOJ/MS51a, 1879; see also [Church of England] Memorandum on the Marriage Law of 1879, and Enos Nuttall's open letter to the editor, 31 October 1879, in *Daily Gleaner*, 3 November 1879. Also, Memorial on the New Marriage Law in *Daily Gleaner*, 1 December 1879.

After the Colonial Office had added its voice to some of these criticisms, the law was amended in 1880 to extend the hours from 6 am to 8 pm, to reduce the Governor's licence fee to £5, and to allow marriage officers to operate outside their parish.[54]

Still the people showed very little enthusiasm for legal marriage, and the church and elite society in general became obsessed with what was considered a grave sin and social evil in their midst. Some thought that 'concubinage' should be outlawed and made a criminal offence 'punishable with extreme penalties'.[55]

Reflecting a less draconian attitude, however, in 1885 'An Old Minister' claimed that he used to publish banns of marriage between persons who were living together without either their knowledge or consent, and by so doing he was able to induce a number of couples to be married either in the church or in their houses, who would otherwise never have been married. 'And no evil consequence of my proceedings has ever come to my knowledge.' He thus suggested that every marriage officer should be authorised to publish the banns between persons whom he knew had been living together for three years, and also be authorised to declare publicly in church, unless the banns had been forbidden, that the parties were legally married. In his view, 'A little coercion would ... do no harm in this matter.'[56] By the end of the century, however, several persons considered the very publication of banns itself to be a deterrent to marriage and advocated its removal,[57] because they had an impression that it caused embarrassment to the parties if they were cohabiting out of wedlock.

Another seemingly viable option was to adopt the Scottish marriage code, a step that the *Gleaner* advocated. In Scotland there were two forms of marriage recognised by law: 'regular' and 'irregular'. In both cases it was the deliberate consent or contract of the parties, and not the ceremony, that constituted the marriage. Marriage was a civil contract and all that was required was consent deliberately expressed or implied: *consensus non concubitus facit matrimonium*. Regular marriages were contracted by a priest after proclamations of banns. Irregular marriages were not; but although they only required the

---

[54] CO Minute of Edward Wingfield, 5 May 1880, appended to CO 137/495, Newton to Hicks Beach, 10 April 1880, no. 88. Further minor amendments were made by laws 16 of 1893 and 3 of 1896. All these laws were consolidated by law 25 of 1897. See CO 137/581, Blake to Chamberlain, 10 June 1897, no. 236.
[55] Letter by 'Azrael', *Daily Gleaner*, 7 February 1898; and 'Legitimacy' to Editor, *Daily Gleaner*, 26 March 1900. As late as 1918, 'Young Bachelor' was making a similar proposal (see his letter in *Jamaica Times*, 10 August 1918).
[56] Letter by 'An old minister', *Daily Gleaner*, 5 June 1885.
[57] See Letter by C.H. Coles, *Jamaica Times*, 20 July 1901.

consent of the two parties, they were binding in law and dissoluble only by divorce or death. But even the *Gleaner* was ambivalent about whether it would be prudent to treat 'mere' living together in Jamaica as marriage. 'We have always to remember that we are dealing with a people who are largely ignorant of the moral principles that govern more advanced peoples... To say to a couple who have been living together that they are legally married would not educate them to a proper sense of the highest relations of life and how these relations should be rightly contracted.'[58] The 'unadvanced' Jamaican people may have been able to create long-standing relationships of commitment and nurturance, but they were not about to be supported in their 'sinful' behaviour by the authorities, who were anxious that they enter into 'proper' liaisons. Some part of this concern about the mating patterns of the people had to do with how the elite thought it reflected on themselves, as part of an 'uncivilised' community determined to carry on what they would have labelled as one of the worst aspects of the culture of slavery.

The problem of 'concubinage' (and its twin 'evil', illegitimacy/'bastardy') became the centre of controversial public debate by the turn of the century, as was reflected in the plethora of letters and editorial commentaries in the press.[59] So concerned were the elites with these twin 'sins' that in 1903 the legislature pressed Governor Hemming to appoint a commission of clergy and laymen to enquire into the working of the marriage and registration laws.[60]

After due investigation, the Marriage and Registration Commission reported that the causes of 'concubinage' and illegitimacy were mainly 'temperamental' and economic, and that the remedies must be gradual, working via education and industrial progress to improve the moral and living standards of the people. Specifically with regard to marriage, the commission recommended that the publication of the banns be reduced from three times to one; that the marriage licence fee be reduced to 2s. 6d.; and that the licences be made issuable by any clerk of court or Justice of the Peace instead of only by the Governor.

---

[58] *Daily Gleaner* (editorials), 9 February 1889 and 25 April 1903.
[59] See, for instance, *Jamaica Times*, 7 April and 9 June 1900, 20 July 1901. The illegitimacy rates rose from 59.3 per cent in 1878 to 72.14 per cent in 1920.
[60] This commission consisted of Justice E.A. Northcote (chair), Archbishop Enos Nuttall (Anglican), Bishop Gordon (Roman Catholic), T.B. Oughton (acting Attorney-General), Rev. T.B. Webb of MLC for Trelawny, Hon. J.V. Calder, Hon. Alexander Dixon, J.V. Leach (Resident Magistrate, St Catherine), S.P. Smeeton (Registrar General), Rev. Dr W. Clarke Murray, Rev. S.R. Brathwaite, W.H. Plant (Principal of Titchfield High School), Mrs Mary Macnee (the sole woman). Mr G.M. Wortley of the Colonial Secretary's office served as secretary to the commission. See *Daily Gleaner*, 9 May 1903; Hemming to Chamberlain, no. 434, 28 July 1903, JA 1B/5/18, vol. 57.

These recommendations were embodied in Law No. 28 of 1905. Very interestingly, however, without offering reasons, the commission rejected the idea of adopting Scottish law in Jamaica.[61]

If the *Gleaner* could be regarded as representative of a broad cross-section of elite opinion, it seems that not many members of that elite thought that the new law would lead to much change; and they were right. The provisions hardly seemed to influence the attitude of the people to marriage, as the numbers appeared to fluctuate without reference to the legal facilities made available. They continued to live and function according to their own circumstances, ideas and ideals without regard to the law. As the *Gleaner* observed, 'It is impossible to believe that there can be many persons in the island who have a wish to get married, but are deterred by the expenditure of the few shillings required to secure a legal and binding marriage.' The licence fee was but a minute fraction of the cost of covering 'numerous carriages, more numerous guests, a silk gown for the bride, a coat for the bride-groom, a big dinner with a lot of wine and other things thrown in. These are considerations that entirely outweigh the legal expenses involved...'[62]

The newspaper was correct to believe that the marriage situation would not conform to elite notions unless there was a fundamental alteration in the values of the people, i.e., their full acculturation to the Victorian (Christian) culture. Thus with specific reference to the women, there was a concern that 'their ideas of morality are not as advanced as those of their European sisters; they differ from the latter temperamentally; and the same code of social ethics cannot be applied to them. They are among the majority and are influenced by the ideas and feelings which govern the majority; and until those ideas and feelings undergo some alteration ... no effective pressure can be brought to bear upon them'.[63]

In the latter part of the nineteenth century and into the twentieth, elite society sought to impress upon ordinary Jamaicans the idea that the institution of legal marriage was the only acceptable form of conjugality. For reasons of their own, the people embraced alternative means of establishing unions and the majority would not marry. In 1920, therefore, 'polite society' was no closer to getting the 'unwashed masses' to conform to its ideals of marriage than had been the case in 1865.

---

[61] CO 137/641, Olivier to Lyttelton, 15 September 1904, no. 471, and encl: Report of the Marriage Commission and Appendices. The report was also printed in the *Daily Gleaner*, 29 July 1904. For the new law, see CO 137/645, Swettenham to Lyttelton, 21 June 1905, no. 314.

[62] *Daily Gleaner*, 14 April 1905.

[63] *Daily Gleaner*, 16 October 1905.

This persistent failure or unwillingness of the Jamaican people to enter legal marital relationships does not imply 'resistance' or even 'opposition'[64] to the idea of 'marriage'. What was at issue was the difference in the way marriage was conceived by elite and mass respectively. While both classes shared the view that 'marriage' was an important institution in the life cycle, and may even have agreed that a church wedding was essential, they disagreed about the lifelong compulsion of cohabitation that legal marriage seemed to impose. They also disagreed about the purpose of marriage. For the elites, increasingly keen on aping the British Victorian middle-class ideal, marriage was the foundation of, and thus preceded, the family. For the masses, whose ideas about 'marriage' were largely shaped by their experience on the slave plantation, it was not necessary for, and thus very often followed, the formation of the family. If for the elites the two forms and ideas of marriage were deemed mutually exclusive and incompatible on moral grounds, that was hardly the case for the masses. For there is evidence that the latter held legal Christian marriage as an ideal once they felt confident in their partners, and they were even prepared to go to enormous expense to celebrate it. *They* certainly did not either resist or oppose it. On the other hand, however, they felt no sense of shame or inferiority about their non-legal conjugal unions despite the denunciations of the elites. In this context, such 'opposition' and/or 'resistance' as there was came not from the masses towards the Victorian model, but rather emanated *from the elites* towards the lower-class practice of so-called 'concubinage'. The people were quite content to live their lives according to their own ideas and customs and, when they felt the time was right, to legalise their marriages, complete with a lavish church wedding. It was the 'cultural elites' who, despite their power to legislate on 'moral' issues, were rendered impotent on the marriage question and resorted to ranting and raving, resistance and opposition to an institution (participated

---

[64] Following Michel de Certeau, Richard D.E. Burton has made a distinction between 'resistance' and 'opposition' in post-emancipation Caribbean society. In his conceptualisation, resistance must utilise cultural elements from outside the dominant system, and it should also lead to a fundamental change or overthrow of that system. In his view, Afro-Creole cultures in the Caribbean since emancipation are 'cultures of opposition' because they employ the institutions and other cultural materials of the dominant culture, modify but do not transform them, and then turn them against the dominant culture in order to contest it. See Richard D.E. Burton, *Afro-Creole: Power, Opposition and Play in the Caribbean* (Ithaca: Cornell University Press, 1997), pp. 6–9. This is not, however, an appropriate forum to discuss these interesting ideas in depth. Here we shall confine our discussion to show that despite its political and social power, elite Jamaica found itself 'resisting/opposing' the 'subterranean power' of the black majority, whose ability to adhere to their traditional ideas, practices and customs threatened to undermine the civilisation that the elites were seeking to construct.

in by the majority) which they felt reflected negatively on, and even threatened to undermine, the type of civilisation that they were attempting to construct in the Caribbean.

What this demonstrates is that distinctions between 'resistance' and 'opposition', however useful they might be as analytical tools, do not suffice to explain the cultural dynamics of the post-emancipation Caribbean. Resistance/opposition was certainly a reaction to 'power', but not simply to that of the dominant system. The cultural elites did monopolise the power of the state, the church, the press and 'the commanding heights of the economy', all of which they employed to try to impose their culture and morality on the society at large. But 'power' so conceived is by no means all-embracing, particularly in a situation like that of Jamaica, where the elites formed a tiny minority of the population and were thus incapable of strictly enforcing their will on the masses. On the other hand, although excluded from the established institutions of 'power', the Afro-Creole masses were by no means powerless. Their 'power' was 'subterranean'[65] and lay essentially in their numbers. Although not united or organised as a corporate group, they were integrated by a shared cultural expression which was manifested in their beliefs, values, behaviour, customs and practices. It was the pervasiveness of this culture of the lower-class majority which constantly threatened to undermine and potentially overwhelm the elite cultural order. That was the threat which those who possessed conventionally defined 'power' found themselves resisting/opposing lest they be submerged in 'a sea of blackness' by the 'cultural power of numbers'. The concepts of 'resistance' and 'opposition' should not, therefore, be viewed simply in a context of responses by subordinate socio-cultural groups to a dominant system, for 'power' (particularly as it relates to cultural expression) is never the exclusive preserve of any single group in society.

---

[65] Kamau Brathwaite, *Contradictory Omens: Cultural Diversity and Integration in the Caribbean* (Kingston: Savacou Publications, 1974), employs this term to represent the culture of the Afro-Creole masses.

12 | The cloaking of a heritage: the Barbados Landship

Marcia Burrowes

when I die
sail me thru
these paved highways
like a napolean
like a nelson
with my navy of land lovers
with my pride in my pocket
with my pain in my penny-whistle

(Winston Farrell, 'tribute')[1]

Introduction

The Landship is a Barbadian community group located mainly in the plantation tenantries and villages for most of its existence. Coming to prominence in the late nineteenth century, most Landships were Friendly Societies whose trademark was to wear British naval livery and perform naval 'manoeuvres' during their parades. They were very popular among the working classes and enjoyed especial prominence in the late 1920s and early 1930s.

However, Landships have had an uneasy existence in Barbadian society. Their critics have accused them of mimicking the coloniser, that is, of being black labouring-class Barbadians who dressed in British naval uniforms and tried to become British. They have argued that such an accusation was highly feasible, for at that time Barbados was 'Little England', an outpost of empire in the British West Indies. What the Landship demonstrated was black allegiance to the colonial ideal.

This chapter presents alternative readings of the group. It argues that as a cultural form the Landship demonstrates one of the ways labouring-class Barbadians coped with colonisation in the post-emancipation period. What was interpreted as mimicry was instead a form of cultural camou-

---

[1] Winston Farrell, *Tribute* (Barbados: Farcia Publication in association with the Commonwealth Liaison Unit of Barbados, 1995), p. 7.

flage that enabled Landship members to manoeuvre within the constraints of plantation society. By adopting the clothes of the colonial master, they devised ways of creating pockets of resistance within colonial space.

In 1931, an article in *The Advocate News* highlighted the occurrence of an unusual social event in Barbados. Entitled 'Little England's Navy En Fete', the article opened as follows:

> Little England's navy was to fete last Thursday. Responding enthusiastically to the invitation of Mr. C.B. Brandford of No. 2 Bay Street, the Admirals and Commanders of about 23 units of the landship movement led a band of their officers and sailors and red cross nurses, numbering well over 300, in a well-organised train excursion to Belleplaine.[2]

What then ensued was a report of a train excursion to the Barbados countryside, in which a large number of persons from the labouring class and some from the middle class mingled and mixed for the day. The writer dubbed the event a 'social pepperpot', for among this gathering was an Oxford graduate, students of the arts and humanities and some females 'whose dress and bearing bespoke some standard of taste and degree of culture'. All present had an enjoyable time as they ate and drank and danced to the music of Bromley's Band in the Railway Shed.[3] The main event of the day was the parade of the units of the Landship:

> During the day the men paraded on the spacious pasture at Belleplaine firstly in companies from each ship and subsequently in mass formation, and although there is much room for improvement in their drill and manoeuvring, their turn out, on the whole, was impressive.

What can be noted is that before embarking upon this description of the parade, the writer found it necessary to make a special plea to his readership for understanding and tolerance of the group. 'At first blush one is tempted to raise a smile of derision at what appears to be merely stupid mimicry and regular antics. But there is a deeper significance and a worthier motive underlying this movement.' He then argued that what the 'ships' were noted for was the high instance of discipline among their members. Thrift and unity were also virtues closely adhered to in the movement. Moreover, a Landship parade provided 'an enjoyable

---

[2] 'Little England's Navy En Fete', *The Advocate News*, 10 October 1931, p. 4.
[3] Bromley has become a legend in Barbadian folk history. A sanitary inspector, he operated a brass band and was notorious for his train excursions to Belleplaine at which his band would play. His band specialised in tuk band songs. See Trevor Marshall, Peggy McGeary and Grace Thompson, *Folk Songs of Barbados* (Jamaica: Ian Randle Publishers, 1996 [1981]), p. 69.

spectacle for hundreds of country-folk whose life is one of unvarying monotony and soul-killing drabness'.

Though it is now several decades since this report, the group referred to in the article continues to 'sail' on in Barbados. The majority of 'units' of the present-day Landship have come together under the leadership of Captain Vernon Watson. There is now officially one 'ship', called *The Barbados Landship*. There are still individuals known as Admirals and Commanders who go on parade in their medals, gold tassels and peaked caps with naval emblems. There are also nurses, policewomen and other costumed representatives of naval, military and civil organisations. No longer organising impressive excursions to the countryside, *The Barbados Landship* is in great demand to appear and do its marching routine at cultural events around the island. In 1997, the Government of Barbados acknowledged that the Landship was part of the Barbadian heritage and thus an important cultural and national institution.[4]

Yet the Landship continues to present the same dilemma to which the writer of the 1931 article referred. The accusation of playing the 'monkey game' and of being an exercise which is 'a mock, farce, a poor joke' continues to haunt the group. This is so despite recent research. Their role as a Friendly Society is now generally accepted, with Aviston Downes emphasising that the initiative for the Society came from within the black working classes and not the clergy. Trevor Marshall has argued that their marching routine is composed of African-Caribbean dance steps, while Curwen Best sees the tuk band, the musical band that accompanies the Landship, as an integral component of Landship identity. Landship and tuk band together become 'a distinctively African-Bajan phenomenon'. Yet for some Barbadians, the Landship is an embarrassment and a colonial artefact that suited a time when Barbadians were good at aping the colonisers in 'Little England'.[5]

---

[4] Note the comments of the Minister of Education, Culture and Youth Affairs, Mia Mottley. See 'Landship part of we culture', *The Sunday Sun*, 23 February 1997, p. 30.

[5] For the stinging criticism of the Landship, see Lawson Bayley, 'Shocking State of Affairs', *The Sunday Advocate News*, 9 February 1975, p. 4. For the Landship as a Friendly Society, see John Gilmore, *The Barbados Landship Association: 130 years: 1863–1993* (Barbados: the National Cultural Foundation and the Audio Visual Aids Department, 1993); Aviston Downes, 'Searching for Admiral Moses Wood: Oral Tradition and the History of the Landship', *Journal of the Barbados Museum and Historical Society*, vol. XLVIII, pp. 64–78; also Downes, 'Sailing from Colonial into National Waters: A History of the Barbados Landship', *Journal of the Barbados Museum and Historical Society*, vol. XLVI, pp. 92–122. For the revelation of the African-Caribbean dance steps, see Trevor Marshall, 'A Ship on Land?', in Rachel Wilder (ed.), *Insight Guides: Barbados* (Hong Kong: APA Productions Ltd., 1990) p. 65. For the comments on the tuk band, see Curwen Best, *Roots to Popular Culture: Barbadian Aesthetics: Kamau Brathwaite to Hardcore Styles* (London: Macmillan Caribbean, 2001), p. 53.

This chapter raises questions about the identity of the Landship and its role in the post-emancipation colonial Barbadian society. Its main focus is the period of its inception to the 1930s. Though some attention will be paid to the historic development of this group, the main task is to address the question of colonial mimicry and the resulting identities of the colonised.

In pursuing this agenda Stuart Hall reminds us that in the creolisation process, it is more the norm to find examples where the cultures of the colonised and the coloniser have been successfully synthesised. What may appear to be acculturation, as is the case at first glance with the Landship, is still an example of creolisation precisely because the British and African cultures have been mixed. It has been the tradition to argue that a Caribbean cultural form must have an easily recognisable 'African' component to be creole. Hall argues that this tradition can be misleading:

> The important pockets of survival in their pure form are massively outweighed in our culture by the way African-derived cultural practice and meanings have survived, by being *synthesised* with other elements in the cultural mix.[6] (My emphasis.)

Homi Bhabha argues that even in situations where the colonised have worked assiduously towards the target culture, the act of colonial mimicry does not result in a true image of the coloniser, but a distorted one:

> Colonial mimicry is the desire for a reformed, recognizable Other, *as a subject of a difference that is almost the same but not quite*. Which is to say, that the discourse of mimicry is constructed around an ambivalence; in order to be effective, mimicry must continually produce its slippage, its excess, its difference.[7]

What is also produced by this act of mimicry is usually a critique of the foibles and failings of the coloniser. Bhabha calls this critiquing process the menace of mimicry: 'The *menace* of mimicry is its *double* vision which in disclosing the ambivalence of colonial discourse also disrupts its authority.' As Childs and Williams put it, mimicry, 'as a repetition

---

[6] Stuart Hall, 'Thinking Diasporically: Home Thoughts From Abroad', in *The Distinguished Lecture Series,* University of the West Indies, Cave Hill Campus, as recorded by the Educational Media Services, Learning Resource Centre, Care Hill Campus, 18 November 1998.

[7] Homi K. Bhabha, *Location of Culture* (London: Routledge, 1995 [1994]), p. 86.

that is "almost but not quite" the same as the original, queries not only the definition but the self-identity of the "original"'.[8]

It will be argued here that the Landship is an example of the process of synthesis described by Hall. When the cultural form is assessed, it becomes possible to reveal some of the components that are normally hidden from view. However, to be the Landship, the cloak or the Royal Navy uniforms and all the accompanying rituals are vital components of its identity. This is because it is a synthesised cultural form. It needs the cloak, with all confined within, for its identification.

In pursuit of origins

The popular understanding is that in 1863, a Barbadian seaman called Moses Ward, or Moses Wood, created the group now known as the Landship. A former member of the Royal Navy, Moses opted to re-enact on land the discipline and camaraderie he had experienced at sea. He and his friends dressed themselves in the uniforms of the British Royal Navy and adopted the appropriate titles held by naval officers. A corresponding hierarchy was duly created. To complete the enterprise, it was decided that each group or 'ship' would be named after a British vessel, preferably a British man-of-war. With this evolved the following Landship names: *Iron Duke*, *Dreadnought* and *Nelson*. Consequently, there arose in Barbados the advent of a ship on land, or, as is more popularly observed, the ship that never goes to sea.

In pursuing some understanding of the Landship, the first of several pitfalls is the question of the origins of the group. Though popular discourse affixes the name Moses Ward or Wood as its founder and the date 1863 as its commencement, there is no clear evidence to support this. For example, other years, all within the late nineteenth century, have been given as possible launching points.[9] With regard to the name it is possible that the Ward alternative only arose through an error in

---

[8] Ehabha, *Location of Culture*, p. 88; Peter Childs and Patrick Williams, *An Introduction to Post-Colonial Theory* (London: Prentice Hall, 1997), p. 132.

[9] Indeed it was only in 1972 that the date 1863 made an appearance in the writings, just in time for the 109th anniversary of the movement. Gilmore gives both 1863 and 1868, but goes along with 1863. See Gilmore, *The Barbados Landship Association*, p. 2. Both dates are also given in the *A-Z of Barbadian Heritage*. See H. Fraser, S. Carrington, A Forde and J. Gilmore, *A-Z of Barbadian Heritage* (Jamaica: Heinemann Publishers Caribbean Limited, 1990), pp. 97–8; Hilton Vaughan gave an estimate of the 1890s. See Giraud Robinson, 'The Barbados Landship: Origins, Structure and Economic Aspects' (unpublished Caribbean Studies thesis, University of the West Indies, Cave Hill, 1977), p. 3.

transcription and that the founder was indeed Moses Wood.[10] Downes has located Moses Wood, but was unable to solve the mystery surrounding Landship origins.[11] Then there is the question of his racial composition and his country of origin. It has been contended that he was a white Englishman who made his home in Barbados, a coloured Barbadian of Cardiff and Southampton who retired in Barbados, as well as a black Barbadian seaman born in Barbados who returned home.[12] Again this needs clarification. The result of these pockets of obscurity in the genesis story is that much of it cannot be verified. The issue of how the movement began remains to be resolved.

There is, however, evidence to suggest that Landships, or a similar cultural form, indeed existed in the 1870s. There are references to a cultural practice called 'marching' as a form of entertainment. At the Harvest Home celebrations in St John, it was reported that the labourers were 'accommodated with marchings and dancing'. These 'marchings and dancing' were the norm at these events and were highly entertaining. This chapter will demonstrate that the naval 'manoeuvres' performed by members of the Landship when they are on parade are a series of vigorous dance and marching movements to the music of drums and a form of wind instrument such as the penny whistle or the flute.[13]

Nevertheless, when pursuing the origins of the Landship, we find the earliest evidence of their launching is in 1898, when two ship-

---

[10] It was in the 1953 Wells report on Friendly Societies in the West Indies that the name 'Wood' first appeared. Wells wrote: 'Mr. Vaughan tells us that Landships are said [...] to have been started in Barbados by Moses Wood, a Barbadian seaman, who lived in Cardiff and Southampton.' In 1964, Louis Lynch appears to be paraphrasing what Wells had written, but puts in the name 'Ward' instead. Lynch writes: 'Wells says it was introduced by Moses Ward, a Barbadian seaman who lived in Cardiff and Southampton.' F. and D. Wells, *Friendly Societies in the West Indies: Report on a Survey and a despatch from the Secretary of State for the Colonies to the West Indian Governors dated 15th May, 1952* (London: Her Majesty's Stationery Office, 1953) #253; Louis Lynch, *The Barbados Book* (New York: Taplinger Publishing Co., 1964), p. 224.

[11] Wood was born in 1860 and so could not have founded the movement, if it did begin in 1863. However, the oral tradition strongly suggests a Wood connection. Whether he played a key role in later events or whether the movement was indeed founded at a later date is to be debated. See Downes, 'Searching for Admiral Moses Wood', pp. 66–74.

[12] For the claim of white Englishman, see Bayley, 'Shocking State of Affairs'. For coloured Barbadian, see A.F. and D. Wells, *Friendly Societies in the West Indies: Report on a Survey and a despatch from the Secretary of State for the Colonies to the West Indian Governors dated 15th May, 1952* (London: Her Majesty's Stationery Office, 1953). For Black Barbadian, see Marshall, 'A Ship on Land', p. 65. Aviston Downes goes along with the Cardiff and Southampton version. See Downes, 'Sailing from Colonial into National Waters', p. 101.

[13] 'St. John Correspondent', *The Times*, 7 July 1875, p. 3.

societies appear on the list of registration of Friendly Societies published in the Official Gazette. These are the *Ship Nelson* and the *Victory Naval*. This, however, does not mean that these Landships were created at that time; rather that they came forward, or were made to come forward, to be registered as Friendly Societies from 1898 onwards.[14]

The *Ship Nelson* is the more famous of the two. Mention was made of it in the 1953 Wells report on Friendly Societies. It is also one of the Landships known to the majority of the present-day members. The *Ship Nelson* Friendly Society was dissolved on 1 April 1905 after only seven years in existence. It, or another ship bearing its name, was 'raised' again at a later stage. The *Barbados Landship Review*, the magazine that celebrated the achievements of the Landship movement, lists the *Nelson* as a member of the Landship Association in 1932.

Another early Landship was the *Rosetta*, which came to the fore as an unregistered Friendly Society. With a model ship as its insignia, it had 17 members, many of whom were boatmen. Its officers did not wear naval uniforms. The *Rosetta* had been formed in June 1901, just one month before its officers were arrested. Having broken the provisions regarding registration as stipulated in the Friendly Societies Act, Admiral Alonzo Duke, a boatman by trade, and Paymaster Walter Wiltshire, a tailor, were ordered to pay a £1 fine and 1s. 6d. in costs, or face 14 days in prison. Ironically, the very impulse for launching this ship-society, which Admiral Duke said was to keep them 'above the frowns of this world', had also brought them into disrepute with it.[15]

The *Rosetta* was one of the many Landships that found themselves in breach of the law during this time. In 1901, Landships were also in breach of the Uniforms Act, which outlawed the use of military uniforms by civilians. This was the era of Governor Hodgson, who launched a campaign to eliminate what he termed 'bogus Friendly Societies'. Hodgson utilised the authority of the police and the Registrar of Friendly Societies in his attack on these early ship-societies. Many suffered persecution and were forced to dissolve.[16]

Yet Landships continued to 'sail'. For example, in 1907 the *Dauntless* was launched, followed by the *Indefatigable* and the *Renown*

---

[14] Indeed the Friendly Society Act of 1905 made further adjustments to the previous Acts and as a result, several groups were made to register as Friendly Societies or otherwise face legal sanctions.
[15] See the proceedings of the trial as given in *The Barbados Agricultural Reporter*, 18 September 1901, p. 3. Also Bonham Richardson, *Panama Money in Barbados: 1900–1920* (Knoxville: The University of Tennessee Press, 1985) p. 224; Downes, 'Sailing from Colonial Waters', pp. 108–9.
[16] Downes, 'Sailing from Colonial Waters', pp. 107–9.

in 1908. By 1912, the *Queen Mary* and the *New Zealand* had also been launched. They were all registered as Friendly Societies during this period.[17] These Landships were also listed in the 1932 *Landship Review*. Moreover, in 1997, the *Queen Mary* and the *Indefatigable* had members within *The Barbados Landship*.

Special mention must be made of the launching of the *Queen Mary*. In April 1912, Mr J. Gittens Knight, the Registrar of Friendly Societies, refused the application of the *Queen Mary* of Brittons Hill, St Michael. He argued that the area was 'already sufficiently supplied with registered Societies'. The *Queen Mary* persisted with its application and was successful. In May 1912 it registered as Friendly Society No. 468. The Society paid examining fees valued at £1.[18]

Taking possession of the air

By the 1920s, Landships found themselves sailing into the era of socialist ideas and a burgeoning labour movement. These changing times signalled changes in their status within the society. No longer the object of harassment by the authorities, Landships increased in size and number. They also found favour among some members of the middle class whom Hilton Vaughan called 'benevolent outsiders', who helped them with 'time, money and advice'.[19] One such group was the Bridgetown Brotherhood, who invited Landship persons to have meetings with them at Bethel Church in Bridgetown and discuss their hopes and problems.[20] With such favourable social winds blowing their way, the late 1920s and the early 1930s formed the heyday in the Landship experience.

Band Major Daniel Hope of the *Cornwall* has been a member of the Landship since 1935. He has always been the 'flute man', the person who blows the flute or penny whistle for the tuk band. A resident of Carlton, St James, Band Major Hope remembers when, in the 1920s, there were at least two Landships in each of the 11 parishes in Barbados. The city parish, St Michael, had many more. In the 1930s, the 'ships' were so large that at times two tuk bands would be used to play for the march and the

---

[17] CO/32/35 to CO/32/48.
[18] CO/32/47 and CO/32/48.
[19] See Hilton Vaughan, 'Some Social and Political Tendencies,' in J.M. Hewitt (ed.), *Silver Jubilee Magazine: 1910–1935* (Barbados: 1935), pp. 31–3 and 57–61 (p. 60). Hilton Vaughan was a black lawyer who became one of the leading historians in Barbados.
[20] George Bernard, *Wayside Sketches: Pen Pictures of Barbadian Life* (Barbados: Advocate Co., 1934), p. 15. Also S. Victor Johnson, 'Socio-Cultural Implications of the Barbados Landship' (unpublished Caribbean Studies thesis, University of the West Indies, Cave Hill, 1976–77), p. 5; Downes, 'Searching for Admiral Moses Wood', p. 68.

parade. One would lead the group while the other would be placed in the middle. The Landships of the northern parishes (St James, St Peter, St Lucy) would visit each other and, on occasion, parade together. He distinctly remembers that in the parish of St Peter there were Landships in Speightstown, Mile and a Quarter and Black Bess. The *Cornwall* would visit these and other Landships around the island.[21]

In 1998, the oldest active member of the Landship was Lieutenant Lloyd Adams of the *Director*. He was 89 years old. Known fondly as 'No. 1', Adams recalled that in 1919, when he was ten years old, he used to 'follow dem about'. At that time he was called 'the skylight boy' because of his young age. He was not a member of any particular ship but would attach himself to any one of them parading through his area, or he would travel to where he could view them on parade. As a child, he was attracted to them by the music of the tuk band; he would follow them and do the dance steps. When he was old enough he joined the *Cornwall* of St Michael. He too believed that the 1930s were the period when there were many Landships throughout the island.[22]

There is evidence to support his claim. For example, in August 1930, 145 Landship members, led by Commander Carter of the *Hood*, marched to St Mary's Church and participated in the Sunday service. The Landships involved were the *Renown*, *Victory*, *Royal George*, *Warspite* and *Spark*. Canon W.G. Murray led the service and preached a sermon entitled 'Can anything good come out of Nazareth?' This biblical echo was in response to those who condemned the Landship because its members came out of poor circumstances. It also enabled the canon to project a more positive future for the group. It was reported that the sermon was inspiring to the listeners. After the service, the members returned to their docks.[23]

That the Landship was definitely on the march becomes clear again in August 1930 when a series of articles appears in the *Barbados Advocate*, entitled 'That Terrible Tom Tom'. Though the first 'correspondent' assumed the drumming heard late into the night was that of the cadets, it was quickly clarified that it was the 'Landship Army' marching through the residential streets near the Garrison. The complaints were mainly about the 'strumming and drumming' that reportedly could be heard until midnight. One 'correspondent' agonised as follows:

> One does not desire to interfere with recreations and amusements of other people, but we also deserve some considera-

---

[21] Personal interview with Band Major Daniel Hope, 19 May 1998.
[22] Personal interview with Lieutenant Lloyd Adams, 14 May 1998.
[23] 27 August 1930, *Barbados Advocate*, p. 10.

tion. And I think this is something more than reasonable liberty – to take possession of the air for half and three quarters of a mile in all directions and fill it with the monotonous hammering of that terrible tom-tom.[24]

Despite a call for the application of the law against noise on the public streets, Landships continued to thrive. In August 1931 they were the highlight of the Carnival entries in Queen's Park. The admirals rode in a gaily-decorated hackney carriage while the other members of the crew rode in donkey carts. This prompted the writer to comment that 'even among Landships there are differences in station'.[25]

Again in 1931, an article entitled 'Monster Landship Parade' appeared in the *Barbados Advocate*. Gordon Belle, who wrote under the pseudonym of George Bernard, was its author. The article recorded the events of a parade held on 9 November 1931 in which 'the combined Landships under the command of Lord High Admiral Walcott turned out to parade *en masse*'. Held at the famous black cricket ground, the Empire Club, the parade was witnessed by over a thousand spectators. The Landship that seemed to impress the crowd the most was the *Warspite*. It contained the young male recruits called the 'Blues'. The No. 3 Company, under the leadership of Commander Hunte, also gained great applause for its march past.[26]

Sir Frederick Clarke addressed the parade. Sir Frederick was the speaker of the House of Assembly and one of the few members of the plantocracy admired by the general populace for his knowledge and impartiality.[27] Dr Hugh Cummins, a prominent member of the educated middle class, delivered the vote of thanks. The parade ended with three cheers being raised for Sir Frederick and another set for the visitors. The

---

[24] *Barbados Advocate*: 27 August 1930, p. 10; 29 August, p. 12; 3 September, p. 10; 5 September, p. 11.
[25] *Barbados Advocate*, 5 August 1931, p. 8.
[26] George Bernard, 'Monster Landship Parade' *The Advocate News*, 12 November 1931, p. 5. Belle was a Landship devotee who spent much of his time not only reporting on the activities of the Landships, but also engaged in the task of persuading the public to view them in a more favourable light. It was against the law for a civil servant to write for a public forum. For Belle's references to the Landship, see Bernard, *Wayside Sketches*, pp. 15–18.
[27] Clennel Wickham, a black journalist who wrote scathing commentaries about the local plantocracy, found Sir Frederick Clarke 'a triumphant exception. He is most decidedly the right man in the right place [...] His knowledge of parliamentary law and procedure is altogether admirable, his patience is exhaustless, and his impartial ruling over the House of Assembly for the past generation, can never be too highly esteemed.' See Clennel Wickham, *Pen and Ink Sketches by a Man with a Fountain Pen* (Barbados: Barbados Herald, 1921), p. 5.

British National Anthem was played and the Landship Companies were dismissed.

By 1931, a central authority, called the Barbados Land Ship Association, governed the various units. Its headquarters were in Bridgetown. Among the activities of the Association was the publication of the magazine called the *Barbados Landship Review*. In it such details as the names of Landships, as well as the dates of parades, weddings and funerals, were recorded. Landships were now addressed by the prefix 'BLS', another addition to the nautical image. The Secretary of the Association was Mr E.L. Millington. In an article in the newspaper he thanked the police for their role in protecting its members along the November 1931 march. Special thanks were accorded to Sergeant Major Goodman for his assistance in training the crews.[28]

With an Association organising their public appearances, the Landships reached the zenith of their activities. In February 1932, a total of 15 Landships, comprising 575 officers, nurses and 'blues' (young male recruits), attended the 11 o'clock church service at the Cathedral. The Governor of Barbados, Sir William Robertson, and the Governor of the Windward Islands, Sir Thomas A. Vans Best, attended the service. The Dean of the Cathedral officiated. After the service there was a parade that was inspected by the two Governors and the Dean. The Governor of Barbados addressed the units, advising them to 'continue the good work' and to 'grow up to be loyal citizens'.[29]

Mr Charles Daisley, a prominent member of the middle class and a member of the Barbados Land Ship Association, gave the main address:

> Mr. Daisley replied on behalf of the ships, thanking His Excellency and assuring him that the B.L.S. had two special objects to carry out – firstly to create "strikes" and secondly to give the Police "Troubles". With regard to the first object he said that it was the intention of the Association to "strike" the bad ways of living among their followers and to do all that lay in the power to become loyal citizens. The second object, he said, disclosed the intention of the Association to live up to everything that pointed to "uplift" and to become such loyal citizens, that the Police would experience great "troubles" in finding convicts in Barbados, more especially among Land Shipmen.[30]

---

[28] *Barbados Advocate*, 18 November 1931, p. 10. See also Lynch, *The Barbados Book*, p. 223.
[29] *Barbados Advocate*, 8 March 1932, p. 8.
[30] Ibid.

The Governor thanked Mr Daisley for his remarks and the parade marched off to the dock of BLS *Rodney* at Bannister Land, where they were dismissed.³¹

Though it would have proved difficult to top the February parade, the Barbados Landship Association managed to do just that. In 1932, over 600 Landship members competed at an athletic meet which was held at Queen's Park on Easter Bank Holiday. There were various events, including 100- and 200-yard races. The prize was a mahogany shield bearing the inscription 'B.L.S. Association Shield'. BLS *Hudson* was the victorious Landship. The Dean of the Cathedral was once again involved, this time distributing the prizes. When that task was completed, the Dean stood on the table that had held the trophies and addressed the gathering. He congratulated the ships for the keenly contested events and called for three cheers for Dr Cummins, Captain Goddard and Sergeant Major Goodman. The Landships were then dismissed.

Ironically, after this very public burst of activity, reports on the Landship rapidly dwindle after 1932. Landships continued to 'sail', but not in the public eye. Vaughan accounts for this: 'But with increased depression, membership fell off, finances dwindled, the magazine expired, and the friends of the movement were for the most part too worried over their own affairs to attend to the "ships".'³² Nonetheless, Landship activity continued in the tenantries and villages throughout the 1930s.

In October 1937, the Landships sailed to their most important rendezvous. They were part of the official welcoming committee for Marcus Garvey when he made his one-day visit to Barbados. Arriving at Bridgetown in the early hours of the morning, Garvey was taken to Liberty Hall for his first engagement.

> At the entrance of the Hall there were 24 men and women dressed in the uniform of the Barbados Land Ship "York". These formed a Guard through which he passed while the African National Anthem was played on a Coronet. Mr. Garvey and his Secretary then entered the hall while

---

³¹ *Barbados Advocate*, 4 June 1932, p. 10. It is important to note that this February 1932 parade appears to be the grand parade to which Hilton Vaughan refers. It was held at the Cathedral and the Governor did take the salute. Though the numbers are much fewer than the 3000 men and 800 women that Vaughan alludes to, the total of 575 is still very impressive for the time. This Landship Cathedral parade outnumbered the total mustered by the cavalry, the police and the cadets for the King's Birthday Parade held in June 1932. That official parade had only 424 persons on display. For the discussion by Vaughan of the grand parade, see 'Some Social and Political Tendencies', p. 60.
³² Vaughan, 'Some Social and Political Tendencies', p. 60.

another anthem was sung by the congregation. Mr. Garvey made a short speech thanking those responsible for the arrangements made for his reception, and expressed how pleased he felt at seeing so many faces.[33]

To be part of such a historic event was a fitting tribute to the Barbados Landship. Moreover, forming the guard of honour for Marcus Garvey while the African National Anthem was played authenticated other components of their identity. By dressing in the uniforms of the Royal Navy, the Landship had succeeded in closely guarding key components of their identity that would have been frowned upon by the colonial authorities.

Reading the Landship

Clifford Geertz posits that culture is an 'acted document' which can be read to see what it says. Thus cultural forms can be read as 'texts, as imaginative works built out of social materials'. When the cultural form or text is read, the emphasis is more upon discovering what is being said than on giving an account of the form. Such readings lead to a greater understanding of the people of that culture 'without reducing their particularity'.[34]

This chapter seeks to present alternative readings of the Landship. Traditional readings have emphasised the act of dressing in the uniforms of the British navy and adopting its norms and practices. For example, when penning his articles on the Landship, Gordon Belle chose to emphasise their adoption of British naval culture. His intention was to demonstrate to the Barbadian public that Landship members were well behaved, disciplined subjects who actively showed their allegiance to the colonial ideal. In this way they were 'Little England's navy', safeguarding the principles of empire.

This early view of the Landship, with its emphasis on the adoption of British navy rituals and norms, became the guiding tool for perception of the movement. In the 1953 Report on Friendly Societies in the West Indies, the Landships' adoption of British naval culture received close attention:

> The societies' meeting rooms were got up to look like ships, with, for example, masts and wires on the roof; members wore dress resembling naval uniforms and there were

---

[33] Police Report, October 1937. Many thanks to the publishers of the Garvey papers for this data.
[34] Clifford Geertz, *The Interpretation of Cultures: Selected Essays* (London: Fontana Press, 1993 [1973]), pp. 10, 14 and 449.

ceremonies reminiscent of naval drill and routine. Sometimes the insignia included a model ship. Mutual aid was combined with the ceremonial.[35]

Recent publications continue to make use of the traditional readings of the group. In the 1996 publication of the *Dictionary of Caribbean English Usage*, the Landship is described as follows: 'A group of usually rural men and women formed basically as a Friendly Society; it functions exclusively on land, but is organised and best known as *a ceremonial copy of the British Navy*.'[36] (My emphasis.)

In evolving alternative readings, this chapter does not deny that British naval rituals played a role in the formation of Landship identity. Rather it argues that concentrating predominantly on the adoption of naval culture has resulted in other readings being obscured from view. What results is that the *cloak of the Landship*, that is, the naval uniforms, the use of British names for the ships, and other practices, have dominated the analysis. Other readings have not been actively pursued. The task at hand is to seek these narratives within the Landship story.

For example, Trevor Marshall has argued that the Landship parade was a form of Barbadian masquerade:

> For most Barbadians, the landship was masquerade on a small scale as the 'sailors' and 'ratings' went through their 'manoeuvres' and 'duties' on board 'ship'. These Landship parades became a feature of public holiday entertainment as the bands travelled through several villages and parishes, playing popular tunes, and inviting persons to contribute their own compositions, however innocent or suggestive in lyrics, or simple or intricate in melody.[37]

When the Landship parade is seen as masquerade, a new reading of the cultural form evolves. Masquerade brings in the element of spectacle and the occupation of the street, a public space closely guarded from the labouring classes during colonial times. This chapter has shown how the Landship claimed the street for their parades. Their marching and

---

[35] F. and D. Wells, *Friendly Societies in the West Indies: Report on a Survey and a despatch from the Secretary of State for the Colonies to the West Indian Governors dated 15th May, 1952* (London: Her Majesty's Stationery Office, 1953), #261.

[36] Richard Allsopp, *Dictionary of Caribbean English Usage*, with a French and Spanish supplement ed. Jeanette Allsopp (Oxford: Oxford University Press, 1996).

[37] Trevor Marshall, 'Notes on the History and Evolution of Calypso in Barbados' (unpublished seminar paper, Department of History, University of the West Indies, Cave Hill, 1985), p. 24.

drumming in August 1930 disturbed the elite residents of the Garrison and the surrounding areas. Moreover they were able to 'take possession of the air for half and three quarters of a mile in all directions.'[38] The Landship, as masquerade, occupied the streets. And while Marshall argued that the Landship was masquerade 'on a small scale', the evidence of parades numbering 500 participants changes this perspective. These were large masquerade bands marching and dancing in the streets. It means that for a brief moment in the early 1930s, the Landship, as masquerade, danced in and gained access to key areas of colonial space.

Furthermore, as masquerade, their uniforms functioned as *costume* for the spectacle. Landship members were aware of this and made every effort to tailor the rigid naval look. For example, at the carnival parade in 1931, all were decorated, including the horse pulling the hackney carriage. Yet it was the officers who were spectacular on parade. The white shirts and trousers were starched until they were stiff. There was also a dazzling array of ceremonial cords, badges and stripes in colours such as purple and yellow, all along the shoulders and on the trousers. Officers carried real swords. Note the following description of Lord High Admiral Walcott at the November parade in 1931:

> The dominant figure in the field, however, was the Lord High Admiral Walcott, who cut a truly impressive appearance in his uniform. His head was covered by a cork hat such as Nelson wore, in the crown of which a slight breeze played through a plume of black and white feathers. The rays of the sun drew sparklets of fire from the gold epaulets which emblazoned his shoulders, and over his left shoulder and across his manly breast was thrown a scarlet sash embroidered with gold braided edges. Yellow stripes adorned the sides of his black trousers, and he carried his sword in a manner befitted of his rank.[39]

Though Lord High Admiral Walcott utilised the crisp white of the naval officer's uniform, the additional trimmings and colours added an African-Caribbean flair. The result was that the very stiff, starched image of the British navy was transformed and became costume for the masquerade. Such a deliberate adjustment can be read as a psychological rejection of the stiffness and sterility of colonial entrapment. Transforming the naval uniform in this way freed Landship members from the constraints of colonial rule.

---

[38] See footnote 24 for the full text.
[39] Bernard, 'Monster Landship Parade', p. 5.

This then leads to another reading of Landship activity. A key element of a Landship parade was performance. With their naval uniforms transformed into *costumes*, Landship members were themselves transformed from cane cutters, lightermen, sailors, washerwomen and maids, to dancers, actors and musicians. Performing for the general public was, and still is, one of the highlights of being in the Landship. Present-day Landship members speak of doing 'a good performance' and of the extra lift a large and enthusiastic crowd gives them when they are on parade. Similarly, at the 1931 gathering in Belleplaine, the Landship parade did provide 'an enjoyable spectacle' for the spectators. Their performance momentarily alleviated the 'unvarying monotony and soul-killing drabness' that was the reality of post-emancipation plantation existence in Barbados.[40]

The inclusion of the tuk band for the Landship masquerade is another aspect of the narrative that has been overlooked by commentators. The music of the tuk band accompanies the members for the performance. Captain Watson, of the present-day Landship, explains the importance of the tuk band:

> The band is made up of four pieces of instruments; the bass drum, the kettle drum, the flute and the steel. The essence of that is the drum provides that sound or that beat which the members listen to and which guides them in their movements or drill. The kettle provides what you call the rhythm which the drums follow. And the flute provides the melody, which is accompanied by the steel... The bass drum is very important. The bass drum provides the beat. We will find it very difficult to drill with a kettle alone. It's this bum bum, this beat, this bass beat, which we listen to and move by.[41]

The tuk band as a musical entity predates the Landship by at least a century. Yet the question remains to be answered as to how this musical entity became such an integral component of this cultural form. Curwen Best has argued that 'the tuk band created the rhythms of the sea for the landship – slow, medium or fast, echoing the states of the ocean, and literally creating a more visibly and audibly intriguing spectacle to the patrons for whom the landship performed'.[42] In this way the tuk band became known as the 'engine' of the Landship. On odd occasions

---

[40] See footnote 2 for the full text; personal interview with Lieutenant Lloyd Adams, 14 May 1998.
[41] Personal interview with Captain Vernon Watson, 5 June 1997.
[42] Best, *Roots to Popular Culture*, p. 53.

Landships have performed without their uniforms, but it is highly unusual for them to perform without their tuk band.

Landship parades include other theatrical elements that challenge British naval traditions. In the early twentieth century, women were included in the Landship movement. Called nurses or 'Stars', a Garveyite echo, these women further broke naval tradition when they performed during the parades:

> The nurses, for the most part self conscious and with lips tightly pursed, did not quite measure up to the standard set by their brothers and their effort must be judged rather by what they attempted than what they accomplished. It may be mentioned that half a dozen of them were unable to withstand the heat of the sun and the prolonged standing, and had to be assisted off the field. On such occasions the ship's doctor was always a prominent figure and never moved without his medicine wallet.[43]

So intent was Gordon Belle on dismissing the presence of the women in the parade that he was unaware of the importance of the event he described. The act of feeling faint and needing help from the ship's doctor was/is all part of Landship drama. It provided role-play for the 'Stars' who were otherwise not central in the very male ceremony. It also injected humour into the traditionally stiff trappings of the military and naval parade. The 'feeling faint' routine is still a part of a Landship performance today and is very entertaining.

Then there is the dancing of their 'naval manoeuvres'. In Landship terminology, these movements are known as the drill. Once the parade is in full swing, there is a further display of unconventional naval manoeuvres. Rather than utilise the rigid marching routine associated with naval displays, the Landship manoeuvres became energetic dance steps. Crowd favourites were, and still are, the 'wangle lo', in which the performers, with hands on hips, bend their knees and, using a circular motion with their hips, slowly lower their bodies to the ground. This dance is performed to the rhythms of the tuk band. These Landship dancers bring their bodies up slowly and 'go down' once again. The other manoeuvre that delighted the crowd was called 'rough seas', which some Landship members now call 'hand exercise'. The Drill Master calls, 'Yuh gine rock out de ship now.' In a motion similar to the action of sails spinning on a windmill, the entire Landship dances around the parade square, rocking their bodies from left to right, their hands doing the action of the windmill sails.

---

[43] Bernard, 'Monster Landship Parade', p. 12.

Recent research has demonstrated that these 'naval manoeuvres' are reflective of an African-Caribbean heritage. Best has argued that the 'physical movements of the landship became a medium through which they were able to perpetuate the rhythms and dances of Africa'.[44]

Consequently, another reading of the Landship can be pursued. This cultural form practised the traditions of the masquerade and danced to the drum rhythms of the tuk band in the post-emancipation period, as their ancestors had done during slavery. Moreover, these activities took place in the public space, a space normally barred to the labouring classes, particularly for the performance of the masquerade. By adopting the uniform and the rituals of the Royal Navy, the Barbadian Landship devised a form of cultural camouflage. This camouflage allowed them to covertly practise their ancestral traditions in the colonial period:

> let my children know
> how i have manoeuvred
> a century or more
> of rough seas
> from the hole of my ship
> to the deck of my buggy
> from pond-grass and plantations
> to a new lan-
> guage of drums borrowed
> rhythms that now cash
> my own mortgage[45]

Running your hands over the cloak

Kamau Brathwaite has long established that when we are seeking to understand traditions in the Caribbean community, the search should begin with the folk. They were the people who survived despite oppression and who were able to adapt and recreate new traditions. In addition, they 'devised means of protecting what has been gained (miraculous, precarious maroonage)' and they 'begin to offer to return some of this experience and vision'.[46]

The cloak of the Landship was one of those devices. In this instance, the cloak was not only the literal adoption and wearing of the

---

[44] Best, *Roots to Popular Culture*, p. 53.
[45] Farrell, *Tribute*, p. 8.
[46] Kamau Brathwaite, *Contradictory Omens: Cultural Diversity and Integration in the Caribbean* (Jamaica: Savacou: 1985 [1974]), p. 64.

British naval uniforms, but also the use of British ship names and all the accompanying naval and military rituals. It originated in colonial Barbados when the labouring classes had to exercise what Kamau Brathwaite has called 'psychological maroonage'.[47] Because of the limitations set by emancipation, the constraints imposed by the size of the island and the monocrop sugar economy, there was little option for the emancipated labourer but to stay and work on the plantations for very low wages. What these Landship members exercised was a psychological freedom through the adoption of this cloak. As the Landship they were able to sail and march and dance to and in their own reality. Their use of the colonisers' uniform allowed them to do this.

Furthermore, what they did to the uniform assisted in the construction of a Landship reality, and thus their own emancipation. Everything was done *in excess* on their uniforms. There were several gold and purple cords on the officers; large bunches of yellow plumes on their cork hats and medals of every kind. Yet, in the majority of cases, the result was not caricature but blend. It was the synthesised cultural form of which Hall speaks. What the Landship did was to add a Caribbean flair to a very pristine British naval livery. The effect was to produce 'a partial vision of the colonizer's presence; a gaze of otherness'. This partial presence was the basis of colonial mimicry.[48]

What resulted was a cloak that interrogated the coloniser while it seemed to bestow praise. Unfortunately, the other members of the colonised society, in this case Barbadian society, were encouraged to view the cloak as the coloniser saw fit. Over time, the cloak as a means of bestowing praise upon the coloniser was deemed to be the only interpretation:

> The ways in which black people, black experiences, were positioned and subject-ed in the dominant regimes of representation were the effects of a critical exercise of cultural power and normalisation. Not only, in Said's 'Orientalist' sense, were we constructed as different and other within the categories of knowledge of the West by those regimes. They had the power to make us see and experience ourselves as 'Other'.[49]

---

[47] Kamau Brathwaite, *Bajan Culture Report & Plan* (Barbados: UNESCO/Ministry of Education and Culture, March 1979), p. 7.
[48] Bhabha, *Location of Culture*, p. 88.
[49] Stuart Hall, 'Cultural Identity and Diaspora', in Patrick Williams and Laura Chrisman (eds.), *Colonial Discourse and Post-Colonial Theory* (New York: Harvester Wheatsheaf, 1994 [1993]), pp. 392–403 (p. 394).

As a result, instead of seeing the Landship as a cultural document that critiqued colonialism, Barbadian society chose to make the Landship become the Other. In doing this, the society failed to recognise that it was being made to see life through the eyes of the coloniser. It had also become the Other.

Index

abolition of slavery   xv, 24–6, 30n.24, 104, 142, 159
Acaau, Jean-Jacques   99–101
Adams, Lieut. Lloyd   223
Adas, Michael   151, 153
Advocate News   216–17, 223
African diaspora   187–8
Afrocubanismo movement   170–2
Anglican Church   xxiii, 75, 128, 185, 202, 209, 225, 226
Antigua   69–72, 76, 80, 81, 106, 182
Antorcha, La (Cuba)   169, 170
Apprenticeship period (1834–38)   27–31, 62–3, 66–8, 84, 104–5, 109
Ardouin, Beaubrun   98
armed forces
  in Dominica riots   113
  in Haiti   96, 101, 102
  in Jamaica riots   115
  in Suriname riots   148, 149, 155
  in Trinidad riots   126–8, 130–6
  see also militias; West India regiments
Arrindell, Attorney-Gen. William (British Guiana)   47
arson attacks   112, 117, 127, 146
Asians *see* Chinese immigrants; Indians; Javanese
asylums *see* orphanages; reformatories
avoidance protest   151–2, 153–4

Bahamas   80
Barbadian newspaper   25, 26
Barbados
  coercion of labour   105–6, 108–9
  emancipation in   104–5
  emancipation era politics   20–38
  Landship   215–34
  prisons   67, 72, 75–6, 77–8, 80, 82
  punishments   72, 82, 106
  reformatories   75, 75–6, 81
  slave revolt (1816)   23, 24, 26
  strikes and protests   112
  young offenders   69, 72, 75–6
Barbados Advocate   223–6
Barbuda   182

Barkly, Gov. Henry (British Guiana)   47
Barnett, Mary   41
Barthélémy, Gérard   98, 102
Beckles, Hilary   21
Belgrave, Jacob, Jr (Barbados)   25–6
Belize   184–6, 189, 191
Belle, Gordon   224, 227, 231
Bencomo, Juan René Betancourt   177
Bermuda   80
Besson, Jean   197–8
Best, Curwen   217, 230, 232
Bhabha, Homi   218
blanqueamiento   163, 177
Bloch, Marc   90
Bogle, Paul   8, 9–10, 11, 12
Bolland, O. Nigel   21
Bowcher-Clarke, Robert   34
Boyer, President Jean-Pierre   95
Brathwaite, Henry   35
Brathwaite, Kamau   232–3
Bremen, Jan   152
Brereton, Bridget   63, 110
Bridgetown   24, 25–7, 28–9, 33, 223–7
Britain
  abolition of slavery   xv
  and penal reform   40–4, 65–6, 70, 73, 81
  recognition of Haiti   93n.10
  see also Colonial Office
British Guiana (Guyana)   33, 106, 112–13, 116, 189
  young offenders in   39–63
British Honduras *see* Belize
Bronkhurst, H.V.P. (missionary)   45
brujería   165, 168–70
Bryan, Patrick   42, 197, 202, 203
Burton, Richard   182–3, 193, 213n.64

cabildos de nación   160, 161
Cabrera, Lydia   175–6
Cape Colony   42, 42–3, 58
Carbonel, Walterio   172
Caribbean identities   193, 194
Carlyle, Thomas   44
Carnival   137–41, 224

236 Index

Carpenter, Mary   40–1, 73
Carpentier, Alejo   184
'centipede gangs'   45, 60
children   62–3, 80, 110
  see also young offenders
Childs, Peter   218–19
Chinese immigrants   180
  in British Guiana   46, 54
  in Suriname   143, 146, 149
  in Trinidad   120, 124
Chisholm, Linda   42–3, 55, 58
churches   xxii–xxiii
  celebration of emancipation   104–5
  and conflict resolution   11–13
  and conjugality   202, 204
  and Landships   223
  racial segregation in   26
  see also Anglican Church; Roman Catholic Church
civil rights, free coloureds demand   22, 24–5, 27–31, 37
Clarke, Sir Frederick   224
Colebrooke, Gov. William Macbean George (Antigua)   69–72
  as Gov.-Gen. of Windward Is   83
Colonial Office
  and free coloured elites   29
  overrule legislature   83, 201
  and prisons   67, 72–3, 84
  and public order   43, 132, 136
Communist Party (Cuba)   167
conjugality in Jamaica   197–214
contracts of employment   89–90, 97, 109, 143
corporal punishment   3, 72, 79, 82–4
courts
  prosecutions   5–6, 14–15
  sentences   3, 66, 72, 76, 82, 85, 155
  trials   6–9, 65, 144
Couva   124
Crais, Clifton   12
Craton, Michael   21
creole culture   xxi, 179–96, 218
crime   45, 50–1, 60, 145–6
  see also young offenders
Cuba   xvi, xxiiin.11, 159–78, 194n.47
cultural practices, opposition to   137–41, 164–5, 167–70
Cummins, Dr Hugh   224
Cummins, Thomas   28, 30, 31, 34

Daily Chronicle (British Guiana)   60
Daily Gleaner   201, 205–7, 210–11, 212
dancing   223, 231–2
Danish colonies   xv
Darling, Lieut.-Gov. Charles (St Lucia)   117

Day, Thomas (British Guiana agent)   33
de Certeau, Michel   182–3, 213n.64
de Kom, Anton   151–2
De Lisser, H.G.   202, 203
Delgado, Martín Morúa   163
Dessalines, Jean Jacques   94
Dissenters   xxiii, 11–12
district commissioners (Suriname)   144, 147–9
Dominica   104, 106, 107–8, 113–14
douglas   191–2
Downes, Aviston   217
Dutch colonies   xv
  see also Suriname

East Indians see Indians; Javanese
education   xxiii–xxiv, 45, 46, 73, 74–5
El Dia   169
El Nuevo Criollo   168
elites   xviii–xxv
  and colonial authorities   149–50
  and conjugality   197–214
  fears of revolt   xiv–xv, xx–xxi, 130–1, 137–41
  free black and coloured   xxv, 20–38
  in Haiti   89, 92, 93–4, 99
  opposition to cultural practices   xxi–xxiv, 17, 120–1, 137–41, 164–5, 167–70
  use of law   xxiii–iv, 5, 17, 209–12
  see also planters
emancipation see abolition of slavery
emigration see migrant labour
ethnic identities   187–96
Eyre, Gov. Edward John   80, 83, 84

Falmouth Post (Jamaica)   6–7, 7–8
festivals   137–41
Fick, Caroline   94
financial crisis (1848)   114, 128–9
Foucault, Michel   78
France   xv, 93n.10, 95
  see also French Creoles
franchise reform
  in Cuba   162–3
  free coloured demands for   22–3, 25, 27–31, 32, 36, 37
Franklin, Joseph   24
free people of colour   xxv, 20–38, 159
French Creoles   137, 140
Friendly Societies   217, 221–2, 227–8
funeral in Belize   184–6

'Gagging Act' (Barbados)   33–4
Gardner, William James   207
Garraway, Joseph (Grenada)   30
Garvey, Marcus   166, 226–7

Geertz, Clifford 227
Georgetown 55, 60, 61–2
Gittens Knight, J. 222
Gleaner 201, 205–7, 210–11, 212
Glissant, Edouard 183–4
Gómez, Juan Gualberto 160–1, 163
Gordon, George William 8
Grenada 11
Grey, Gov. Charles (Jamaica) 115, 116
Guerre Nègre, Dominica 113–14
Guha, Ranajit 3–4
Guillén, Nicolás 166, 171
Guyana *see* British Guiana

hair cropping 80, 125–6
Haiti 89–103, 184
  revolution xiv–xv, xx, 89, 90–1, 92
Hall, Stuart 187, 218, 219
Harris, Lord, Gov. of Trinidad 125–9
Harris, Thomas, Jr 28, 29, 32, 34
Havana 170
Hay, Douglas 6
Hayne Smith, Attorney-Gen. William 46, 47n.40, 48
Haynes, Douglas 4
head shaving 80, 125–6
healing, traditional 165
Hemming, Gov. Augustus 211
Henry Christophe 93
Heuman, Gad 8
Hewitt, Margaret 41
Hincks, Gov. Francis (British Guiana) 48
Hindus/Hindustanis 138, 142–55, 190
  see also Indians
Hodgson, Gov. Sir Frederick 221
Holt, Thomas 44–5, 79, 107
Hope, Major Daniel 222–3
Hosay 137–41

indentured labour xix
  in British Guiana 46, 47, 116
  emigration from Barbados 31–4
  in Suriname 142–55
  in Trinidad 119–20, 122, 134, 140
Indians 180
  in British Guiana 46, 53, 119
  in Suriname 142–55
  in Trinidad 120, 123, 134–5, 137–9, 189–90, 191–2
industrial schools 41–2, 46, 48, 52–3, 73, 75

Jamaica
  alternative justice in 9–13
  celebration of emancipation 105
  coercion of labour in 80, 106–10

courts and sentencing 3–9, 83
marriage and conjugality 197–214
obeah and myalism 13–17, 19
prisons 67, 78, 79, 80, 82, 84
riots 114–16
strikes and protests 111–12
voluntary organisations 73–4
young offenders 42, 58, 74–5, 76, 81
  see also Morant Bay rebellion
James, Winifred 204
Janvier, L.J. 95
Javanese 142–55
juvenile offenders *see* young offenders

Keate, Gov. Robert (Trinidad) 121, 124
Kennedy, Joseph (Barbados) 29, 35
Kingston, Jamaica 6–7
Kirke, Henry (Demerara magistrate) 45
Kolff, Dirk 155
Kortwright, Gov. Cornelius (British Guiana) 52
Kusha Haraksingh 189

labour
  apprenticeship 29, 62–3
  coercion of 80, 105–10, 119–20
  on plantations 43–4, 97
  see also indentured labour
Lachatañeré, Rómulo 171, 175
Lal, Chimmam 153
landholding xviii–xix, 96–7, 98, 112
law/legal system
  elite use of xxiii–iv, 5, 17, 209–12, 221, 224
  popular attitudes to 3–13
Lazarus-Black, Mindie 13, 14, 182
Leyburn, James 91
Liberal (Barbados) 24, 28–9, 32, 33, 34
Liberal Party (Barbados) 35
Livingstone, W.P. 201
Louis, Michael 117
Lovelace, Earl 192–3
Loving, Henry 30

McDowell, Lieut.-Gov. (St Vincent) 83
MacGregor, Gov. Sir Evan (Barbados) 30, 31
Machado, President 166
McNeill, James 153
Macphail, Gov. John (Antigua) 70
Madeirans 143
Manigat, Leslie 100
Manners-Sutton, Gov. John (Trinidad) 122, 135–6
Maroons 90, 97, 112, 152
marriage in Jamaica 197–214
Marshall, Trevor 217, 228–9

Marshall, Woodville   117
Marti, José   161–2
Masters and Servants Ordinance (Trinidad)   119, 122
May, Margaret   40
mental illness   67–8
messianic movements   151–2
migrant labour   31–4, 166
  see also indentured labour
militias   23, 28, 113, 134–6
Mintz, Sidney   91
missionaries   xxii–xxiii, 45, 186, 207
Montserrat   106
Moore, Brian   116, 191
Morant Bay rebellion (1865)
  events preceding   8–9, 81
  reaction to   3, 83n.42, 122, 134, 135
Morning Journal (Kingston)   6
Murray, Canon W.G.   223
music   173, 190, 216, 220, 228, 230
Muslims   138–9, 146
myalism   13, 15–17

National Association for the Advancement of Colored People (NAACP)   166
negrista poetry   171
Nevis   106
New Times (Barbados)   28–9, 30
newspapers
  in Barbados   24, 28–30, 216–17
  in Cuba   160–1, 168–70
  in Haiti   101
  in Jamaica   6–8, 205–7, 210–11
  in Suriname   145
  in Trinidad   133–4, 139
Nicholls, David   100
nonconformist churches   xxiii, 11–12
non-cooperation   145, 151, 153–4

obeah   13–17, 19
Onderneeming School, British Guiana   39–40, 42, 49–63
orisha   184
orphanages   46, 47–9, 74–5
  see also vagrants
Ortiz, Fernando   164, 167, 169n.30, 172–3, 195, 196
Ortner, Sherry   4, 5

pan–Africanism   166
parades   167, 220, 222–7, 228–32
Partido Independiente de Color   165, 169
pass system   95, 97, 143
Patronato   159
peasant communities   xviii–xix, 12–13, 91–2, 96–7, 98

people's courts   9–13
Pétion, President Alexandre   94
Pinchbeck, Ivy   41
Piquet Rebellion (Haiti)   99–102
plantations   43–4, 93–5, 115, 145–55
  see also indentured labour
planters
  coercion of labour   105–8, 143, 155
  fears of uprisings   117, 122–4, 128, 134–6, 146–7
  financial crisis among   114, 128–9
  and free coloureds   22–3, 34–5
  and indentured labour   31–4, 143–55
police
  in Haiti   95–6
  and parades (Barbados)   225
  and public order (Trinidad)   124, 126–8, 130–1, 133, 136, 140
  and riots on plantations   148
Port of Spain   80, 124–30, 133–4
Portuguese immigrants   46, 54, 116, 120
Prakash, Gyan   4
Prescod, Samuel Jackman   21, 28–9, 31, 32, 34–6, 37
press *see* newspapers
Pringle, Captain J.W. (prison inspector)   66, 67
prisons   40, 66–8, 75–8, 125–6
  discipline in   82–4
  inspectors   3, 66, 67, 77, 78
  official visitors   51, 60
  see also reformatories
prostitution   77
public spaces, gatherings in   9, 25, 35, 101, 122, 126–7
  see also parades
Puerto Rico   xvi
Pullen-Burry, Bessie   204
punishment   72, 79–84
  in prisons   3, 70, 72, 82, 83–4
Puri, Shalini   190

Ramchand, Kenneth   194
Ratu Adil cult   151–2
Rawson, Gov.-Gen. of Windward Is   84
Raygaroo, Jumpa   148
rebellions
  Barbados (1816)   24
  in Dominica (1844)   113–14
  Piquet Rebellion, Haiti (1844)   99–102
  see also Morant Bay rebellion; riots
re-enslavement, fears of   108, 111–12, 113–14
reformatories   39–64, 69–75, 80
Rennie, Lieut.-Gov. William (St Vincent)   80, 84

rents 105–6, 108, 111
resistance 4–5, 182–3, 213–14
Reybaud, Maxime 100–1
riots 115–16, 124–30
Roach, Nathaniel 28, 30, 31
Robertson, Gov. William (Barbados) 225
Robinson, Gov. William (Barbados) 81; (Trinidad) 136
Robotham, Don 10
Rodney, Walter 46, 112
Rodwell, Gov. Cecil (British Guiana) 57
Roman Catholic Church xxii–xxiii, 75, 128, 169, 186–7
Rose Hall Industrial School 62
Roseberry, William 18
Royal Navy 141, 219, 227, 228

St Domingue *see* Haiti
St Lucia 82, 106, 110, 116–17
St Vincent 76, 77n.30, 78, 80, 83, 84, 106
Santo Domingo xv, xvi
Schlossman, Steven 52
Schuler, Monica 10, 15
Scorpion, HMS 127
Selvon, Sam 189, 193–4
Sharpe, Attorney-General Henry (Barbados) 26–7, 35
Sheller, Mimi 8n.23, 9
Simmonds, Lorna 112
slave society, dismantling of xiv–xvii
slavery *see* abolition of slavery
Smith, Gov. Lionel (Barbados) 26, 30; (Jamaica) 106
Smith, M.G. 181
sociedades de color 160
Spanish colonies xv–xvi, 163
State Supervision 142
Stern, S.J. 99
Stoler, Ann Laura 146
Stony Hill Reformatory 42, 58
strikes and protests 110–17, 147–51, 154
sugar trade 114, 115, 128–9, 159
 see also plantations
suicide 153
Suriname 142–55
symbols of resistance 100, 101–2

task system 150–1
taxation 114, 115–16, 116–27, 129
Tejera, Diego 162n.8
tenancy-at-will system 105
Thorne, Joseph (Barbados) 33, 34

Tobago 106, 111
tourism 173
transculturation 195–6
treadmill 82, 84
Trinidad
 civil unrest in 80, 124–36
 economic problems 118–19, 128–9
 ethnic groups in 121–2, 128, 137–9, 189–90, 191–2
 festivals in 137–41
 indentured immigration 119–21
 penal institutions 75, 76, 78, 83–4
 young offenders 76, 77, 83–4
 see also under Indians
Trinidad Press 133
Trinidad Sentinel 133–4
Trotman, David 43
Trouillot, Michel-Rolph 90, 92, 98, 99
tuk bands 216n.3, 217, 222–3, 230–1

United Negro Improvement Association (UNIA) 166
United States of America xvi, 93, 114–15, 162, 170
Urrutia, Gustavo 166–7, 171, 174–5

vagrants 43, 49, 65, 66, 69
Vans Best, Sir Thomas 225
Varona, Enrique José 161
Vaughan, Hilton 222, 226
violence 68–9, 78, 145–6, 154
Virgin Islands 80
vodou 100, 184, 186
voluntary organisations 73–4
volunteer forces 134–6

wages 114, 116, 129, 140, 147–51
Walcott, Derek 190
Watson, Captain Vernon 217, 230
West India Committee 136
West India Regiments 113, 115, 130, 133, 134
Williams, Patrick 218–19
Wilmot, Swithin 109
witchcraft *see brujería*
women and girls
 and alternative justice 9, 13
 destitutes 73–4
 and marriage 203–4, 205–8, 212
 prisoners 67, 69, 71, 76–80, 85, 125
 punishments 80, 84, 106, 125
 withdrawal of labour 96, 109–10

Young, Gov. William (British Guiana) 45
young offenders 39–64, 65–86